HANGED AT NORWICH

NEIL R. STOREY

T0322568

The
History
Press

Norwich Guildhall, historic centre of justice for the city, pictured in the early twentieth century.

First published 2011
Reprinted 2016

The History Press
The Mill, Brimscombe Port
Stroud, Gloucestershire, GL5 2QG
www.thehistorypress.co.uk

© Neil R. Storey, 2011

The right of Neil R. Storey to be identified as the Author
of this work has been asserted in accordance with the
Copyrights, Designs and Patents Act 1988.

All rights reserved. No part of this book may be reprinted
or reproduced or utilised in any form or by any electronic,
mechanical or other means, now known or hereafter invented,
including photocopying and recording, or in any information
storage or retrieval system, without the permission in writing
from the Publishers.

British Library Cataloguing in Publication Data.
A catalogue record for this book is available from the British Library.

ISBN 978 0 7524 5865 6

Typesetting and origination by The History Press
Printed in Great Britain

CONTENTS

ACKNOWLEDGEMENTS

I have been granted privileged access to numerous public and private archives and collections in the preparation of this book; to all those, too many to mention, who have opened their doors and collections to me, I say a very genuine thank you. It has been proved, yet again, that when researching some of the darkest tales from Norfolk's past I have met and renewed the acquaintance of some of the nicest people. I wish to extend my personal thanks to all of them and to my students for their creative thoughts and interest, but I would like to express particular gratitude to the following, without whose help, kindness, enthusiasm, generosity and knowledge this book would not have been so enriched:

My friend and esteemed fellow crime historian Stewart P. Evans and his good lady Rosie; James Nice; Robert 'Bookman' Wright; BBC Radio Norfolk; the late Syd Dernley; Andrew Selwyn-Crome; John Forbes; Dr Vic Morgan; Helen Tovey at *Family Tree* magazine; the Norfolk Family History Society; Clifford Elmer books; Les Bolland books; Norfolk Probation Service; The Tolhouse Museum, Great Yarmouth; The Shirehall Museum and Bridewell at Walsingham; Wymondham Bridewell Museum; Dr Tim Pestell; Ian Flint and Marilyn Taylor at Norwich Castle Museum; The Galleries of Justice, Nottingham; Dr John Alban and all the helpful staff at the Norfolk Record Office; the University of East Anglia Library; the encyclopaedic knowledge of Michael Bean and Clive Wilkins-Jones; the superb staff at the Norfolk Heritage Library, Norwich; Thetford Library (Thetford Norfolk Studies Collection) and my friends amongst the past and present serving officers of Norfolk Constabulary, especially Peter Pilgram and the late John Mason at the Norfolk Constabulary Archive.

Finally, and by no means least, I thank my family, especially my dear son Lawrence and my beloved Molly for their love, interest and support in the research for this book.

The photographs and documents in this volume are mainly from originals in the author's archive unless otherwise annotated to: Norfolk Library and Information Service (NLIS), The National Archives (TNA:PRO), Norfolk Record Office (NRO). The death heads illustrated are on display at Norwich Castle Museum and were photographed by the author with permission. Any omissions in acknowledgement or infringement of copyright are unintentional and no offence was intended.

INTRODUCTION

Norwich Castle has maintained a commanding presence over the city of Norwich since the eleventh century. Built as a royal seat of power and governance, part of it was used as a prison from the time of its completion; a purpose to which the whole building was given over in 1345. It was finally vested in the Magistrates of Norfolk as a county gaol by Royal Grant, confirmed by Act of Parliament in 1806. Executions are recorded on some of the earliest surviving records of Norwich. Across the county, up until the eighteenth century, public executions tended to be conducted where there were seats of county and borough justice. Norwich Castle was used to hold the prisoners who were awaiting trial and those who were under sentence from the Assizes for the County of Norfolk; these were held at Thetford at Lent and Norwich in the summer. The executions of those condemned at the Norfolk Assizes were usually conducted in Norwich or on Melford Common (also referred to as Magdalen Common) in Thetford.

For crimes committed within the walls of the city of Norwich, there was a separate City of Norwich Assizes, held in the Tolbooth (otherwise known as the Tolhouse) in the market place. Originally built for the collection of market tolls, it was used for court hearings and as a prison from the thirteenth century until it was replaced, in 1413, by the Guildhall. Prisoners were held in a purpose-built gaol at the east end of the Guildhall known as 'Little Ease.' In 1597, the city's new 'Common Gaol' was established at a new

Norwich Castle, ancient gaol for the county of Norfolk, pictured in 1813.

Norwich Guildhall in the mid-nineteenth century.

location nearby, in the former Lamb Inn on St Giles Street. Those condemned by the City of Norwich Assizes were executed upon the city gallows, usually on the Castle Ditches, until the new City Gaol was opened in 1827. King's Lynn and Great Yarmouth also hosted Assizes under their own jurisdiction; their prisoners were held at the Lynn Gaol or Yarmouth Tolhouse, with executions being conducted within their own boroughs, usually in the Tuesday Market Place at Lynn or at the White Gate in Great Yarmouth.

There are also instances of condemned criminals, such as rioters and murderers, being brought back to the locale of their deed, or residence, and being publicly executed there to show justice being done and to act as a stern warning to others. Both County and Borough Assizes used local men as executioners until the early nineteenth century, when improved transport links, a decrease in capital sentences and the desire to improve the standards of executions, saw most English provinces employ the executioner appointed by the Gaol Committee of the Court of Alderman for the City of London and Middlesex.

One of the earliest gallows recorded in Norwich stood about a quarter of a mile outside the city's Magdalen Gate, located upon 'a triangular piece of ground where the road forks leading to Catton on the left and Sprowston on the right.' It was recorded as being used as early as the fourteenth century; the usual place for burial of those executed upon the Magdalen Gallows was at the churchyard of St Margaret in Combusto, a long-lost church of Norwich, that stood at the northern end of Magdalen Street; it ceased to function in the fifteenth century. During excavations of the site, in 1987, a number of the graves revealed the occupant had been buried in a prone position (face down), head to the north and feet to the south (the normal Christian pattern is head to the west and feet to the east). Some had been thrown in pits with little ceremony and the remains of fastenings were found about them, indicating they had been buried in their clothes rather than placed in a shroud; a number of the remains were found with their hands behind their backs, implying they had been tied.

The Magdalen gallows were pulled down and burnt by Kett's rebels in 1549. When the insurrection was put down, the gallows were 'made new' – and to ensure people fully understood the consequences for such behaviour, thirty rebels were hanged, drawn and quartered there. The Magdalen (or 'Maudlyn Gallows' as John Kirkpatrick recorded them in the eighteenth century) were still in use in 1616, when a Roman Catholic priest, Thomas Tunstall, was hanged, drawn and quartered 'at the gallows out of Magdalen-gates.'

His head was then set on a pole and displayed upon St Benedict's Gate, with his quarters hung from four other city gates. In 1561, the corner of Town Close, 'between the two great London Roads', was made the common place of execution for criminals. A gallows was also occasionally erected in Norwich Market Place for those condemned to death by the City Assizes and when particular examples were to be made to the populace. In 1549, a temporary gallows was erected at the Market Cross in the Market Place, where forty of Kett's men were executed after the rebellion. A gallows was also erected there 100 years later, during the Civil War, to terminate the lives of those who raised riot and insurrection in the name of the King.

Although this book concentrates on execution by hanging in Norwich, it would be negligent not to mention that during the fifteenth and sixteenth centuries, Norwich was also a place of execution for heretics and those who transgressed religious law. The Bishop had his own prison in the cellar of the Palace Gate and trials would be conducted before an Ecclesiastical Court. Those found guilty of the most severe transgressions of religious law would be killed by being burnt at the stake at the Lolland's Pit; this was situated without Bishop's Bridge. The number of those suffering this terrible fate reached a pinnacle during the reign of 'Bloody' Mary Tudor (1553-58), when forty-eight poor souls were condemned to the flames during her short reign.

During the seventeenth century the regular place for executions in Norwich moved to the locale of the Castle; those condemned to death by the Assizes for the County of Norfolk being executed upon the gallows on Castle Hill, while those from the City of Norwich Assizes would be hanged on the gallows at the Castle Ditches. Under the 'Bloody Code', of the eighteenth century, there were over 200 capital offences and by 1810 there were an unprecedented 220 crimes that carried the death penalty for offences as diverse as murder, highway robbery, burglary, arson, piracy, sodomy, pick-pocketing above the value of 1s, shoplifting goods above the value of 5s, firing hay stacks or destroying a pond containing fish. In the face of such draconian laws it must be remembered that, although the criminal may have been found guilty of a capital offence and sentenced to death, many did not actually end up on the gallows, their sentence being commuted to a prison sentence or transportation. They were occasionally given the choice of joining the army instead of keeping their date with the executioner. At some Assizes in Norfolk as many as thirteen people had the death sentence passed upon them, but it was unusual

Magdalen Gate, viewed from within the city wall in about 1720 by Henry Ninham, from a drawing by John Kirkpatrick.

Norfolk)
TO WIT. }

A CALENDAR

Of all the Prisoners being in the Gaol of the said County, (as have been committed for trial at the next Assizes, or at the next Gaol delivery of the said County), to be tried at the Assizes to be holden at the Castle   Norwich, in and for the said County, on Tuesday, the 17th day of December, A.D. 1844, before the Honorable Sir John Williams, Knight, one of the Justices of our Lady the Queen, assigned to hold pleas before the Queen herself, and the Honorable Sir John Taylor Coleridge, Knight, one other of the Justices of our said Lady the Queen, assigned to hold pleas before the Queen herself, Justices of our said Lady the Queen, assigned to deliver the aforesaid Gaol of the Prisoners therein being.

NoBill	R. W.	1 JAMES HARRIS, aged 29, (on bail),	Committed September 26, 1844, by G. B. L. Knight, Esq. charged on the oath of Benjamin Bunting, of Framingham Pigot, Gentleman, and others, with having, on the 29th November, 1838, about one o'clock in the morning, burglariously broken and entered the dwelling-house of the said Benjamin Bunting, at Framingham Pigot aforesaid, and stolen therefrom a liquor stand, glass decanter, mourning ring, two decanter slides, a bell, two plated waiters, and a broach, his property.
1 Im —	R. Imp.	2 JOHN HARVEY, aged 9, (on bail),	Committed October 4th, 1844, by the Right Hon. and Rev. Lord Bayning and the Rev. Thos. Paddon, Clerks, charged on the oaths of John Howe, of Colton, farmer, and others, with having, on the 11th September last, at Colton aforesaid, set fire to a stack of wheat, the property of the said John Howe.
15 yr —	R. W.	3 GEORGE DYE, alias FITT, aged 17,	Committed October 21, 1844, by John Wright, Esq. H. S. Partridge, Esq. and Rev. T. P. Slapp, Clerk, charged on the oaths of Daniel Watson, of Larling, innkeeper, and others, with having, on the night of Sunday, the 25th of August last, at Larling, set fire to a wheat stack, the property of the said Daniel Watson.
1 Im —	N.	4 WILLIAM LOCKETT, aged 45,	Committed November 1, 1844, by Robert Copeman, Esq. charged on the oath of Brooks Crane Shephard, of Banningham, farmer, with having, on the 31st October last, at Banningham aforesaid, stolen a peck of wheat, the property of Robert Shephard, of Banningham aforesaid, farmer.
6 Im —	R. W. Imp.	5 FREDERICK HOUSEAGO, aged 16,	Committed November 5, 1844, by G. B. L. Knight, Esq. charged on the oath of Maria, the wife of William Harvey, of Bixley, labourer, with having, on the 28th October last, at Trowse Newton, stolen a striped waistcoat, the property of Samuel Chapman.
1 Im —	N.	6 THOMAS SUTTON, aged 31,	Committed November 7, 1844, by Robert Copeman, Esq. charged on the oath of George Rayson, of Buxton, carpenter, with having, on the 2nd of the same month, at Buxton, stolen a bushel of potatoes, his property.
7 Years.	{ R. W. Imp. N. R. W.	7 ROBERT HARROD, aged 19, 8 WILLIAM JENKINS, aged 17, 9 JOSHUA ARTIS, aged 17,	Committed November 7, 1844, by J. T. Mott, Esq. charged on the oaths of William Drane, of Alby, and others, with having, on the 6th of the same month, at Alby, stolen a half-crown, three sixpences, and a two-penny piece, the property of the said William Drane. And also with previous convictions for felony.
15 yr —	R. W. imp.	10 ROBERT PARKER, aged 18,	Committed November 6, 1844, by the Rev. T. P. Slapp, Clerk, and H. N. Palmer, Esq. charged on the oaths of Joseph Palmer, of Wilby, farmer, and others, with having, on the 8th September last, at Wilby, set fire to a wheat stack, the property of the said Joseph Palmer. Stands further charged with having, on the 27th October last, at Wilby aforesaid, set fire to a wheat stack, the property of Joseph Palmer and another.
NoBill —	R. imp.	11 ROBERT DYE, aged 20,	Committed November 8, 1844, by the Hon. and Rev. Robert Wilson, Clerk, charged on the oath of Leonard Patrick and others, with receiving cheese, well knowing the same to have been stolen.
Remanded	R. W.	12 CHARLES SADLER, aged 32, (on bail.)	Committed November 9, 1844, by the Rev. Edward Postle, Clerk, charged on the oath of George Basey, of Ashby farmer, with having, on the 4th of the same month, at Ashby, stolen five chickens, his property.
7 Days	N.	13 ROBERT GREEN, aged 30,	Committed November 9, 1844, by the Rev. A. E. L. Bulwer, Clerk, charged on the oath of John Norman, of Swannington, bricklayer, with having, on the 5th of the same month, at Swannington, stolen a fork shaft, his property.
6 Im —	R. imp.	14 THOMAS BRIGHTMAN, aged 18,	Committed November 9, 1844, by Joseph Scott Esq. charged on the oaths of Ann Cannell, of Cringleford, and others, with having, on the 7th of the same month, at Cringleford aforesaid, stolen three flannel petticoats, three pairs of cotton stockings, the property of Abraham Cannell, of Cringleford aforesaid, farmer.
15 yr —	R. W.	15 JOHN RUTLAND, aged 33,	Committed November 11, 1844, by James Gay, Esq. charged on the oath of Daniel Dix, of Twyford, farmer, with having on Sunday the 10th of the same month, at Guist, set fire to a barley stack, his property.
14 yr —	R. W.	16 CHARLES BAXTER, aged 52,	Committed November 12, 1844, by the Hon. and Rev. William Wodehouse, Clerk, charged on the oath of Benjamin Newson, of Hingham, butcher, with having, on the evening of the preceding Friday, at Hingham, stolen from his shop a piece of mutton, his property.
14 Days —	N.	17 JAMES BELL, aged 25,	Committed November 16, 1844, by the Rev. William Manning and Temple Frere, Clerks, charged on the oath of Cornelius Gibson, of Burston, farmer, with having, some time in the month of September last, at Diss, stolen a spade skeppet, his property.
6 Im —	R. W.	18 JAMES HAMMOND, aged 16,	Committed November 25, 1844, by H. R. Upcher, Esq. charged on the oath of Charlotte Farrow and others, with having, on the 21st of the same month, at Felbrigg, violently assaulted the said Charlotte Farrow, with intent to ravish her.
3 Months	R.	19 LEONARD ALDIS, aged 22, (On bail.)	Committed November 27, 1844, by Sir Edmund Bacon, Baronet, and the Rev. Edward Postle, Clerk, charged on the oath of Robert Smith, of Rockland St. Mary, tile-maker, with having, on the 24th of the same month, at Claxton, stabbed and wounded him, with intent to maim him.
Acq —	R. W.	20 JOHN MALLETT, aged 22,	Committed November 28, 1844, by W. R. Cann, Esq. charged on the oaths of Samuel Breeze, of Kimberley, labourer, and others, with having, on the 18th of the same month, at Wicklewood, stolen from the person of the said Samuel Breeze, a sovereign, half-sovereign, and purse, his property. Also charged with a previous conviction for felony.
15 yr —	R. W.	21 WILLIAM MEDLAR, aged 37,	Committed December 3, 1844, by W. F. L. Bulwer, and C. W. Marsham, Esqrs. charged on the oaths of Robert Samuel Thorne, of Burgh next Aylsham, farmer, and others, with having, on the morning of the 26th of November last, in Burgh next Aylsham aforesaid, set fire to a stack of wheat, the property of and in the stack yard of Robert Samuel Thorne.
1 Im —	R. W. imp. and R. W. imp.	22 GEORGE STOREY, aged 27, and 23 WILLIAM PALMER, alias STRIKE, aged 20.	Committed December 10th, 1844, by Rev. W. J. Jex Blake, Clerk, and J. H. Holley, Esq. charged on the oath of Nathaniel Printer, of Banningham, dealer, and others, with having, on the 8th November last, at Skeyton, cut and wounded the said Nathaniel Printer, with intent to do him some grievous bodily harm.

Norfolk Assize Calendar for 17 December 1844.

for more than two of them to hang and these would have tended to be repeat offenders, those who had used extreme violence or who had committed murderer.

All crimes that could receive a capital sentence were ultimately brought before the Courts of Assize, periodic criminal courts held around England and Wales presided over by the judges of the King's Bench Division of the High Court of Justice. The judges served in the seven circuits of England and Wales on commissions of 'oyer and terminer'; setting up court and summoning juries at the established Assize Towns. The Norfolk Circuit of Assizes rotated around the counties of Buckinghamshire, Bedfordshire, Huntingdonshire, Cambridgeshire, Norfolk and Suffolk, together with the County of the City of Norwich and the jurisdictions of Ely, Kings Lynn and Great Yarmouth. It should be remembered that justice was not always swift; if a suspect was brought into custody for a serious crime shortly after the last Assizes, he or she would face the judicial process of appearing before local magistrates or Coroner's court, then a long wait before their trial at the next county Assizes. Even in the nineteenth century the *Norfolk Chronicle* riled: 'The late city calendar furnishes no less than three cases of exceptional long confinement before trial; namely one person for more than twelve months, who has been acquitted and two others in custody upwards of eleven months against whom no true bills were found.'

Norfolk Assizes in Norwich were held at the Shire House or Shirehall. The first Shire House in the city dated from the thirteenth century; known as the King's Hall, it stood on Garter Hill (between the thoroughfares that became known as Golden Ball Street and Orford Street). A new Shire House was built against the north wall of the castle keep in 1579. It was destroyed by fire in 1746, and a new building was promptly erected on the same site, opening in 1749; a further vestibule was added in 1784. In 1822-3, this Shire House was taken down to make way for the new castle gaol buildings and a new Shirehall was erected 'in the ditch' at the base of the castle mound, fitted out with two courts and appropriate facilities for the County Assizes and the Quarter Sessions, all to designs by the architect William Wilkins Jnr. The prisoners would be brought to and from the courtrooms via a subterranean passage from Norwich Castle Gaol. The Shirehall was enlarged in 1887, when waiting rooms for witnesses, twenty-one new cells for men and four waiting cells for women were constructed. The Shirehall, although not used for its original purpose, is still extant today.

In *The History of Norwich* (1814), Philip Browne describes the formalities observed when the Assizes were held in the city:

When the day appointed by the judges for holding the Assizes is come, the two City Sheriffs, with their Under Sheriffs and officers and the High Sheriff of the County of Norfolk, with his Under Sheriff and Sheriff's Men, led by their Marshall, with trumpets and banners, go to meet His Majesty's judges as far as the bounds of the city (generally at Eaton), where the judges are received by the High Sheriff in his carriage, and so escorted by the cavalcade on horseback, through the city, to the Shire-house on Castle Hill: being come to the foot of the bridge, the City Sheriffs with their retinue, wait on the Castle Ditches and the High Sheriff, with the judges, enter the Shire-house and open the

Act vesting Norwich Castle to His Majesty's Justices of the Peace for Norfolk, July 1806.

ANNO QUADRAGESIMO SEXTO

GEORGII III. REGIS.

C A P. LXXXVI.

An Act for enabling His Majesty to grant the Castle of *Norwich*, with the Common Gaol, Castle Hill, and certain Land adjacent thereto, in the County of *Norfolk*, and for vesting the same in His Majesty's Justices of the Peace for the said County, for the Use thereof; and for other Purposes relating thereto. [12th *July* 1806.]

WHEREAS the Castle of *Norwich*, with the Common Gaol, Castle Hill, and circumjacent Ground, containing about Six Acres One Rood and Thirteen Perches, is Part of the County of *Norfolk*, although surrounded by the City and County of the City of *Norwich*: And whereas the King's most Excellent Majesty, in Right of His Crown, is seised in Fee Simple of the said Castle, Castle Hill, Common Gaol, and circumjacent Ground: And whereas from Time immemorial the Assizes and Quarter Sessions of the Peace for the said County of *Norfolk* have been holden at the Shirehouse within the said Castle, and the Public Records of the said County are deposited, and the public Business of the said County hath been transacted there, and the Common Gaol and Prison of the said County of *Norfolk* adjoins to and forms a Part of the said Castle: And whereas by Letters Patent under the Great Seal of *Great Britain*, bearing Date on or about the Eighth Day of *April* in the Year One thousand seven hundred and seventy-three, the King's most Excellent Majesty was graciously pleased, with the Advice of the First Commissioner of the Treasury, and Chancellor and Under-Treasurer of the Exchequer, and the Commissioners of the Treasury, to demise, grant, and to farm let, unto *George* Earl of *Orford, Horatio* Lord *Walpole, Edmund Rolfe* Junior, *Anthony Narris,* and *Edward Bacon,* Esquires, and the Survivor of them, and the Executors and Administrators of such

Survivor,

Crowds gather outside the Shirehall for a glimpse of some of the characters involved in the Stanfield Hall murder trial 1849.

several commissions; after which, being joined by the City Sheriffs, they proceed to the Guildhall, at the porch of which the High Sheriff, with his posse, wait in like manner and the judges being, by Sheriffs, conducted into the court, the several commissions are then read; after which the judges are again conducted by the City and County Sheriffs to their lodgings.

The next day the same procession is made to the cathedral church, where the judges are received by the corporation, when, the loud organ playing, they are conducted into the choir. After the service for the day has been sung and an anthem performed, the assize sermon is preached by the High Sheriff's Chaplain. After the service, the Corporation, with one of the judges, proceed to Guildhall and the High Sheriff with the other, to the Shire-house, where the business of the Assizes is commenced and continued till all is concluded.

The Assize week would draw many people to Norwich from across the county, for the festivities that arose around them. Public dinners and breakfasts were held at the great inns of the city, the theatre was open every evening and concerts, entertainments, singing, music, illuminations and firework displays were staged in the garden without St Stephen's Gate.

Under a system that dated back to Henry II, Assizes for the County of Norfolk were held at Thetford at Lent and the Summer Assizes were held Norwich. Holding Norfolk's county Assizes in two separate locations was never a very practical arrangement, especially as the Assizes held at Thetford meant the transport of prisoners, by road, to the town, which was a considerable distance from Norwich. After numerous petitions, one of the earliest dating from 1649, and on no less than five subsequent occasions between 1781 and 1820, the matter was brought before the House of Lords by Lord Suffield, when he presented a petition from Norfolk magistrates in 1824. The document stated that the prisoners were carried in open carts through the towns and villages guarded by soldiers and pointed out 'it was not long since that they were exhibited as sights, one shilling being charged to see convicts of the second and third degree and two shillings or more for condemned felons.' The facilities at Thetford were also criticised, for they consisted of 'a dungeon thirteen feet below the surface of the ground, measuring eighteen feet six inches by nine feet and eight and a half feet in height... in this cell upon one occasion no less than seventeen persons were placed to sleep.' The air to ventilate this cell was admitted through a hole only eight inches square and it was recorded 'even the turnkey, whose business it was to open the door, ran back the moment he did so, owing to the excessive stench that was emitted.' The Lord Chancellor intimated the subject was under consideration, but it was unanimously decided against by the twelve judges.

As the nineteenth century progressed, the number of Borough Assizes were reduced across the county and consequently the last executions conducted outside Norwich were at King's Lynn, when Sgt Peter Donohue of 30th Foot was executed on 13 November 1801, for uttering counterfeit Bank of England notes. At Great Yarmouth, the last person executed was John Hannah (70), who was executed on 6 September 1813, for the murder of his wife. While, following the Norfolk Assizes at Thetford, three men were condemned, namely James Reeve for rape, Miles Wiseman for shooting at and wounding a gamekeeper and Robert Gibson for sheep stealing; all three went to the gallows, in the town, on 10 April 1824. After this date all Norfolk executions, public or private, were carried out at Norwich. The Norfolk Assizes remained divided between Norwich and Thetford until 1831, when they were adjourned to Norwich; with the passing of the

Prisoners under transport during the sixteenth century.

Norfolk Assizes in session at the Shirehall in the late nineteenth century.

Norwich Assize Bill in the House of Commons, the Lent Assizes were formally removed to the city in 1832. This situation remained until 1972, when the Assize Courts were abolished nationally, along with Quarter Sessions and replaced by a single permanent Crown Court.

By the mid-nineteenth century executions had evolved into major public spectacles, regularly attended by thousands of spectators. The execution of those under sentence of death from the County Assizes was carried out on Castle Hill, upon the 'new drop' scaffold used in Norfolk for the first time at noon on 6 April 1805. The condemned was Leeds Mays, who had been tried and found guilty of horse stealing at Norfolk Assizes. The 'new drop' operated with a trapdoor released by the executioner, which would plunge the felon to their doom on the end of the noose, rather than the less sophisticated twist of a ladder or pull away of a cart. These gallows were further improved in the mid-nineteenth century with the introduction of double doors that fell simultaneously with the withdrawal of a bolt, later modified to fall with the push of a lever.

The 'new drop' gallows were erected, when required, on the bridge behind the porter's lodges to the Castle. Premium prices were paid by those who wished to obtain a good view of the proceedings from the comfort of rooms at an inn, private house or atop a church tower. With the arrival of the railways in Norfolk, carriages and even special trains were laid on to bring spectators from London and across the country to watch an execution at Norwich. It was even known for the prison authorities to move the scaffold up the hill, closer to the castle, to allow a better view if a sizeable crowd was expected.

Public executions contained elements of both civic occasion and public entertainment, and they drew vast crowds who ate, drank, revelled and jostled for the best view of the felon's final moments 'on the drop.' On Castle Hill such events could be particularly disorderly, as they were sometimes conducted on market days, when the babble of the crowd would be interspersed with the noises of the livestock. On other occasions, executions would occur at the same time as fairs, and although attempts were made to maintain silence and decorum from the time that the condemned was led out until the execution had been carried out, it was frequently commented in the newspapers of the time that the music, gongs, bells and hubbub of the fair often commenced again before it was considered decent to do so.

The formality of the occasion was observed by the civil, police and prison officials involved. During the mid-nineteenth century, the short space between the gate of the Castle Gaol and the scaffold would be lined on one side by the magistrates of the county and representative of the press on the other. Shortly after the appointed hour, the great door of the prison would open and the Sheriffs, attended by their javelin men, would lead out the solemn procession, followed by the Chief Constable of the County Police, followed in turn by the Chaplain, reading loud and clear from the appropriate portion of the burial service. The condemned, with arms pinioned, would follow the Chaplain, attended on one side by the Governor of the Castle Gaol and the executioner on the other, with a number of the turnkeys following behind. The bell of St Peter Mancroft would toll the death knell, the procession almost moving in time with each slow, mournful ring.

Upon arrival at the scaffold, an expectant hush would fall over the crowd; as the condemned man or woman mounted the steps of the gallows, cries of 'hats off' would come from the crowd (hardly a mark of respect: the call requested that headgear be removed to allow a better view for those further back). Once upon the gallows' trap, the executioner would ensure the legs of the condemned were fastened; he would then pull a white hood down over their head, place the noose and adjust it around the neck so the eyelet of the spliced rope fell below the angle of the jaw (the submental position), usually under the left ear. Once all was prepared, the executioner would step swiftly over to push the lever that would release the trapdoors and the condemned would be plunged into eternity. The crowd and reporters would mark the efficiency and mercy of the executioner by noting how swiftly the signs of life departed from the felon. Sometimes, if the condemned was 'dying hard', the executioner would descend below the scaffold and attach weights to their 'client's' legs; they were even known to pull or swing upon the legs to hasten their end.

A massive crowd await the of the execution of James Rush, the Stanfield Hall murderer, 21 April 1849.

The Church of St Peter Mancroft whose great bell tolled for the executions at Norwich Castle, c. 1881.

What happened to the remains of the executed felon depended on the sentence pronounced by the judge. The bodies of particularly violent or murderous criminals, would often be taken down and parboiled, before they were tarred and placed in a metal 'cage' formed around their body. The body would then be removed and gibbeted for all to see. They were often placed near the scene of their crime, as a stern warning of what can happen to those who transgress the law. Many of these gibbeted remains swung for years afterwards; the last of them in Norfolk were taken down by order in the early nineteenth century, after it was decided by local magistrates that they were 'unsightly.' The locations of gallows and gibbets were noted on early maps such as Faden's Map of Norfolk (1797), which recorded such structures near Holt, Martham, Wereham, Methwold, Bradenham Heath, Badley Moor near East Dereham, on the North Denes at Great Yarmouth, Burnham Westgate, Weeting, Diss and Thetford. Although the names of those who swung, or the deed that brought them there, may be lost to common memory, their legacy remains in names such as as Gallows Hill, Gibbet Lane and Gibbet Piece across the county today; even Heigham Street in Norwich was once known as 'Hangman's Lane'.

The development of greater anatomical and surgical knowledge from the late seventeenth century on meant anatomy schools required fresh cadavers for teaching purposes and thus many executed felons were passed to surgeons to be 'dissected' and 'anatomised'. During this, the body would be opened and a dissection of the body parts and organs carried out, followed by the 'anatomisation of the skeleton'. The bones were boiled clean, wired together and used for teaching purposes. In 1752, the Murder Act came into force. This Act allowed the bodies of murderers to be conveyed immediately to the surgeons as an alternative to being gibbeted. Dissection was described as 'a further terror and peculiar Mark of Infamy'; whether gibbeted or passed to the surgeons, the law was clear: 'in no case whatsoever shall the body of any murderer be suffered to be buried'. The rescue, or attempted rescue, of the corpse of an executed felon became a crime punishable by transportation for seven years.

Others, often those hanged for lesser offences, would be given over to their family or friends to arrange burial: indeed, some families earned good money by charging interested people to come and view the corpse of their executed relative in their home. Others were conveyed to the usual place of burial for executed felons (and those who died while imprisoned at Norwich Castle Gaol), under the toll of the bell of St Michael-at-Thorn on Ber Street, where the body would be interred in the churchyard. It is somewhat ironic that this graveyard was also the burial place for prison officials, including gaoler John Gardner, who was buried there on 24 October 1652, and Hangman Michael Smyth, who was laid to rest a short distance from a number of his victims on 12 April 1678.

The Anatomy Act of 1832 brought an end to the practice of automatically handing over the bodies of executed felons to surgeons. Until April 1837, burial of the executed was conducted either 'within the castle precincts' or at St Michael-at-Thorn; Charles Daines, 'the Hempnall Poisoner', was the last executed felon to be buried there. One notable exception to this rule was Peter Taylor, who was executed on 23 April 1836 for his complicity with the Burnham Poisoners Frances Billings and Catherine Frarey. Both the women's bodies were interred at the Castle, but Taylor's body was acquired by Norfolk & Norwich Hospital Surgeon Mr Donald Dalrymple and turned into a skeleton, used for the instruction of anatomy. After 1837, all of those executed in public, either upon the Castle Hill or privately within the Castle (up to George Harmer, the last man to hang there, on 13 December 1886), were buried within the castle precincts.

Those condemned to death by the Norwich City Assizes were executed upon a scaffold erected on the Castle Ditches; they were escorted there in due form, and in procession from the City Gaol, on St Giles Street. The formal procession was described at the execution of John Crome in 1787, led by an Under Sheriff on horseback. Following him were:

Four Sheriff's Officers, the Sheriff in a Chariot, Twelve Constables, Four Sheriff's officers, the Malefactor in black with a hatband and the executioner dressed in black jacket and long trousers with a black cap, in a cart covered with black baize. [Followed by] The Turnkey on horseback, with a black wand, [then] a Mourning Coach with the Chaplain [and finally] a Hearse with the Coffin.

On other occasions more officials would be in a mourning coach, and the malefactors would be displayed in an open cart, sitting upon the coffins that were to receive their executed bodies.

Over the years, the old Norwich Gaol was criticised for being insecure and unfit for purpose as a common gaol; it was frequently rife with sickness and disease, which often proved fatal for a number of its inmates. The new City Gaol 'without St Giles's Gates' (technically in Heigham Hamlet) was completed in 1827 and became the new site for the execution of Norwich City's felons. The first – and only – public execution conducted there was that of John Stratford, 'the Norwich Dumpling Poisoner', on 17 August 1829,

William Calcraft, public executioner 1829-1874.

who was hanged by newly appointed executioner William Calcraft, on a gallows erected on top of the main entrance lodge on the corner of Earlham Road. Ironically, Stratford had supplied a large quantity of metalwork and fittings to the contractors building the gaol, and he ended his life upon a set of gallows he had helped to construct.

The only other man to be hanged at Norwich City Gaol was William Sheward, who was privately executed on 20 April 1869 by William Calcraft with no public viewing, save a few invited members of the press. Preliminaries, in preparation for the execution, were dealt with by the Prison Governor, John Howarth. He ordered the scaffold erected at the extreme end of the south-east angle of the prison by Mr Foyson, who also supplied the 'drop' used for executions at Norwich Castle Prison. Norwich City Gaol was closed in May 1878 and the prisoners were moved to the County Gaol at the Castle.

William Calcraft took up the position of public hangman in 1829 and served continuously for the next forty-five years, becoming Britain's longest-serving public hangman. He carried out all the executions in Norfolk during his tenure. Born at Great Baddow, Essex, in about 1800, he was the eldest of twelve children. Maintaining his trade as a cobbler, Calcraft worked all over the country – and did so in front of crowds of thousands. He hanged both men and women, sometimes swinging three or four at the same time in the early years of his career. When Calcraft worked in Norwich, he boarded outside the prison walls – at The White Horse on the Haymarket for engagements at the Castle, and at The Norfolk Hotel on St Giles Street for City Prison engagements.

As the nineteenth century progressed, the number of offences that carried the death penalty was reduced and the pressure against the vile spectacle of public execution (and the behaviour of the crowd) gathered momentum and acquired some high-profile supporters, such as the authors William Makepeace Thackeray and Charles Dickens. There were also those who sought to bring about the complete abolition of capital punishment, such as the statesman John Bright. Among them were a number with strong Norfolk connections, such as Elizabeth Fry, the prison reformer; her brother, Joseph John Gurney; Amelia Opie; Thomas Fowell Buxton; and Lord Suffield. Rather than completely abolish executions, authorities compromised and removed executions away from the eyes of the general public.

The last public execution in Norfolk was conducted upon Castle Hill, Norwich on 26 August 1867, when Hubbard Lingley was executed for shooting his uncle, Benjamin Black, at Barton Bendish. The officiating executioner was William Calcraft, who also went on to carry out the last public execution nationally on 26 May 1868 when he hanged Michael Barrett, the perpetrator of the Clerkenwell bombing, in front of Newgate Prison, London. On 29 May 1868, the Capital Punishment (Amendment) Act was passed, bringing an end to public hanging. The Act required executions to be carried out behind prison walls. This Act did however allow the Sheriff of the county in which the execution took place the discretion to admit newspaper reporters and other witnesses, including relatives of the victim, to the execution.

William Calcraft retired in 1874 and his place was taken by William Marwood, a cobbler from Horncastle, Lincolnshire. Duly appointed as official hangman by the Sheriffs of London and Middlesex, he received a retainer of £20 per annum, plus a further £10 for each execution he carried out, plus travelling expenses. He was also able to keep the condemned person's clothes – but, unlike Calcraft, he did not receive a salary. Marwood was, however, the first British executioner to put his mind to the methods, especially the efficiency, of his craft.

Carrying out experiments with sacks, he worked out the optimum points upon which an executed person's vertebrae can be dislocated, taking into consideration their height and weight. He laid out the 'table' that helped an executioner to work out the suitable length of rope, or 'drop', to break the condemned person's neck: too short a drop could strangle; too long a drop could actually tear open the neck of the prisoner (or worse).

The 'scientific' methods Marwood applied to the craft of executioner were adopted by the Home Office as standard practice from the 1870s and were in use, with only minor modifications, until the last British executions, less than 100 years later, in 1964. It should not be forgotten that up to the 1870s, all British executions, even on the 'new drop' of the early nineteenth century, involved the death of the condemned by strangulation rather than dislocation of the vertebrae; it is hardly surprising Marwood took great pride in the remark: 'Calcraft hanged them – I execute them!'

Marwood took advantage of Britain's magnificent railway system from the time of his appointment and carried out most of the executions in Britain and Ireland. With executions being conducted behind closed doors, the work

The White Horse on Hay Hill, about 1885, much as it would have looked when hangman William Calcraft lodged there when he worked in Norwich.

William Marwood, public executioner 1872-1883.

of the executioner, and his experiences with notorious criminals during their last moments on the gallows, took on an unprecedented mystique. Marwood would draw crowds when he 'held court' at inns where he lodged in the city. When he came 'on business' to hang William Abigail, in May 1882, it was reported that, 'he posed as a public character to sundry persons... He exhibited the ropes which terminated the existences of Lefroy and Lamson and certain technicalities of his methods were also explained.'

Executions 'behind the walls' of Norwich Castle, still drew crowds to watch the black flag rising, which signified that the sentence of death had been carried out. Within the prison, the execution of William Abigail is typical of the way in which executions were conducted at the time, and was recorded by one of the reporters who personally witnessed it:

After breakfast the condemned man was led from his cell by a warder and escorted by the Governor, Mr Under Sheriff Francis, the Chaplain and the surgeon; he passed along a covered way to the bathroom, where he was met by Marwood, who at once pinioned him. The mournful procession then started for the gallows, erected on a level with the corridor, the Chaplain meanwhile reciting the prayers for the dying, to which the convict responded most fervently, clasping his hands. The sun was shining brightly as the convict, supported by the executioner and having a warder on each side, stepped into the open air. The solemn service proceeded, the bell of St Peter Mancroft church tolling and whilst the condemned man was repeating the words 'Lord Jesus, receive my spirit,' the bolt was withdrawn and he died without a struggle.

On 2 August 1887 all prisoners from Norwich Castle were transferred to a new purpose-built Her Majesty's Prison Norwich, on Prison Road (now Knox Road) and after centuries as the county gaol, Norwich Castle ceased to be used as a prison.

The new HMP Norwich constructed its gallows in a coach house on the east side of the building. To reach it, the convict would have to walk about 30 yards from the condemned cell in the central corridor. The executions conducted here were subject to a protocol that demanded efficiency and professionalism, explicitly described in *Rules and Standing Orders for the Government of Local Prisons*.

Upon the receipt of the prisoner under sentence of death, the Governor was duty bound to notify the High Sheriff, who was responsible for carrying out the sentence, and the Secretary of State on the day the sentence was pronounced, with any special recommendation of the jury being fully set out in his correspondence. A detailed newspaper report of the trial, from a reliable rather than sensational newspaper, would be attached, along with a copy of the entry relating to the prisoner in the confidential before-trial calendar. Any observations relating to matters of importance, either suggested to the Medical Officer by the evidence given at the trial, or by information obtained subsequently from the Director of Public Prosecutions, would also be forwarded as soon as possible, as would the notification of the date set for the execution.

The Governor would also contact the Prison Commissioners asking to be furnished with the list of candidates reported as competent for the office of executioner, with information as to the conduct and efficiency of each of them and the regulations to be observed in carrying out the sentence. On receipt of these papers, the Governor would transmit the list of candidates to the High Sheriff, together with the memoranda issued by the Secretary of State in reference to executions – specifically the conditions to which any person acting as executioner or assistant executioner should conform.

Permanent warders were assigned to watch the prisoner, and, unless absolutely necessary, no one else was permitted to come into contact with the condemned. The condemned would also be allowed private exercise and fed as the Governor or Medical Officer decreed. A Chaplain would have free access to visit and could be called for by the condemned. Any other visitor could only have access to the condemned having obtained an order from the Governor, or a Prison Commissioner.

The Governor would then have to ensure the scaffold and all necessary appliances were in good order. He would have obtained the necessary equipment upon request from the stock held at Pentonville Prison. The items would be sent in two boxes, one small box containing the chains for adjusting the rope, the rest of the equipment in what looked like a long wooden toolbox, painted grey and fastened with a sturdy retaining bar and padlock. Inside this larger box was:

1. The rope.
2. The pinioning apparatus.
3. The cap.
4. A bag capable of containing sand to the same weight as the prisoner in clothes. (The bag was made to an approved pattern with a very thick neck well padded on the outside with soft canvas to obviate any damage to the rope. The instructions sternly insisted that 'no unnecessary experiments should be carried out either with the rope or bag.')
5. A piece of chalk (to mark the rope or floor with a 'T' so as to position the feet of the condemned as necessary)
6. A few feet of copper wire.
7. A rule, or graduated pole, 6ft long.
8. A piece of pack thread (just strong enough to support the excess coils of the rope without breaking).
9. A tackle to raise the bag of sand, or the body, out of the pit.

A week before the execution the rope was tested by a competent officer in accordance with directions; in case of any defect, a new one was obtained. The Governor was authorised to

To be submitted to the High Sheriff.

Memorandum of Conditions to which any Person acting as Executioner is required to conform.

1. An executioner is engaged and paid by the High Sheriff, and is required to conform with any instructions he may receive from or on behalf of the High Sheriff in connection with any execution for which he may be engaged.

2. A list of persons competent for the office of executioner is in the possession of High Sheriffs and Governors: it is therefore unnecessary for any person to make application for employment in connection with an execution, and such application will be regarded as objectionable conduct and may lead to the removal of the applicant's name from the list.

3. Any person engaged as an executioner will report himself at the prison at which an execution for which he has been engaged is to take place not later than 4 o'clock on the afternoon preceding the day of execution.

4. He is required to remain in the prison from the time of his arrival until the completion of the execution and until permission is given him to leave.

5. During the time he remains in the prison he will be provided with lodging and maintenance on an approved scale.

6. He should avoid attracting public attention in going to or from the prison ; he should clearly understand that his conduct and general behaviour must be respectable and discreet, not only at the place and time of execution, but before and subsequently ; in particular he must not give to any person particulars on the subject of his duty for publication.

7. His remuneration will be £ 5 for the performance of the duty required of him, to which will be added £ 5 if his conduct and behaviour have been satisfactory. The latter part of the fee will not be payable until a fortnight after the execution has taken place.

8. Record will be kept of his conduct and efficiency on each occasion of his being employed, and this record will be at the disposal of any High Sheriff who may have to engage an executioner.

9. The name of any person who does not give satisfaction, or whose conduct is in any way objectionable, so as to cast discredit on himself, either in connection with the duties or otherwise, will be removed from the list.

10. The apparatus approved for use at executions will be provided at the prison. No part of it may be removed from the prison, and no apparatus other than approved apparatus must be used in connection with any execution.

11. The executioner will give such information, or make such record of the occurrences as the Governor of the prison may require.

*Memorandum of Conditions
for the executioner, c. 1950.*

pay the executioner £5 for the performance of the duty required of him, to which would be added £5 'if his conduct and behaviour have been satisfactory.' Under similar terms, the assistant executioner, was paid a total of £2 2s. An allowance was also made for 'reasonable travelling expenses' – normally a third class railway fare and such cab fares shown to be absolutely necessary. The Governor would also provide proper food and lodging for the executioner and his assistants, while they were required in the prison.

The Governor would also ensure the Medical Officer, Sheriff, Chaplain and Coroner were provided with the correct papers to sign, to confirm the judgement of death had been executed upon the offender; the same papers were displayed on the prison door after the execution. He would also ensure the persons required, or entitled, to attend the execution were attended to.

On his arrival at the prison, the day before the execution, the executioner was furnished by the Governor and Medical Officer with all necessary information as to the height and weight of the culprit, his general condition, age and whether he was likely to offer any resistance. The executioner would observe the prisoner from an unseen location and then, armed with all this information, he would calculate the length of the drop required according to the 'Table of Drops', and his own experience. The Governor and Medical Officer might recommend a departure from the table, if there were special reasons for a departure, such as a medical problem, injury or the prisoner's size or weight. If the executioner disagreed with the other officials, he would be entitled to ask that the amendment to his calculations be annotated and signed by the officials that demanded it.

In the first quarter of the twentieth century, the old execution sheds that caused a host of logistic difficulties, and suffered from maintenance problems, were disposed of in favour of purpose-built execution suites. The number of prisons where executions could be carried out was also reduced but Norwich remained a hanging prison, and after the closure of Ipswich Prison in 1925, male prisoners were transferred to Norwich and those who were capitally convicted in Suffolk were brought to Norwich for execution.

Like most other execution suites, the Norwich facilities had the condemned cell directly next door to the execution suite. The close proximity of condemned man and gallows meant that work in the execution chamber would be performed with as little noise as possible, all those involved keeping their conversation minimal and voices low, while the executioner and his assistant wore plimsolls. The night before the execution, the executioner, having worked out the agreed drop, would set up the gallows using the test sack filled to correspond to the weight of the condemned in the presence of the Prison Governor. The bag would then be left hanging on the rope down the open pit all night, to ensure the rope was stretched. Early on the morning of the execution, the executioner and his assistant would return, pull the sand bag out of the pit and mark out the prescribed drop on the rope, allowing thirteen inches for the neck. If the rope had stretched, they adjusted the chains high in the chamber ceiling where the rope was fixed with a 'D' ring. They would also pull up the trapdoors and set the release lever with the safety catch on. The rope was then coiled and the excess tied with pack thread so the noose would hang at a convenient height to be easily slipped over the head of the condemned.

As the appointed time for the execution approached, the executioner and his assistant, with two warders in escort, would gather in front of the condemned cell's door. The prison Governor, Medical Officer and Sheriff would wait outside the door of the lobby area; the Chaplain was usually inside the condemned cell with the prisoner. The Governor would check his watch, and as the chimes of the prison clock marked the hour, so the life of the condemned would be tolled out also.

Upon a given signal, at the appointed time, all would enter their relevant doorways. The Governor and officials would move through the lobby area and flatten themselves against the wall of the execution chamber. The executioner would lead in the condemned, who would normally be found sitting with his back to the entrance door at this time. He would often stand up automatically, but before he had a chance to turn around his hands would be pinioned by the executioner. Meanwhile, the other door in the condemned cell – which the condemned, had they asked, was told led to a store room – opened into the lobby area and the prisoner was led through by the executioner, followed by the assistant and the warders. If the condemned offered resistance or was in a state of collapse he would be supported onto the gallows by the warders; two sturdy planks crossed the pit for them to stand on and ropes with hefty knots hung down for the warders to hang onto and steady themselves as the gallows' traps fell. Many of those present were surprised at the size of the pit; in Norwich the gallows were large enough to take two condemned at a time, so when the traps dropped open it appeared 'as if the floor disappeared.'

Once inside the execution chamber the procedural instructions for the executioner and his assistant were:

1. Place the culprit exactly under the part of the beam to which the rope is attached. [This position would have been marked on the traps by the executioner with a 'T' shape in chalk]
2. Put on the white linen cap.
3. Put on the rope around the neck quite tightly (with the cap between the rope and the neck), the metal eye being directed forwards and placed in front of the angle of the lower jaw, so that with the constriction of the neck it may come underneath the chin. The noose should be kept tight by means of a stiff leather washer or an Indian rubber washer or a wedge.

While the executioner is carrying out the above procedure, the assistant executioner will:

1. Strap the culprit's legs tightly.
2. Step back beyond the white safety line so as to be well clear of the trapdoors.
3. Give a visual signal to the executioner to show that he is clear.
     On receipt of the signal from his assistant, the executioner will:
1. Withdraw the safety pin.
2. Pull the lever which lets down the trapdoors.

In reality the lever was normally pushed to avoid slippage. Many executioners also took great pride and considered it most humane to carry out their duties as quickly as possible. It was quite common for them to leave only the merest tip of the safety pin in the lever socket to enable a rapid knock to release it and allow the lever to be pushed. In most cases the execution, from the moment of entry to the condemned cell to the condemned dropping into the pit, took less time than the steady chimes of the prison clock to mark the hour – about twenty seconds. In the 1940s and '50s, Albert Pierrepoint was noted for carrying out his executions in about ten seconds, although when Harry Kirk attempted to emulate this speed during the execution of Norman Goldthorpe at HMP Norwich in 1950, he was to regret his haste. Just one year later, in 1951, Dennis Moore and Alfred Reynolds, who had each murdered their pregnant sweethearts in unrelated incidents, went to the gallows at the same moment on 19 July 1951, gaining them the unenviable distinction of being the last prisoners to hang at Norwich.

Neil R. Storey, 2011

1

CIRCUMCISION OF A CHRISTIAN CHILD

Mosse Abraham, Isaac Parvus and Daiaia le Cat, 1240

Sadly, the relationship between Jews and Christians in Norwich was often turbulent historically, especially after the alleged ritual murder of a boy by crucifixion in 1144, who was later proclaimed St William of Norwich. Almost 100 years later, in 1230, matters had not improved when a custody dispute between the city's Jewish community and one of its male Christian converts resulted in one of the earliest examples of serious crime to survive among the court records of medieval Norwich.

The case revolved around Odard, son of Benedict, a physician (probably a Jewish convert to Christianity), who went out to play in the streets on the vigil of St Giles. It was claimed the boy was then taken by a Jew called Jacob and removed to a house. Once there, Jacob and others held him down and covered over his eyes, while another circumcised him with a knife and gave him the name Jurnepin. The boy was kept in the house for a day and a night before he escaped and wandered along the bank of the river. When he was discovered by Matilda de Burnham and her daughter, the boy was sitting down *plorante et ululante* (crying and howling), and saying that he was a Jew. Matilda took the boy home to her own house, and kept him there all night. When the Jewish townspeople heard of this, they came to her house and wished to take the boy away. Fortunately, the boy was recognised and his whereabouts reported to his father, who came to collect him. A complaint was taken to Richard de Fresingfield, the Constable of Norwich Castle and City Bailiffs by the Jewish townspeople, who claimed Christians wished to take away a Jewish child. The Norwich civil and religious authorities reacted quickly and 'Senioret, a Jew of Norwich', having fled, was outlawed for the felony of circumcising Odard. In 1234, the formal case was brought by Benedict, with thirteen Jews being accused of complicity in the abduction and circumcision of a Christian child. The case was heard before the Prior of Norwich, the Friars Preachers, the Friars Minor and many others. They found all bar one of the accused 'Guilty.' The next stage was a trial before the King, the Archbishop of Canterbury and the greater part of the Barons and Bishops; they decided the case was unprecedented and decided it should be referred to the Church for inquiry by the Bishop. The Jews remained in prison, but agreed to pay a fine of 100 marks for respite of judgement. Further fines were paid as were fees for bail and court hearings until 1240, when a final hearing sent three Jews – Mosse Abraham, Isaac Parvus and Daiaia le Cat – to the gallows and the Jewish house, called the Thor, was pulled down and destroyed.

2

COIN CLIPPING

Vives of Haverhill, Manser Ursell, Henna of Rising, Senior l'Eveske, Fluria de la Selerie and Abraham Deulecresse, 1279

The act of clipping the edges of the hammered coins, putting the coins back into circulation and melting down the collected clippings into ingots or sheet silver was a crime that frequently attracted the death penalty in medieval England. In 1279, a number of Jews were arrested and charged with coin clipping in Norwich. About sixteen of them were found guilty and punished: some forfeited their property; some were hanged and their property escheated to the Crown. The list of those who went to the gallows, and whose property was sold to the citizens of Norwich, contains the name: Vives of Haverhill, Manser Ursell, Henna of Rising, Senior l'Eveske and Fluria de la Selerie. Another to suffer was Abraham Deulecresse, a wealthy Jew executed for coin clipping and blasphemy. His property, Abraham's Hall in St Peter Mancroft, was sold and used as a resource for a perpetual charity set up in the city by Katherine de Kyrkeby in 1332.

3

CATHEDRAL RIOTERS

Thirty citizens of Norwich, 1272

The relationship between the cathedral and the citizens of Norwich was often far from harmonious. During a fair, held on Tombland in June 1272, a mob of citizens drove a group of men of the priory back into the cathedral close after a priory man, armed with a crossbow, shot and killed a citizen. Days and weeks passed, and the citizens of Norwich were outraged that no apparent action was being taken against the prior's man for the death and so an attack was launched against the cathedral. In *Historia Anglicana*, Bartholomew Cotton recounts:

> 1272, on the day following the Feast of St Laurence [11 August], the citizens of Norwich laid siege around the precincts of the monastery. When their insults failed to gain them admittance, they set fire to the main gate into the monastery... they burned the dormitory, the refectory, the guest hall, the infirmary with its chapel and indeed almost all the buildings within the precincts of the monastery. They killed many members of the monastery's household, some sub deacons and clerics and some lay people in the cloister and in the monastery. Others they dragged off and put to death in the city.

After the fire, the citizens entered the buildings and looted them of everything the fire had spared, be they sacred vessels and books or gold and silver, and then the riot dispersed. In the immediate aftermath of the attack on the cathedral precincts, King Henry III came, in person, to ensure justice would be seen to be done upon the 'delinquent citizens.' Alleged participants and ring-leaders of the riot were tried and thirty of them were found 'Guilty.' Those condemned were dragged to the gallows by horses and hanged; they were then cut down and their bodies were burned to ashes.

4

REVIVED AFTER HANGING

Walter Eghe, 1285

One of the earliest records of an execution in Norwich is also one of the most remarkable. Following the theft of some cloth from the house of Richard de la Hoe, a merchant, and other larcenies, Walter Eghe was captured by the officers of justice. Just two days later, on 12 February 1285, he was brought before the bailiffs and citizens at the Tolbooth in the Market Place to face trial. Eghe was found guilty and was sentenced to hang. After being strung up on the gallows his body was cut down by William Stanhard and removed to St George's Church, where he was to be buried in the churchyard. As the body lay, awaiting interment, symptoms of life were observed, and the man who had been suspended from the gallows was speedily restored to consciousness and action. The news of Eghe's recovery rapidly spread through the city and he wisely claimed sanctuary within the church for fifteen days because he could find no means of escape as the officers of adjacent parishes had set a watch upon his place of refuge. On the fifteenth day, Eghe escaped from the church to the cathedral, where he remained in sanctuary until, at his own suit, he obtained the pardon of the King (Edward I), issued on 24 March. The pardon had been issued upon the grounds that the city's rights did not extend beyond *infangthief* (the right to try and, if appropriate, hang a thief found in possession of stolen goods). Despite being rightly convicted for the theft, it appears he had not committed his crime in a way that would empower the city court to order his execution. Eghe then presented himself before the Court armed with the King's Charter, demanding of the bailiffs and citizens upon what authority they had ordered him to hang. The King was so displeased with the law officials of Norwich that he sent John de Lovetot to investigate the matter and took the liberty of the city into the hand of the King, which His Majesty retained until his next parliament when he restored it to his faithful lieges after their 'coming down handsomely.'

5

THREE THIEVES OF FREEBRIDGE

Geoffrey Gaunt, William of Tilney and Roger Barun, August 1308

The 100 accused persons of Freebridge held at Norwich Castle Gaol were tried before William de Ormesby and John le Breton on 7 August 1308. Geoffrey Gaunt, an approver (one who has confessed his crimes and named his accomplices to a Coroner), was tried for being a member of a gang that robbed the home of Semeine Attewnhus, at Great Massingham, in December 1305. They stole a black horse, cloth and jewels worth 40s. William of Tilney was taken on 18 July 1307, having stolen one bundle and one carpet worth 9s from John Walbot of Terrington. Roger Barun of Mapletreestead was taken for breaking into a chest belonging to John of Barningham and carrying off 100s in silver. The same Roger, along with others, broke into the house of the rector of Ingworth and carried off goods and chattels worth 40s. The jury found all three guilty and they were sent to the gallows.

6

MURDER AT TROWSE

Richard Quynchard and Geoffrey Chaloner, October 1309

On 2 October 1309, following their delivery from Norwich Castle Gaol, Richard Quynchard of Blythburgh and Geoffrey Chaloner stood accused before two Justices of the King, William de Ormesby and William Inge. Both men had confessed to killing and robbing Thomas Spark of Yelverton at Trowse on the night of 25 May 1309 and to committing a further robbery upon 'two foreigners', taking cloth and goods worth 8s from them. They named another, Geoffrey Atte Bush of Brampton, as being involved in the murder. In answer to this accusation, Bush made it known to the court that he wished to defend himself in a duel. Quynchard argued that because he was missing two fingers on the right hand he could not duel. Bush then submitted to trial and the jurors acquitted him. Quynchard was hanged for making a false accusation, while Chaloner withdrew his accusation but was still hanged for the murder.

7

ABJURATION OF THE REALM

Adam Waterman, January 1310

Adam Waterman of East Yarmouth was brought before the justices at Norwich on 8 January 1319, having 'abjured the realm' in the church of St Peter Hungate, Norwich. Abjuration of the realm was often taken by fugitives who had taken sanctuary and meant the person taking the oath swore to leave the country directly and promptly, never to return to the Kingdom, unless by express permission of the sovereign. One of the earliest recorded formal abjurations was:

> I swear on the Holy Book that I will leave the realm of England and never return without the express permission of my Lord the King or his heirs. I will hasten by the direct road to the port allotted to me and not leave the King's highway under pain of arrest or execution. I will not stay at one place more than one night and will seek diligently for a passage across the sea as soon as I arrive, delaying only one tide if possible. If I cannot secure such passage, I will walk into the sea up to my knees every day as a token of my desire to cross. And if I fail in all this, then peril shall be my lot.

Adam Waterman had clearly not left the country and was confronted by Roger of Morley, Coroner for the city of Norwich, who showed the record of the abjuration to the court. Waterman was sent to the gallows.

8

THE THIEF AND HIS LOVER?

Hugh and Agnes of the Kirkeyard, March 1311

Hugh of the Kirkeyard was brought before justices William de Ormesby, William de Colney and Richard de Walsingham on 1 March 1311. He was accused of causing the deaths of Reginald Hare and Richard Turbern of West Rudham, and also of a burglary at the house of Leonta Orgoil, in which he carried off cloth worth 10s. Found guilty and sentenced to death, he was followed by Agnes of Kirkeyard, who had been taken for 'receiving the aforesaid Hugh and his thefts.' She was also found guilty and they were hanged upon the same gallows.

9

STEALING FROM CHURCHES

Richard Thurkyld, Matilda le Palmere, Hugh le Bakestere and Beatrice, daughter of Adam, March 1316

Richard Thurkyld of Northwold, Matilda le Palmere, Hugh le Bakestere of East Tuddenham and Beatrice, daughter of Adam of Yelverton were taken on suspicion, having been found in possession of a missal, a gradual and other diverse ecclesiastical ornaments from the churches of Ketteringham, Swainsthorpe and Markshall. Thomas, Dean of Norwich and his clerk attended the court with letters from the Bishop. All the accused were convicted and the spoils were returned to their respective churches. Hugh was released to the Bishop but Richard, Matilda and Beatrice were all sent to the gallows.

10

MEN OF THE GREAT RIOT

Nineteen townsmen of Bury, 1327

Angered by the power of the monastery, a great affray occurred between the townspeople and monks of Bury St Edmunds in Suffolk in 1327. The citizens rioted destroying the Abbey gate and inflicting severe damage on the Abbey buildings, smashing many of its windows. Once inside the Abbey the townsmen carried off gold and silver chalices, church plate, books, vestments, utensils, and money; even the Prior, Peter de Clapton, and twelve monks were taken prisoner and held in a house in the town. The rioting was protracted and the Abbey was soon besieged. At the end of October, commission was granted to the Earl of Norfolk, Thomas Bardolf, and others to take, if necessary, the *posse comitatus* of both Norfolk and Suffolk to arrest those besieging the Abbey and to imprison others guilty of criminal acts in these affrays. Four justices were also appointed to hold a special Assize at St Edmunds, on the complaint of the Abbot, who supplied the names of about 300 alleged offenders, including three rectors, nineteen Chaplains (or assistant parochial clergy), a merchant, six drapers, four mercers, two butchers, a tailor and two taverners.

Twenty were summarily hanged, while thirty carts full of the townsmen were carried to Norwich where a further nineteen were hanged and the rest confined. Nearly 200 persons remained under sentence of outlawry for five years as their case dragged on in the King's courts. The matter was only resolved in 1331 when an agreement was formally drawn up. The massive fine of £140,000 was imposed on the defendants for their remission, whereby they would pay the Abbey the sum of 2,000 marks during the next twenty years, in sums of 50 marks at a time. The great seal was affixed to this covenant and the defendants were conditionally discharged.

11

ANOTHER GALLOWS CHEAT

Henry le Satere, 1345

In an incident that echoes the case of Walter Eghe sixty years earlier (*see* Walter Eghe, 1285), Henry le Satere was hanged upon the gallows without Magdalen Gate for felony. He was cut down by a clerk named Thomas Davy and removed to the churchyard of St Margaret in Combusto for burial. Before he was laid in the ground, however, le Satere revived. Perhaps Davy had cut him down too soon or was involved in some chicanery during the execution; either way, Davy was imprisoned for his role in the matter. The ultimate fate of Henry le Satere remains unknown.

12

KETT AND HIS REBELS

Robert and William Kett and others, 1549

On the weekend of 6 July 1549, many folk from Wymondham and its surrounding villages gathered to celebrate the feast of the translation of St Thomas à Becket. The recent enclosures of land around the town proved to be an emotive subject and on the evening of Monday 8 July, a group of townspeople tore down the enclosure fences of Mr Hobart of Morley. They then marched to Hethersett to destroy John Flowerdew's estate fences but Flowerdew bribed the mob to rip down Robert Kett's enclosures instead. However, when they arrived at Kett's land, Kett went one better and joined with the mob himself, helping them to tear down his own fences before leading them back to Flowerdew's house where they smashed his enclosures.

The following day, the rioters assembled again in Wymondham and decided to march on Norwich, with Robert Kett at their head and Kett's brother, William, at his right hand;

their numbers swelled as hundreds of protestors joined the march en route. On Wednesday 10 July, the rebels attempted to enter the city of Norwich, but the Mayor, Thomas Codd, and the City Council refused them entry fearing accusations of collaboration and that the rebellion would spread to their city too. Sir Roger Wodehouse of Kimberley went to the rebels with carts containing beer and food in an effort to pacify them and urged them to disperse. The carts were seized and Wodehouse was taken prisoner. Staying outside the walls, the Rebel force made camp upon Mousehold on 12 July and established a council comprising a representative of both the Norfolk and Suffolk hundreds, from which the rebellion was drawn. Sitting under the later titled 'Oak of Reformation', the council issued warrants as 'the King's friends and deputies' to assemble food, cattle, weapons and people on Mousehold Heath. They also drew up a twenty-nine point charter of demands based almost entirely on righting the wrongs done to commoners over the previous decades. A Royal herald came to Kett's Camp on 21 July and read aloud terms for a general pardon. Kett refused, saying they had offended no laws and required no pardon. The herald denounced Kett as a traitor and any fiction of Royal sanction having been exposed, the Norwich authorities closed the city to the rebels; the following day the rebels stormed the city and, meeting little opposition, it was soon under their control. Mayor Codd and many of the City Fathers were taken prisoner.

A Royal Army under the Marquess of Northampton was despatched to the city and arrived on 31 July. The rebels fell back to Mousehold, but returned again the same night; the fighting that ensued continued to the early hours, resulting in about 300 deaths, including Lord Sheffield's.

A considerably larger force, estimated to have comprised up to 14,000 men including mounted gentry and mercenaries under the then Earl of Warwick, arrived at the city on 23 August. Another herald was sent to Kett offering pardons and but was again rejected. Three days of intense fighting then commenced. The rebels took to heart the old Norfolk prophesy:

Robert Kett under the Oak of Reformation, Mousehold, 1549.

The country Gnoffs, Hob, Dick and Hick
With clubbes, and clouted shoon,
Shall fill up Dussyndale
With slaughtered bodies soon.

So to Dussin's Dale they went for their final battle. Unfortunately for them, the terrain was perfect for Warwick's cavalry; with the mercenaries and the finest artillery that the royal armouries could muster, the Earl's forces smashed the rebel lines and claimed a bloody victory, with as many as 3,000 rebels slain.

The following morning, the Earl of Warwick began to hear the cases of many of the prisoners his forces had captured. Justice was swift; many were executed on the city gallows outside the Magdalen Gate. Nine of the rebel leaders, including Miles, Kett's Master Gunner, were strung up on the 'Oak of Reformation', cut down again, their bowels pulled out and burned before their faces, then their bodies were beheaded and quartered. The heads and quarters were then set up on poles on the tops of the towers and gates of the city as a warning to all. A further forty-nine rebels were hanged on a specially erected gallows near the cross in the Market Place, thirty on the gallows outside Magdalen Gates and many more in the towns and villages from whence the rebels came. In total, some 300 suffered.

The worst fate awaited the Kett brothers. Robert fled the battlefield and was captured, exhausted, at Swannington (the man who apprehended Kett was awarded 20s by order of the Privy Council on 3 February 1550). Together with his brother William, the Ketts were transported to the Tower of London, tried at the King's Bench and convicted of high treason. Returned to the county, the Ketts were delivered to Sir William Windham, High Sheriff of Norfolk. On 9 December 1549, Robert Kett was paraded through the streets of Norwich, brought to the foot of the Castle, weighted with irons and drawn up by a rope fixed about his neck to a gibbet erected upon the battlements. He was left hanging there 'till his body was intirely wasted.' His brother William suffered a like sentence at Wymondham, his body being 'left to consume' from the West Tower of Wymondham Abbey.

13

THE NORWICH CONSPIRACY

John Throgmorton, Thomas Brook and George Redman, 30 August & 2 September 1570

The great 'Stranger' immigration of 1567 brought a substantial Flemish and Walloon community of Protestant weavers to the city of Norwich. In the main they seem to have been welcomed, but there were dissenting voices. Norwich merchant grocer George

Certayne verſis / wꝛittene by Tho=
mas Bꝛooke Gētleman / in the tyme of his impꝛyſōment /
the daye before his deathe / who ſuffeꝛyd at Noꝛwich / the. 30. of Auguſt. 1570.

Languiſhe / as I lye /
And death doth make me thꝛall /
To cares which death ſhall ſone cut of /
And ſett me quyt / of all.

Yett feble fleſhe would faynt /
To feale ſo ſharpe a fyght /
Saue Fayth in Chꝛiſt / doth comfoꝛt me /
And fleithe ſuch fancy quyght.

Foꝛ fyndyng foꝛth howe frayle /
Eache woꝛdly ſtate doth ſtande /
I hould him blyſt / that fearyng God /
Is redd of ſuch a band.

Foꝛ he that longeſt lyues /
And Neſtoꝛs yeares doth gayne /
Hath ſo much moꝛe accompte to make /
And fyndyth Lyfe but vayne.

What cawſe ys then to quaple /
I am called befoꝛe /
To taſt the Joyes which Chꝛiſts bloode /
Hath bowght and layde in ſtoꝛe.

No no / no greter Joye /
Can eny hart poſſes /
Then thꝛowgh the death to gayne a lyfe /
Wyth hym in blyſſednes.

Who ſende the Quene long lyfe /
Much Joye and contries peace /
Her Cowncell health / hyꝛ fryndes good lucke /
To all ther Joyes increaſe.

Thus puttyng vppe my greaues /
I grownde my lyfe on God /
And thanke hym with moſt humble hart /
And meakelye kyſſe his rodde.

Finis / q' Thomas Bꝛooke.

☞ Seene / and allowyd / accoꝛdynge to the Quenes
Maieſtyes Iniunction.

God ſaue the Quene

☞ Impꝛynted at Noꝛwich in the Paryſhe of Saynct Andrewe /
by Anthony de Solempne. 1570.

Broadside of verses written by Norwich conspirator Thomas Brooke upon his imprisonment in 1570.

Redman of Cringleford spoke out in the city against the 'Strangers', claiming they were taking the jobs and livelihood of the citizens of Norwich. He demanded that they should be sent home, and if they were not he threatened to 'string up the Sheriff' and 'levy a force.' Joined by Norwich gentlemen John Throgmorton and John Appleyard, the Sheriff of Norwich and Thomas Brooke of Rollesby, they formed two groups. Redman raised a force in Cringleford, while the other was levied at Harleston Fair where they raised a number of men 'with sound of trumpet and beat of drum', and publicly declared the cause of their rising, namely, to expel the Strangers from the city and realm. Magistrates were informed of these actions; John Throgmorton was first to be apprehended, followed by a number of the others and the rising was put down before it really got started.

Those accused of conspiring to raise the force were held at Norwich Castle until they were tried before Lord Chief Justice Sir Robert Cattyn on 17 July 1570. Ten were indicted on charges of high treason, others with contempt. Found guilty of contempt, John Appleyard and four others were condemned to suffer imprisonment, and forfeit their goods and lands, but they could consider themselves fortunate not to have lost their lives. A number of the other conspirators were condemned to death, but only three of them were to go to the gallows for high treason. John Throgmorton, who had stood mute throughout his arraignment, confessed to being the chief conspirator upon the gallows, insisting that none had deserved to die but himself, for that he had procured them. Nonetheless, he was joined in his fate by Thomas Brooke on the 30 August, with George Redman following them to the gallows on 2 September 1570. All three suffered the dreadful fate of being hanged, drawn and quartered.

14
THE ROMISH PRIEST

Thomas Tunstall, 13 July 1616

Thomas Tunstall was born at Whinfell, Kendal, Westmorland; he was described as Carleolensis – that is, born within the ancient Diocese of Carlisle – and was descended from the Tunstalls of Thurland Castle, Tunstall, Lancashire. Among his ancestors was Cuthbert Tunstal, Bishop of Durham. Britain had split with and outlawed the observance of the Roman Catholic religion, so Thomas Tunstall took the College oath at Douay, France in 1607, received minor orders at Arras in June 1609 and left the college as a priest in August 1610. Roman Catholic worship was still an offence against the state, but a number of priests risked journeying to England in secret so that they could lead worship among the wealthy families who could afford to maintain and hide them; hence a number of country houses have priest holes hidden within their walls.

Tunstall returned to Britain under the alias of 'Richard Dyer', but was almost immediately detected and apprehended. He then spent the next five years in various prisons until he affected a successful escape from Wisbech Castle by rope. Tragically, he cut his hands so severely in the escape that he had to call upon the charitable protestant Lady L'Estrange to tend his wounds. Unfortunately for Tunstall, she was the wife of local magistrate Sir Hamon L'Estrange. When L'Estrange discovered his unwanted guest, despite his wife's entreaties, he had Tunstall committed to Norwich Gaol. Tried at the next Assizes, Tunstall was found guilty of high treason and condemned to be 'hanged, drawn and quartered.' This horrific punishment was enacted upon the Magdalen Gallows, outside Magdalen Gate, Norwich. Aware of his gruesome fate, it is said Tunstall pointed out he was a Friar by vow, though not by act, of the order of St Benedict and requested that his head be set on a pole and displayed upon St Benedict's Gate, with his quarters hung from four other city gates. The saintliness of Tunstall's demeanour on the scaffold left a profound impression on the people of Norwich, especially those who harboured loyalty to the old Catholic faith; his memory was maintained and Thomas Tunstall was beatified in 1929.

St Benedict's Gate, c.1720. The head of Thomas Tunstall was displayed on a pole here in 1615.

15

THE GREAT BLOWE RIOTERS

*Christopher Hill, Anthony Wilson, William True,
Henry Goward, Edward Gray, Thomas and John Bidwell
and Charles Emerson and others, 1648-9*

In 1647, Britain was in the grip of Civil War but Norwich had managed to stay out of any major actions by declaring for Parliament. When John Utting, a moderate man, was made Mayor of Norwich in 1647 he did not maintain the draconian hard line of the Puritans and by 1648 it was soon a common belief his sympathies lay with King Charles I. Leading city Puritan official Sheriff Thomas Ashwell and Alderman Christopher Baret,were concerned enough to ride to London and present their concerns to Parliament. A pursuivant was despatched to Norwich with orders to take Utting into custody and bring him to Westminster, leaving Baret to deputise in his absence. No doubt recalling the removal of Mayor William Goslyn from office and his imprisonment in 1642, many people in Norwich were not going to tolerate such behaviour again and immediately sent a petition to parliament 'testifying his good government and behaviour.' But on Sunday, 23 April 1648, with the pursuivant still in the city and with rumours abounding that the Mayor was to be carried away, groups of citizens began to gather and shout abuse at Baret and threatened to hang Sheriff Ashwell and the pursuivant on the Castle Mound.

By late evening a huge crowd, some of them armed, had assembled in the Market Place and a password, 'For God and King Charles', was given out. Despite technically being deposed from office, Mayor Utting publicly appealed for calm. On Monday 24 April crowds gathered on Chapel Field and marched to the Market Place where the pursuivant was lodged at the King's Head. The terrified official was smuggled out of the building and escorted beyond the city gates, but by the time he had escaped the crowd had began to riot and set about the house of Sheriff Ashwell, and others, who had taken their complaint to London. A request for help to quell the riot was sent to the nearest troop of cavalry, who were stationed at East Dereham under the command of Charles Fleetwood. The rioters resolved to repulse the troops but knew their improvised weapons, such as bill hooks, pitch forks and spits, were inadequate, so they raided the arsenal at the headquarters of the County Committee, not far from St Peter Mancroft Church on what is now known as Bethel Street. When the cavalry arrived, the fighting was most intense around St Stephen's Street and more arms were looted from the Committee House. However, in their haste to break open some of the powder casks and carry off the contents, rioters had spilt quantities of gunpowder through the building; one rioter even described how he had filled his hat with gunpowder swept up from the stairs. A number of the rioters retired to the Committee House, when suddenly – although hardly surprisingly – the gunpowder within was ignited

Pamphlet relating the story of the 'Great Blowe', 1648.

and the building exploded with the force of about ninety barrels of gunpowder. To give an idea of the scale of this blast, Guy Fawkes and his conspirators planned to use just thirty-six barrels of gunpowder to blow up the Houses of Parliament. The explosion ranked as one of the largest in the seventeenth century: forty rioters were killed and over 120 were injured by the blast, some of them mortally. In the immediate vicinity of the explosion a large number of adjoining houses were also destroyed, along with the windows of St Peter Mancroft and St Stephen's churches; the blast sending timbers, tiles, wood, plaster, stone and lead debris showering down across the city.

After this cataclysm the riot soon came to an end and many rioters were arrested and thrown into the Castle Gaol. They lay there until a Special Commission was arranged to try the 108 Norwich rioters at the Guildhall on 25 December (Parliamentarians treated Christmas Day like any other and wanted to prove the point). At the trial, nine were acquitted, twenty-four were fined £30 and sentenced to remain in prison until their fines were paid and eight, convicted of being the ringleaders of the Norwich insurrection, were sentenced to death. They swung upon the gallows at the Castle Ditches on 2 January 1649. They were all lesser tradesmen and artisans: Christopher Hill (brazier); Anthony Wilson (blacksmith); William True (dyer); Henry Goward (saddler); Edward Gray (oatmeal maker); brothers Thomas and John Bidewell and Charles Emerson (no trade recorded). They all received great sympathy from the crowd, for, as Christopher Baret was keen to point out, several gentry ringleaders escaped unpunished.

16
FOR KING CHARLES II

Major Francis Roberts, Lieutenant John Barber and others, 1649

The year following the execution of Charles I, in January 1649, was marked by counter attacks and dissent against Cromwell and his parliamentary forces. Royalist actions had been fought in Ireland and Scotland, while Leveller inspired mutinies had occurred and the ringleaders had been executed. 'Free-born' John Lilburne had already published a

The South Prospect of Black-friers Church in Norwich.

Blackfriars and St Andrew's Halls, known as The New Hall, in 1649.

savage attack in which he argued that the Monarchy was preferable to Cromwell's military despotism. In September 1649, he published *An Outcry of the Young Men and Apprentices of London*, inciting the soldiery to rise up in support of the Agreement of the People and the Leveller martyrs who had been shot for mutiny at Burford. Lilburne was certainly not alone in his views. Seizing upon what they believed as a ripe time, a group of Norfolk Royalist supporters attempted an insurrection in favour of King Charles II near Norwich, on 7 October 1649. But the plan was discovered before it had gotten off the ground and the leading conspirators were arrested and imprisoned. They had to wait until December to find out their fate. In his *History of the County of Norfolk* (1806), Francis Blomefield recounts:

> ...three judges were sent down to Norwich by the parliament, who sat at the New-hall [St. Andrew's Hall] as a high court of justice on Friday Dec. 20, in great pomp, with the sword, mace,&c. On Saturday they condemned six, who were executed the Monday following, on a gallows erected between the cross and the well in the market-place; on Tuesday they condemned six more: on Wednesday, being Christmas day, they passed sentence on Mr. Cooper, a minister at Holt, who was hanged there. On Thursday the 26th, five more were condemned: on Friday, Col. Saul and a shoemaker were condemned, and after hanged at Lyn. On Monday, Dec. 30, Major Francis Roberts, and Lieutenant John Barber, and two others were condemned; the two former were hanged on the gallows in the market, and the other two at two several market towns; one Mr. Will. Hobart, who gave witness against Mr. Cooper, was the next day himself condemned, and hanged at Dearham.

17
TWO NORWICH WITCHES

Mary Oliver and Mother Tirrel, 2 January 1649

As the last of the 'Great Blow' rioters went to their death upon the city gallows at the Castle Ditches, two old women named Mary Oliver and Mother Tirrel 'of the Hospital' were executed with them, having been found guilty of a very different crime, that of witchcraft. It seems that times of great social upheaval, such as Civil War, can cause such pressure on society that it can break down and the weakest, most vulnerable people can become the vents for the undercurrent of malice; as a consequence the prosecution of supposed witches became prevalent in the mid-seventeenth century.

Despite the surviving records for witch trials at King's Lynn and Great Yarmouth, the known surviving documentation for the Norwich trials is frustratingly sparse. Norfolk antiquarians have noted that Matthew Hopkins, the 'Witchfinder Generall', brought forty men and women before the Norwich Assizes for trial as witches in 1645; some sources state he sent as many as twenty to the gallows. Hopkins also cites the case of 'Meggs, a baker hanged at Norwich Assizes for witchcraft' in his *The Discovery of Witches: In Answer to severall Queries Lately Delivered to the Judges of Assize for the County of Norfolk* (1647).

The concerns of the Norfolk Assize judges had been aroused by the Revd John Gaule of Great Staughton, Cambridgeshire, when he published *Select Cases of Conscience touching Witches and Witchcrafts* (1646), in which he expounded his criticism of Hopkins and other witch finders for their greed, ignorance and methods. He declared them to be worse symbols of rebellion and chaos than the witches upon which they made war. Gaul expounded his conviction and abhorrence that:

> Every old woman with a wrinkled face, a furrowed brow, a hairy lip, a gobber tooth, a squint eye, a squeaking voice or scolding tongue, having a rugged coat on her back, a skull-cap on her head, a spindle in her hand and a dog or cat by her side, is not only suspect but pronounced for a witch.

Hopkins protested that his motives were both godly and sincere and claimed he had been the victim of malicious rumours which he published in *The Discovery of Witches* (1647). He died of consumption the same year but the persecution and prosecution of witches was carried on by others. They saw through the last capital prosecution of witches in the county that sent Mary Oliver to the flames, for the crime of murdering her husband by witchcraft*, and Mother Tirrel to the gallows at Norwich in 1649.

* NB: Most women convicted of witchcraft in England were hanged. The crime of petit treason, such as the murder of a husband by his wife, by whatever means, was punishable by burning at the stake.

18
'OUT OF HER WITS'

Anne Cowstad, 28 September 1659

The nineteenth century saw the creation of the McNaughten Rules (1843), which provided the first serious attempt to rationalise the attitude of criminal law towards mentally incompetent defendants. Before this advance, insanity was not seen as a defence in itself, but a special circumstance in which there was no acquittal. Juries could deliver a special verdict such as 'Guilty but Insane' and a commutation to detention would usually be forthcoming. In the less enlightened times of the seventeenth century, and before, many of those who would have been spared the gallows under the McNaughten Rules ended up on the end of an executioner's rope. Anne Cowstad was one of them. Considered by many to be a woman of odd habits, or to be 'out of her wits', Ann's crime horrified society; she was found guilty of murdering her two children. No mitigation was discussed, no mercy was shown and she went to the gallows on Castle Hill. She was buried in the churchyard of St Michael-at-Thorn, on Ber Street.

19

THE DUELLIST

Thomas Berney, 8 August 1684

Thomas Berney was young man of a good family, who lived in the house of Robert Watts in the parish of St Andrew in Norwich. On Saturday 19 July, he had begun drinking in the company of the High Sheriff of Norfolk and a number of other gentlemen, including Thomas Bedingfield of Oxborough. At about 2 a.m., on the morning of Sunday 20 July, the Sheriff departed; all those who remained were the worse for drink and a dispute arose between Bedingfield and a Mr Bladwell concerning one of his sisters. Berney remarked to Bedingfield that 'it was not kindly done to reflect upon a gentlewoman.' Bedingfield replied by striking him a box in the ear; Berney struck back, and others became involved in trying to part the pair, but Bedingfield and Berney took their fight onto the street and drew their swords. Berney claimed he could remember nothing more than he 'heard the blood pour upon ye stones.' What is known is that Berney fled the scene and Bedingfield was discovered with eight severe wounds upon his body, four of which were found in his back.

A hue and cry was raised, the gates of the city were shut and a search made for Berney. He was duly apprehended and committed to the common gaol and brought before the

Right Hon. Lord Chief Baron Montague at the City of Norwich Assizes on 14 June 1684. It soon emerged that Berney was a hot-headed man and not always very good with money. His friends were aware of this – but if they declined when he asked them for loans he was known to threaten them with his sword and had wounded several in such quarrels. The evidence weighed against Berney, and although he was clearly sober and very penitent, the jury were unmoved; they did not even retire to deliberate but directly found him guilty of murder. Berney was sentenced to death and hanged upon gallows erected at the Market Cross, in the Market Place, on 8 August 1684. An epitaph on Thomas Berney was published at the time of his execution:

> Here lies interred in this pitt,
> Ye relics of a pregnant witt,
> Till vice enamoured of his part,
> Instructed him in his black art,
> Knowing the fattest soil do breed,
> Ye greatest crop of every weed,
> But God in mercy unto him,
> Rouz'd him into a sense of sin,
> And by distressed misery,
> Unto him taught humility,
> When true repentance of the fact
> That drink and anger made him act
> And from ye ladders top I wiss
> He did ascend to heavenly bliss
> He thought his life was not his loss
> To snatch a Crown from off a Cross.

20

BEFORE HIS OWN HOUSE

Robert Watts, 30 August 1701

Robert 'Gaffer' Watts was a 'throwster' in the weaving trade; he was also an incorrigible drunkard with a filthy temper. On 7 January he was drinking at his local, The Globe, where his companions wanted to 'chaff him up.' In an attempt to top all previous jocular stirrings of Watt's infamous jealousy, one of the group claimed he had bedded Watt's wife and said he would prove it by getting the wedding ring from her finger. Unbeknownst to Watts, the boast turned into a wager; if he successfully went to Gaffer's house, found the wife and brought the ring back to the pub, he would receive a gallon of beer. Claiming he was acting at Gaffer's request and that her husband wanted to have the ring to settle a bet, she gave the ring to the man – much out of naivety as for fear of what Watts might do if she refused. He returned victorious to the pub; Watts was incandescent with drink-fuelled fury, and he stormed out from the pub before the deception was revealed, returned home, picked up a knife and stabbed his wife. Then, as a broadside of the story claimed in rhyme:

Trembling and bleeding, up again she flies,
Unto the window, where she vainly tries,
To call assistance; but no hope was near,
And so he cut her throat from ear to ear.

Soon apprehended for this horrible murder, Watts was tried at the City Assizes and was executed before his own house; the last execution of this sort in the City of Norwich, as all future executions for the City were carried out at the standard places of execution.

21
THE TRAGIC WIDOW
OF PUDDING NORTON

Mary Spilling, 14 August 1706

Throughout the eighteenth and early nineteenth century, instances of newborn babies and infants being murdered by their mothers were brought before the courts across the country. The tragic situations that led to these crimes were repeated time and again.

Women and girls attempted to conceal the birth and dispose of newborns, or widowed mothers, left destitute by the disappearance or death of a husband, killed their own children in a fit of insanity, believing it was the only and best option. Although the details are scant, it appears this was the case with Mary Spilling. Mary, a young newly-widowed woman of Pudding Norton, near Fakenham, was tried for the murder of her child at the Summer Assizes, found guilty and executed upon Castle Hill. After being left hanging from the fatal beam for the usual hour, her body was taken down and conveyed in due form for burial in the churchyard of St Michael-at-Thorn, on Ber Street.

22

THE CONSIDERABLE FARMER

John Ringstead, 14 August 1708

John Ringstead was described as 'a considerable farmer', but was tempted to commit a robbery with James Bately, a butcher, at the house of Mr Robins. They broke in and robbed him of £350, a sum that equates to about £37,400 in modern money. Both Ringstead and Bately were tried and found guilty of the crime at the Norfolk Assizes, at Norwich, but Batley was reprieved. Ringstead did not dispute his guilt, but he was at pains to point out he had never been concerned in any other crime of that kind; he went to the gallows on Castle Hill a penitent man.

23

'WITH AS LITTLE CONCERN'

John Perkinson, 9 April 1709

John Perkinson was hanged on Castle Hill for robbing and attempting to cut the throat of Mrs Mary Becham of Setch. He confessed he was concerned in the robbery but claimed it was Jeffery Day that had attempted to cut her throat. The *Norwich Gazette*, recorded Perkinson, 'appeared little daunted at the gallows and died with as little concern.'

24

TWO LOCATIONS ON ONE DAY

James Canham and Deborah Harris, 31 August 1728

James Canham was an unfortunate man; out of a total of six horse thieves tried at Norfolk and Norwich Assizes (three at each Assize), four received capital sentences. Three were reprieved, but Canham was the one left for execution, having been found guilty of stealing a mare from a Mr Bensley of Eaton.

Deborah Harris was brought before the Norfolk Assizes, being found guilty of wilfully and maliciously firing the house of Robert Cubitt.

When Norwich City and the County Assizes both had capitally convicted felons, the executions would be carried out upon separate gallows in the city on the same day, but this was a rare occurrence. In this instance, Canham went to his doom at the Castle Ditches and Harris upon the Castle Hill. The *Norwich Gazette* was somewhat terse in its reporting of these events: 'They that die are poor wretches, capable of leaving no speech worthy printing; therefore if any Grub Street of that kind be cry'd about, I declare it not of my publishing.'

25

BLACK JACK OF THE WEST

James Blade, John Painter and William Wright, 21 March 1737

James Blade, alias John Johnson, known to many as 'Black Jack of the West' (41) was born in the City of York. He was the son of a ship carpenter and he would have learned that trade too, but for his wander lust. During his travels he happened to fall in with a gang of smugglers and made and spent a lot of money. He then took to stealing deer, highway robbery and other wicked practices. One of the most infamous acts he committed was a raid at the King's Head, upon Stanfield High Green near Mileham. The inn keeper, Joseph Juliers, was robbed of money and goods worth in excess of £20; Blade would have murdered those present had he not been dissuaded from that path by his accomplice. After that he kept fairs in Norfolk, with the unlawful game of Pricking at the Girdle (or Old Hatt), also Thimble and Balls, and a newly invented game called The Black Joke, that became known as one of the greatest cheats ever invented. Black Jack also kept his hand in with robberies and thefts.

John Painter (about thirty-five years old, at the time of his execution) was born of poor but honest parents, who died before he was four years old. The lad was 'put out to nurse' by the parish in Wimbotsham, near Downham. Attaining maturity, he worked as a warrener, renting a warren at Brandon, and settled down with a wife and children. Then he fell in with a smuggling gang and worked for them as a servant. He was caught after hiding a parcel of tea in a blacksmith's shop; when he returned for it the following day, the people were up in the house. They secured him and he was sent to Bury Gaol.

After his release he met up with Black Jack of the West, his old friend from the smuggling gang, and joined him in his robberies. It was recorded at the time that Painter 'was a terror to the country people where he lived, who said he had been guilty of a great many robberies to their knowledge.' He was finally brought to justice together with Black Jack, the pair of them accused of stealing some horses from Watton. When they were brought before the Norfolk Assizes at Thetford, Painter denied the robbing of Mr Lome and said the worst thing he ever did was the stealing of rabbits, two or three dozen in a night, from the warrens that lay near him. He confessed the buying of one of the horses that was stolen from Watton, but Black Jack said he was concerned in stealing them. The pair were found guilty of stealing the horse and returned to Norwich Castle. They went to the gallows together, upon Castle Hill. With all of his back history, one would imagine Black Jack of the West would have something to say as he mounted the gallows, but having acknowledged his guilt to the Minister on the morning before his execution he said nothing on the gallows. Painter said nothing either, it was commented at the time 'He died a very hardened creature.'

They were joined on the scaffold by William Wright, a native of Syleham in Suffolk. He had been convicted of highway robbery after cutting off a woman's pocket on the King's Highway, near Dickleburgh. He claimed he committed the act with his brother and only received part of the money, which amounted to one guinea, 6s 6d. He was keen to point out it was the only robbery he ever committed, though then it occurred to him that he had also stolen about a bushel of wheat out of a barn.

The *Daily Gazetteer* concluded:

They all went drest in their shrouds, with the burial-caps stitched under their chins, and without shoes and stockings; but surely three such stupid and indolent wretches hardly ever swung out of the world together before... After they were cut down, Painter was buried in St Michael's at Thorn Church-Yard, but Black Jack and Wright were delivered to the Surgeons, who, I hear, are now picking their bones, in order to their being anatomiz'd.

26

FOR HORSE STEALING

Charles Grimmer, 27 August 1737

Charles Grimmer was a contrite criminal; he and another had been convicted of horse stealing, both had been given the death sentence, but his compatriot had been reprieved, leaving Grimmer for face the hangman alone. At the appointed time for his execution, upon the Castle Hill, he stepped up to the gallows and from there addressed the crowd. He confessed to his crime and said he was sorry for what he had done and hoped those that those he had wronged would forgive him. He begged all young people about him to take warning, and avoid breaking the Sabbath which, he claimed, 'was his utter ruin and destruction.'

27

THE END OF MAYS OF MASSINGHAM

Robert Mays, 15 April 1738

Robert Mays, of Great Massingham, was tried and found guilty of felony and burglary at the Thetford Assizes. Returned to Norwich, he was executed upon the Castle Hill gallows.

28

ANOTHER HORSE THIEF

William Gotts, 19 August 1738

Norfolk is a great agrarian county and horses were highly prized as both a mode of transport and as working animals. Many a livelihood and farm depended on them and so the penalties for those tempted to steal one could be stiff. William Gotts was tried and found guilty for horse theft by the Norfolk Assizes, at Norwich, on 31 July 1738. Executed upon the Castle Hill gallows, Gotts was not the first – nor would he be the last – to hang for this crime in the county. He was buried in Heigham churchyard.

29

ONE LEFT TO HANG

Robert Blake, 12 April 1740

Robert Blake, Thomas Spurdon, John Girling, William Cross and Robert Smith were all tried and found guilty of horse theft at the Norfolk Assizes, held at Thetford on 20 March 1740. Cross, Smith and another man named John Robinson, all of whom had been convicted of highway robbery, were executed at Thetford; Spurdon and Girling were reprieved and Blake was returned to Norwich for execution upon Castle Hill. On the gallows he confessed to his crime and 'died a very penitent man.'

30

TWO COUNTY RIOTERS

Andrew Lister and Robert Bezett, 23 August 1740

The high prices and scarcity of grain caused a number of riots to break out across the country in 1740. Thousands took to the streets in Norwich, King's Lynn, Yarmouth and other locations to protest. The properties and premises associated with millers and bakers were the main targets. In a number of cases the rioters turned nasty; properties were damaged, people were threatened and violence broke out; soldiers were called out to restore order. At Norwich, the troops fired on the crowd killing seven, including the young man assumed to be the ringleader, and wounded a number more. At the Norfolk Assizes two men from the county, namely Andrew Lister, a farmer from Upwell, and Robert Bezett, were found guilty of riot and left for execution. Brought to the gallows on Castle Hill, an eye witness recorded:

They both behaved decently and earnestly and begged those who stood nigh to put them out of their misery as fast as they could, by pulling them by the legs as soon as turned off. Lister denied to the very last his being guilty of what was sworn against him and a little before he was turned off said that he was 'the honestest man that ever died in a halter.' Bezett was 'turned off' first and Lister called out to the executioner to pull his legs. Lister soon followed and both were swiftly 'out of their pains.'

After hanging the usual hour they were cut down. Bezett was returned to his family and Lister was laid in a coffin by his wife, daughter and two of his own servants and carried to the country in a beast wagon and four horses to be buried.

31

THREE ON THE DROP

Jonathan Mattox, Benjamin Smith and Peter Latten, 8 April 1741

Jon Mattox, a Dragoon and a native of Bury (22), and Ben Smith, a Yarmouth gardener, were found guilty and sentenced to death for breaking into a house at Cantley. Having mounted the scaffold at Castle Hill at 9 a.m., both gave speeches confessing their guilt, for which they were about to suffer. Stating they were both sorry for their misfortunes, it was observed 'they behaved themselves very decently at the gallows and prayed devoutly before they were turn'd off the ladder, desiring the spectators to pray for them.' Beside Mattox and Smith was Peter Latten (also recorded as Peter Lattiman), who was executed for horse stealing. After sentence of death had been passed upon him, Latten 'exclaimed very much at his hard usage' and said he was not guilty of the fact laid to his charge, but he did admit he had stolen other horses in his time. He said very little at the place of execution.

32

FOR THE KILLING OF LAUGHTER

Robert Capps, 8 August 1744

Robert Capps was brought before the Norfolk Assizes on 23 July 1744, charged with shooting Joseph Laughter, the Bailiff, who had an action for debt against Capps. Found guilty of the crime, Capps was executed upon the Castle Hill gallows by order of Lord Chief Justice Lee.

33

MAD TOM THE HIGHWAYMAN

Jeremiah Pratt, 12 April 1746

Jeremiah Pratt, alias John Wilson, know to most as 'Mad Tom', was tried at the Norfolk Assizes in Thetford; found guilty of three indictments for horse stealing, he was sentenced to death. After his condemnation, Pratt confessed to robbing the Yarmouth Stage coach on three occasions; the Norwich Stage Coach once, near the windmill at St Stephen's Gates, and to robbing Mr Long of Spixworth, just outside of Magdalen Gates; indeed, he claimed he 'stole more horses than the infamous Turpin.'

In the hope that no other should be punished for the crimes, Pratt requested that those persons who had any horses stolen from them could apply to him at the County Gaol, and they would receive information from him. He told them whether or not he was concerned in the robbery and, if so, where the horses were disposed of. Returned to Norwich for execution, he met his end in front of a large and rowdy crowd upon Castle Hill.

34

RAPIST

Francis Cooper, 5 September 1747

Francis Cooper (18) was brought before the Norfolk Assizes at Norwich on 15 August 1747, tried and found guilty of the rape of a ten-year-old girl. Sentenced to death, Cooper was executed upon the Castle Hill gallows.

35

THE ROBBER AND THE FELON

John Ambrose and John Jarvis, 8 April 1749

John Ambrose and John Jarvis were brought before the Norfolk Assizes, at Thetford, on 18 March 1749. Charged with unrelated crimes, Ambrose stood accused of the robbery of Thomas and William Rouse, of Barton Bendish. Jarvis, on the other hand, was charged with a number of felonies in the parishes of Scarning and North Elmham. Both were found guilty; they were returned to Norwich Castle and executed upon the Castle Hill gallows at 12 noon on 8 April 1749.

36

THE NORWICH POKER MURDERER

Thomas Clarke, 1 September 1750

Thomas Clarke was tried and found guilty of the murder of John Bonney (also recorded as Banning), before the Norwich City Assizes, on 10 August 1750. He killed Bonney by striking him several times on the head with a poker. He was held at Norwich City Prison and, after the usual procession through the city, he was hanged at the Castle Ditches.

37

HIGHWAY ROBBERY

William Cann, 10 April 1751

William and Nathaniel Cann were brought before Norfolk Assizes at Thetford on 14 March 1751, charged with the assault and robbery of Lydia, the wife of John Tibbenham of Filby, upon the King's Highway. Nathaniel was acquitted, but William was found guilty and sentenced to death. Taken back to Norwich, he was executed upon Castle Hill. After hanging for an hour, his body was taken down, prepared, removed and gibbeted near the scene of his crime.

38

STEALING FROM THE STAR

Daniel Wilson, 15 August 1752

Daniel Wilson was tried before the Norwich Assizes, on 28 July 1752. He was found guilty of stealing two silver tankards, one silver pint mug and seven silver spoons from Mr Storey, the keeper of The Star public house on the Haymarket. Wilson was executed upon the City Gallows at the Castle Ditches. His confession was published at 12 noon on the day of his execution and cost one half penny.

39

STEALING SHEEP

James Palmer, 8 September 1753

James Palmer did not do things in moderation: in the days when you could be hanged for the theft of a single sheep or a lamb, he stole a flock of thirty-two, worth £3 12s, from his master, John Beck. Tried and found guilty at the Norfolk Assizes, Palmer was hanged upon Castle Hill.

40

ROBBERY IN THE CITY

Samuel Agar, 31 August 1754

Samuel Agar was a violent robber who assaulted Mr Coleburne in his home by presenting a pistol to his breast and demanding money. Tried before the Norwich Assizes, he was found guilty and was hanged upon the City Gallows at the Castle Ditches.

41

ONE REPRIEVE
BUT NO PARDON

John Hall, 16 April 1755

On 25 March 1755, John Hall was tried and convicted, at Thetford Assizes, of stealing a black mare out of a close belonging to Thomas Eldred of Wendling in September 1751. Hall was reprieved a quarter of an hour before the time fixed for his execution, in the hope he would reveal information of, or confess, to other crimes the authorities had firm belief he had knowledge of. It was to prove a vain hope, as the *Norwich Mercury* recorded:

…he was often pressed to do it but decided he would make no confession and unless he could be assured his pardon, what he knew should die with him. At the place of execution he behaved very decently and met death with great resolution. He fixed the rope himself and some say he threw himself off the cart. He was a jolly, well looking man about forty years of age. After he was cut down he was carried to Wymondham and buried among his relatives.

42

BURGLARY AT HACKFORD

Richard Taylor, 30 September 1757

The Norfolk Assizes, held at Thetford in March 1757, saw six men condemned to the gallows: Thomas Hall and John Mount for horse stealing; John Youngs and John

Walpole for housebreaking; Robert Bustins, for robbing Richard Brandford on the King's Highway, and Richard Taylor for breaking into the House of Robert Leeds at Hackford and stealing eighteen guineas. The judge reprieved the first four before he left the town, leaving Bustins and Taylor for execution. Bustins' sentence was respited, and then commuted along with the other four, who had previously been reprieved. They were sentenced to fourteen years' transportation each. Taylor was left to go to the gallows on Castle Hill alone.

43

NO SECOND CHANCE

Ambrose Towler, 26 April 1758

On 16 March 1758, Ambrose Towler was brought before the Norfolk Assizes at Thetford. He received due trial and was found guilty of a burglary and condemned. He was brought back to Norwich to be hanged; he remained a very penitent man and upon the gallows declared he was going to his death for the first offence he ever committed.

44

TWO ON THE GALLOWS

Samuel Creasy and John Carman, 1 September 1764

Samuel Creasy (aged about 40) was born of poor but honest parents at Oxborough in Norfolk. His crime was stopping Edmund Bullock, of Marham, while on the King's Highway. He struck him upon the left arm with a large stick – breaking the arm – and robbed him of 8s 6d. He was bought before the Norfolk Assizes on 13 August 1764; they found him guilty and he was sentenced to death. From his condemned cell, Creasy was keen to transmit the message that he was regretful of his actions and that he had not been concerned in any robbery, other than the one for which he was to suffer. (*see* 'In his Father's Footsteps', p.70)

John Carman (aged about 38) was brought before the same Assizes. Born at Tuttington near Aylsham, his father was a hog jobbler and apprenticed his son to a weaver named Howlett at Norwich. Carman became a family man and had settled with his wife and children at Haveringland. However, he was caught stealing sheep and was brought before the Assizes, where he was tried and found guilty; he was sentenced to death. He was fortunate to be reprieved and at the following Assizes, at Thetford, he was ordered to be transported for fourteen years. Carman, however, had other ideas and made his escape out of the transport ship, as it lay on the river Thames. But he was found 'at large' and was returned to court. He was sent to the gallows on Castle Hill.

45

A FATE WORSE...

John Holloway, 20 October 1764

John Holloway had been found guilty of felony at the Norwich City Assizes and was sentenced to transportation, but he escaped. However, he was found at large at Epping, in Essex. Brought back to the City Assizes on 13 August 1764, he was found guilty of being 'at large' and was sentenced to death. On Saturday 13 October, a week before the date set for his execution, Holloway attempted to break out of the gaol. Having freed himself from the shackles on his legs, he almost managed to cut through the rivet of the yoke about his neck, but he was discovered. They didn't want to tempt fate, so Holloway was more securely ironed and shackled and kept his appointment with the hangman in the Castle Ditches.

46

TWO NORWICH RIOTERS

John Hall and David Long, 10 January 1767

The bad harvest of 1766 led to a scarcity of wheat, and the hungry people of Norfolk resented the inflated prices and exports of wheat grown in the county being sent elsewhere. On 27 September, riots broke out in Norwich; goods were seized and scattered at the Saturday market, bakers were threatened with their lives, their property damaged, windows were smashed and a mob besieged the New Mills where 'bags and sacks of flour there cut and thrown into the river, the buildings unroofed and greatly damaged.' The mob, then 'actuated with fresh fury, proceeded into many parts of the city ... broke open houses, destroyed furniture, fired a large granary, threw corn, flour etc into the river and were guilty of every outrage which popular madness could suggest.'

The riot was put down by magistrates and local inhabitants without the assistance of the military. Thirty rioters were arrested and imprisoned in the castle. Intent on making some examples of these rioters, they were tried by Special Commission, with sessions at both the Shire House and Guildhall, on 1 December 1766. Despite Lord Barrington advising them to 'hang as many of your prisoners as possible', eight men were sentenced to death

An executed felon having been cut down from the gallows by an official is handed over to his family and friends for burial.

for their part in the riot: Robert Royce for beginning to demolish and pull down the New Mills in the city; James Fleming, John Hall and David Long for the like offence at the dwelling house of Robert Elvin, the baker. Hall and Long were capitally convicted for the second time for demolishing the malthouse of John Clover at Carrow. Then there were James Lincoln, Henry Nobbs and James Codner, who were sentenced to death for beginning to demolish and pull down the dwelling house of Richard Lubbock.

Only the doubly convicted John Hall (46) and David Long (56), went to the gallows on the Castle Ditches. After hanging for the usual hour, their bodies were cut down and carried back in a cart to the City Gaol, where they were deposited in coffins and delivered to their friends for interment.

47

TWO HOUSEBREAKERS

John Jermy and George Woodbine, 4 April 1767

On 12 March 1767, John Jermy was brought before Mr Baron Andrews at Norfolk Assizes. He was found guilty of breaking and entering and was sentenced to death. He had unlawfully entered the dwelling house of Thomas Barker of Wymondham and carried away goods to the value of £10.

George Woodbine was then brought up and found guilty of receiving part of the money from Jermy, in the knowledge it had been stolen; he was also found guilty, and was sentenced to death. Jermy and Woodbine were executed together on Castle Hill. After hanging for the usual time, their bodies were carried away in a hearse to Wymondham for burial.

48

ESCAPE FROM THE CONDEMNED CELL

Gibbon Houghton, 20 April 1768

On 10 March 1768, Gibbon Houghton was tried at the Norfolk Assizes, held at Thetford, and was capitally convicted of driving away eleven weather sheep out of Lanthorn Marsh in Sudbury, Suffolk. On the Friday night preceding his execution, Houghton made an attempt to escape by making a breach through the cell and made it through the roof of the houses in the prison yard. However, not being able to fix the rope to the battlements on the top of the castle he came down again, went into the vault and covered himself all over with the muck from the dung heap. The debtors raised the alarm and the gaol keeper sent a man with a pitch fork into the vault. After running it into the muck several times, it ran dangerously close to Houghton's body, upon which he laid hold of the fork and gave up his attempt to hide. Houghton claimed if he had not been found he would have laid there until he suffocated. His escape was considered a remarkable one, as the cell in which Houghton was held was considered 'one of the strongest in England' and he was certainly the first to escape from it – but he still kept his appointment with the hangman.

49

HORSE THEFT AND ARSON

John Sherwood, 13 August 1768

On 25 July 1768, John Sherwood, described as 'a lad about seventeen years of age', was brought before the Norfolk Assizes at Norwich charged with stealing a colt out of the stable of Robert Maltwood, of Carbrooke, and setting the stable on fire; it burned to the ground, killing another colt within. He was found guilty and was sentenced to death. It was reported that Sherwood acknowledged the crime for which he was to suffer and desired to inform the public he had no other crimes to confess. A reporter from the *Norwich Mercury* witnessed Sherwood's execution conducted at 12 noon on 13 August 1768; Sherwood was:

…courageous and did not appear to be under any anxiety at the approach of death but at the same time behaved himself in a very decent manner. At coming out of prison he

The execution of John Sherwood.

saluted and took affectionate leave of all his fellow prisoners and walked from thence to his place of execution and fervently joined in the prayers of the clergyman who attended him. After hanging the usual time his body was cut down and delivered to his sorrowful mother who came to town on this melancholy occasion. He was carried to Snetterton in order to be interred.

50

BLAME THE WIFE

Cornelius Green, 5 August 1769

Cornelius Green and his wife Constance were gypsies allowed to lodge upon the small farm of Thomas Brundle of Burston near Diss. Tragically, they saw this as an opportunity to rob Mr Brundle of about 20lbs in gold and silver coin, some of his wife's clothes and an array of other items. As a result, poor Mr Brundle was reduced to working as a day labourer. On 7 July 1769, Mr Brundle was working in a field near Downham when the Greens passed by – Mrs Green was even wearing one of Mrs Brundle's dresses. With assistance from fellow workers, Mr Brundle apprehended the Greens.

They were brought before the Norfolk Assizes at Norwich on 17 July 1769. Both Cornelius and Constance Green were found guilty and sentenced to death. In addition, the judge ordered the sum of 'four score pounds' to be paid to Mr Brundle by the Sheriff of the County (being the reward allowed by Act of Parliament for the apprehension of housebreakers). Before the judge left the Assizes, he reprieved Constance, sending her away with the transports instead. Cornelius Green was left for execution.

He was described as an 'ignorant' man and behaved in a very sullen manner from the time of his conviction. At the gallows he asked the hangman to hasten the execution and made a short speech protesting his innocence to the robbery. At the trial, and upon the declaration of his wife, Green protested he had only assisted in the robbery by standing at the door and receiving the stolen items from Constance as she stripped the house. His pleas were almost drowned out by jeers from the crowd, which continued until Green was 'turned off' upon the gallows on Castle Hill.

51

THE HARFORD HIGHWAYMAN

Joseph Barber, 6 April 1771

Joseph and Robert Barber (both in their twenties) were brought before the Norfolk Assizes at Thetford on 15 March 1771. They were found guilty of robbing £27 and assaulting farmer Robert Smith, of Bracon Ash, in a highway robbery staged between Harford Bridges and Swardeston. Both were sentenced to death but Robert was acquitted, ,leaving his brother Joseph to hang. It was recorded that Joseph 'behaved decently' on the gallows on the Castle Hill and expressed contrition for his crime, urging the crowd to 'shun idleness and profanation of the Sabbath, these vices being the first steps to the dissolute life that brought me to my untimely end.' The court ordered that the reward of £40 for the apprehension of these highwaymen should be distributed between Robert Smith, George Knight, Henry Allen and John Harrison.

52

PLUMB THE HIGHWAYMAN

Edward Plumb, 12 September 1772

Edward Plum was brought before the Norwich City Assizes on 18 August 1772, charged and found guilty of robbing Brandeston farmer Mr Bardwell on the King's Highway, at Mile Cross. Executed on the Castle Ditches, it was recorded that Plumb was 'decent and contrite to the end', confessed to his crime and agreed with the justness of his sentence. After hanging for the usual hour he was cut down, put into a hearse and later interred in the churchyard of St Peter Per Mountergate.

53

END OF A CITY BURGLAR

Jacob Cooper, 28 August 1773

Jacob Cooper was brought before Norwich City Assizes, on 3 August 1773, charged with breaking and entering the dwelling house of William Martin and there stealing over £53 in gold and silver coins. Cooper was found guilty, was sentenced to death and went to the gallows on the Castle Ditches. Contrite and decent to the end, after hanging for the usual hour his body was cut down and delivered to his friends for interment.

54

THEY SCOFFED AT THEIR FATE

Jonathan Jex and Henry Jex, 16 April 1774

Labourers Jonathan and Henry Jex, alias Jacques, were brought before the Norfolk Assizes at Thetford on 17 March 1774. They were charged with breaking in and stealing diverse goods from the dwelling house of shopkeeper Robert Boswell, of Stalham, on 13 October 1773. Their haul included 102 printed and linen handkerchiefs, 60 silk handkerchiefs, 13 pairs of worsted stockings, 50 yards of printed linen and cotton cloth, one black velvet waistcoat, 10 yards of Russian linen, 3 linen shirts, 4 linen shifts, a man's hat, a quantity of tea and one iron tobacco box.

Both were found guilty and sentenced to death. Henry (27) was born at Blofield while Jonathan (17), was a native of Pockthorpe and well known in the city by the name of 'Bonny Lark.' The *Norwich Mercury* commented:

These criminals have behaved in a very unbecoming manner from the time of their condemnation, rejecting the services of several clergymen and others who endeavoured to bring them to a full sense of their unhappy state, nor could they be prevailed upon to do anything towards making atonement for their offences. The night before their execution they spent in a most abandoned manner, singing and making a scoff at their approaching fate but at the place of execution behaved decently.

The execution was conducted on Castle Hill before a large crowd. The onlookers made easy prey for pickpockets as huge crowds surrounded the gallows, fighting for a good view, cheek by jowl. At this hanging it was noted a country woman standing near the gallows had her pocket cut open and was robbed of 14*s*.

55

THE LITERARY FELON

Thomas Green, 12 April 1775

Thomas Green (22) was a native of Chester, born to a reputable family. Having received a liberal education, he enlisted into the army but was led astray and deserted. He initially took up highway robbery but soon progressed to burglary around Diss. He was tried at the Norfolk Assizes, at Thetford, on 17 March 1775, and he was found guilty on three counts: firstly, for stealing a pair of leather boots and other goods from John Jones of Bressingham, on 14 December 1774; and secondly for two counts of burglary (specifically, stealing a silver watch and other goods from the dwelling house of John Newby and burgling the dwelling house of George Potter, during which he took a silver watch and other silver accoutrements, goods and monies).

A reporter from the *Norwich Mercury* witnesses the execution and recorded:

Coming out of prison he [Green] excited universal pity by his serene and graceful behaviour. At the gallows he exhorted the populace in a pathetic manner to avoid the vices which had been the cause of his ignominious end and after some short ejaculations he was launched to eternity.

After hanging for the usual time, Green's body was delivered to some of his friends and countrymen, who ensured it was decently buried in St Gregory's churchyard the same evening. Green had resigned himself to his fate from the moment the death sentence was passed and while he waited in the condemned cell, he wrote a short account of his descent into crime as a warning to others. This account, with an account of his execution, was published by William Chase three days after Green had gone to the gallows on Castle Hill and was advertised as 'may be had from Mr Ripshaw of Ipswich and all the Booksellers and New Hawkers.'

THE
LIFE
OF
THOMAS GREEN,

Who was executed on the CASTLE-HILL,
Norwich, on Wednesday *April* 12th, 1775,
for a *Burglary* in a Dwelling-House at
DISS, in *Norfolk.*

C O N T A I N I N G,

An Account of the several ROBBERIES he committed,
and the different Regiments he inlisted into, and
deserted from.

The whole WRITTEN by HIMSELF,

And published at his own Request.

To which are added,

The Copy of a LETTER he sent to Mr. RIPSHAW, Keeper
f Ipswich Goal, after his Tryal; and another wrote to him
before his Execution, by a Person confined in the Castle.

Also an Account of his Behaviour from the Time of his receiving Sentence, to the Day of his Execution.

N O R W I C H:

Printed and sold by WILLIAM CHASE.
And may be had of Mr. Ripshaw, at Ipswich, and of all the
Booksellers and News-Hawkers.

Thomas Green's account of his own life, written in the condemned cell.

56
A MURDEROUS ROBBER

John Rye, 19 March 1777

John Rye was bought before the Norfolk Assizes, at Norwich, on 13 March 1777. He was tried and found guilty of murdering Joseph Snelling, servant to Mr Joseph Barnes of Long Sutton, Lincolnshire upon the King's Highway at Little Fransham. Rye was, as an eye witness recorded, 'launched to eternity unpitied by an innumerable concourse of spectators upon a gallows erected near the Shire House upon Castle Hill.' The *Norwich Mercury* reported:

> The populace expressed the most indignant resentment against this execrable murderer
> by pulling and tossing him whilst hanging and after he was cut down the carcass was
> conveyed, with difficulty, back to the castle where it was kept till evening.

The Norfolk and Norwich Hospital, 1778.

The body was then conveyed to the Norfolk and Norwich Hospital. On Thursday, 20 March, after the head was scalped and the skull sawn through, a lecture was presented by Mr Donne on the brain and its meninges. The following day the heart, lungs and other viscera were dissected. Rye's was the first body to be anatomised in the city, or county, since the passing of the 1752 Murder Act. This mandated the bodies of executed murderers should not be buried, but should be sent for dissection or 'hanging in chains' otherwise known as gibbeting. An account of Rye's confession and robberies were published for one penny.

57
PAPIST ON THE GALLOWS

John Manning, 12 April 1777

John Manning (22), was brought before the Norfolk Assizes, at Norwich, on 13 March 1777. He was charged and found guilty of a burglary in the house of Mrs Jayne Boyden, at East Dereham, where he stole eleven guineas in gold, three gold rings, a plate and diverse other things. The date for his execution was set for 5 April, but he was respited after a petition, signed by several gentlemen of the county, was presented to the judge on his behalf. However, after due consideration the petition was turned down and the execution set for 12 April 1777. Manning was an Irishman and the newspapers were keen to point out 'he died a Papist' and bemoaned the fact that the cleric would be bound to keep the secret of any confession. At the gallows on Castle Hill, Manning did not join in the prayers of the clergyman that attended him, but he maintained an air of decorum and 'seemed to meet death with great fortitude. He was a true penitent.' His body was delivered to his friends and was interred in St Mary's churchyard the following day.

58
FIVE IN FRONT OF 20,000

Thomas Bell, Thomas Boddy, Miles Bridges, Zorobabel Partridge and John Griffin, 3 April 1779

The Norfolk Assizes, held at Thetford, on 11 March 1779 saw five sent to the gallows; an unusually high number, even for the age of the 'Bloody Code.' The first case was that of Thomas Bell, who was capitally convicted of shooting and maiming one of Lord Walpole's gamekeepers. Then there were Thomas Boddy, Miles Bridges, Thomas Partridge and John Griffin, all members of a gang found guilty of a number of burglaries and highway robberies. The five were condemned all swung on Castle Hill gallows before a massive crowd, which was said to be near 20,000. Numerous people had their pockets picked of their handkerchiefs, and one person, it was noted, lost his watch and upwards of 30s.

59
THREE HIGHWAYMEN

Michael Moore, William Fletcher and William Skipper, 7 April 1781

In reality, there were few 'dandy' highwaymen, but there is evidence to suggest that some women were drawn to young criminal types or 'bad boys', especially if they were young and handsome. Indeed, even the sympathies of crowds could sometimes be very much with young criminals, such as Michael Moore, William Fletcher and William Skipper.

The story began back in August 1780 when Benjamin Bell, John Fuller, and Turner Thurrold had been drinking on horseback at the Swan in Swaffham. They were about to head back to their homes in Castle Acre when they were joined by two strangers on horseback who said they were also going on the same road, so they all set out together. When they had travelled less than a mile from Swaffham, the two strangers launched an attack on their travelling companions, demanding their money. Mr Bell jumped off his horse and got into an adjoining close, while Fuller and Thurrold galloped on. All three escaped being robbed.

The highwaymen pursued Fuller and Thurrold but met John Rice, a Swaffham glazier and waylaid him instead, robbing him of his silver watch, and 4s 6d. While in the act of robbing Mr Rice, Mr Galloway, a farrier from Castle Acre, passed them – and when they had done with Rice, the highwaymen set off in pursuit of him. Knocking Galloway off his horse, the highwaymen beat him cruelly then robbed him of his shoes and £1 3s in money. They then returned towards Swaffham, passing Mr Rice. They were about 200 yards from the town when they encountered Mr Jermyn, a considerable farmer of Weasenham. The highwaymen beat him, tore his breeches and robbed him of his hat, boots, spurs, silver watch, around £35 in cash and a banker's bill for five guineas.

One of the highwaymen's horses got away while they were robbing Mr Jermyn; the unfortunate Mr Rice was travelling up the road so the highwayman dismounted him, took his horse and rode into Swaffham in pursuit of the lost horse. Mr Jermyn got back to the town nonetheless and raised the alarm. Several persons instantly mounted their horses and set off in pursuit of the highwaymen. Thomas Marcon, of Swaffham, overtook one of them at the end of the town, but as he lifted his stick to knock the robber off his horse, the fellow threw himself off and escaped into the fields. The fugitive was, however, discovered in a ditch and was properly secured along with the two horses. The other highwayman escaped on Mr Rice's horse, owing to the darkness of the night, but Mr Bowker of Swaffham, in company with Mr Thurrold and Mr Galloway, made a fresh pursuit in the following morning and overtook the highwayman in the middle of the town of Wisbech, where they managed to pull him off his horse and secure him.

Investigations revealed the first highwayman was one Michael Moore, a butcher of Bourne in Lincolnshire. When taken, he was found to have Mr Jermyn's hat on his head, Mr Rice's watch and Mr Galloway's money and pocket-book in his pocket. The other man had Mr Jermyn's watch and two other silver watches in his pocket, with about £30 in cash, with a purse and a gold gauge and key (that belonged to Mr Jermyn). This highwayman gave his name as William Smith (real name William Fletcher), a chimney-sweep by trade and likewise a Lincolnshire man. They were committed to Norwich Castle by James Nelthorpe, Esq.

The gang were soon identified as one that had been responsible for numerous depravations upon the roads of West Norfolk and eastern England. The horses they had been riding were also stolen and were subsequently recognised by two gentlemen, one from Leicestershire and the other from Stamford, in Lincolnshire. One of the watches taken from Smith was also identified as one that belonged to a Leicestershire tradesman, who had been robbed by the gang some time past when they also relieved him of nearly £30. The inhabitants of Swaffham were praised for their 'uncommon spirit and alacrity in pursuing and taking two such dangerous fellows.'

At the Norfolk Assizes, before Alexander Lord Loughborough, on 15 March 1781, William Fletcher, alias Smith (19), and Michael Moore (17), were joined by two other highwaymen from their gang, namely William Skipper, alias John Love (23), and John Ewston, alias Hewston. They were all found guilty of highway robbery and sentenced to death. Ewston was fortunate and received His Majesty's pardon on condition he entered into the service of the East India Co. Fletcher, Moore and Skipper were left to hang.

Penitent and behaving in a manner becoming of their situation, upon the Castle Hill gallows, the *Norwich Mercury* reported:

> …the fatal three acknowledged justly to suffer and asked forgiveness of all whom they had injured. Skipper exhorted all youth to take a proper warning of their untimely end and after a few moments in most fervent prayer they were launched into eternity amidst the sympathetic tears of thousands of spectators.

A postscript may be found in The *Norfolk Chronicle*, of 5 January 1782, that reported John Ewston set out, well guarded, for London, in order to be put on board an Indiaman.

60

IN HIS FATHER'S FOOTSTEPS

Samuel Creasy, 8 September 1781

Samuel Creasy was committed to the Castle by J. Fenn, Esq. in June 1781, charged on the oath of Mary Gage, of East Walton, with having stopped her on the highway in the parish of Wormegay, near Pentney, at about 3 p.m. on the afternoon of Thursday, 21 June 1781. Having robbed her of about 8s in silver, he then ravished (raped) her on the footpath near the River Nar that led from Pentney Mill to Wormegay. Brought before the Norfolk Assizes on 6 August

Illustration featured in the broadsides published after the executions of both Samuel Creasy Senior in 1764 and his son, who followed him to the gallows in 1781.

1781, Samuel Creasy was found guilty of the crimes and was executed upon Castle Hill; he was penitent to the end but should have known the consequences of breaking the law from the bitter experiences of his family. His own father had been executed upon the Castle Hill gallows seventeen years previously, almost to the day, for a highway robbery (*see* 1 September 1764). Creasy's mother was also held in the Castle for robbery, but she had died just before the Assizes.

61

DOWN TO THE PICKLE CASKS

Abraham Carman and Henry Cabell (senior), 5 April 1783

In January 1783, some villains broke into the house of Mrs Hambling, at Alburgh, near Harleston. The family were away in Norwich and thus the burglars took advantage of the time they had and stripped it of just about every moveable object, down to the hangings from the bedsteads and the meat from the pickle casks. They even regaled themselves with wine, leaving several empty bottles behind them. The burglary was only discovered when a neighbour found the imprints of horse's hooves in the orchard.

Abraham Carman of Laxfield, and father and son Henry Cabell (senior) and Henry Cabell (junior), of Mendham in Suffolk, were arrested for the burglary and were committed to Norwich Castle. Brought before the Norfolk Assizes, at Thetford, on 14 March 1783, the three were found guilty and received sentence of death. Henry (junior) was reprieved and sentenced to transportation; initially he was bound for America, but he ended up sailing aboard the *Friendship*, one of the ships in the first fleet of eleven convict ships to sail to Australia in 1787. These convicts and marines are now acknowledged as the Founders of Australia. Henry Cabell (senior) and Abraham Carman were left for execution and went to the gallows on Norwich Castle Hill.

(Author's Note: The story of Henry Cabell (junior) was made into *The Transports*, an acclaimed ballad opera by Peter Bellamy, released on Free Reed Records in 1977.)

62

TWO BURGLARS

William Green and James Trundle, 10 April 1784

William Green and James Trundle were both burglars tried for unconnected crimes at Norfolk Assizes on 19 March 1784. Green was found guilty of burgling the house of Robert Sayer, of Wells, and Trundle for burgling the dwelling of Hannah Bradfield at Sculthorpe; both were sentenced to death and went to the gallows on Castle Hill. They appeared to behave penitently and acknowledged their guilt, but just before they were turned off, Green offered a 'confession' claiming his real name was 'Author Bible.'

63

FOR THEFT OF A HORSE

Simon Tuffs (senior), 4 September 1784

Father and son Simon Tuffs (senior) and Simon Tuffs (junior) were charged with stealing a horse, the property of John Spratt, a miller of Great Poringland. Brought before Norfolk Assizes on 4 August 1784, both were found guilty and sentenced to death but Simon Tuffs (junior) was respited, leaving his father to go to the gallows on Castle Hill.

64

FATAL BEATING AND ROBBERY AT YAXHAM

James Cliffen, 24 March 1785

James Cliffen was brought before the Norfolk Assizes, at Thetford, on 17 March 1785, charged with wilful murder. He had conducted a violent robbery on a footpath at Yaxham in January 1785, when he cruelly beat brothers Peter and Henry Seaman to the ground, robbed them and left them to die. Henry recovered from his wounds but sadly Peter languished a few days before dying from his wounds, making this a case of murder. Cliffen persisted in arguing his innocence to the end upon the Castle Hill gallows; *The Times*

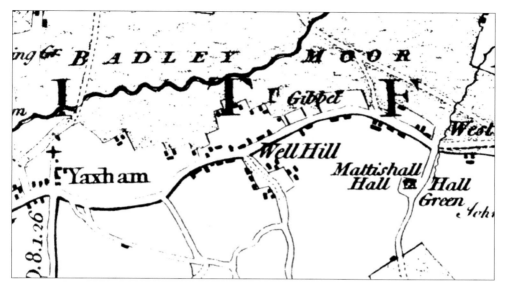

The location of James Cliffen's gibbet on Badley Moor near Yaxham from Faden's Map of Norfolk, 1797.

commented he 'appeared quite hardened and very indifferent about his unhappy situation.' After hanging for the usual time he was cut down, prepared and removed to Badley Moor, between Yaxham and East Dereham, where his body was hanged in chains upon a gibbet made by Samuel Banham for £8 16s.

65

FOUR ON THE DROP

Robert Randall, Robert Cadamy, John Ferrett and William Newland, 2 April 1785

The Norfolk Assizes held at Thetford on 17 March 1785 resulted in four men being capitally convicted and sent to the gallows on Castle Hill. Robert Randall (35) was found guilty of robbing Robert Homan of Easton and Herbert Watts and his wife of Mattishall upon the King's Highway in the parish of Costessey near Norwich. Randall would not put himself on trial, persisting in his wish to plead guilty to the indictment. Robert Cademy (26) went to the gallows for stealing a number of sheep, the property of farmers John Hall of Pinkney and James Parke of Greatend. John Ferrett (30) was condemned for the burglary in the house of Elizabeth Johnson, a widow, at Great Yarmouth and stealing thereout diverse goods, the property of Johnson Wallbank. William Newland (44) had been tried at the 1784 Summer Assizes and had been found guilty of a forgery on the Bank of England, having gone to Yarmouth with forged notes and employed people to go to Ostend and Bruges where, in this latter port, the first note was detected and the men found with it in detained until they could be seen by the Bank's solicitor. As a result Newland was named, traced and arrested. His case had been referred to the twelve judges; where it was confirmed, and he joined the other three on the Castle Hill gallows.

66
CUT THE HAMSTRINGS

Francis Vandergoose, 22 July 1785

Francis Vandergoose was brought before the Norwich City Assizes 18 July 1785 and found guilty of killing his wife by cutting her on the hamstrings. At his execution upon the city gallows at the Castle Ditches, Vandergoose behaved with becoming fortitude and acknowledged the justice of his punishment, but he denied any intention of murdering his wife. After hanging for the usual time his body was cut down and delivered to the surgeons at the Norfolk & Norwich Hospital.

67
THE SMUGGLER
AND THE THIEF

Peter Bullard and Joseph Loads, 6 August 1785

Peter Bullard (31) – tried under the alias of Benjamin Barwood – and Joseph Loads (20) were tried at the Norfolk Assizes on 18 July 1785. Bullard was charged with stealing a horse, while Loads was accused of stealing several pieces of silver coin, a watch and other items – the property of William Salmon, a yeoman of Ingham. Both were found guilty and sentenced to death; they dictated their confessions in the condemned cell. Loads was born at East Ruston. Despite the attempts of his parents to keep him on the straight and narrow, he 'became acquainted with lewd women' and soon became a drunkard and robbed Mr Salmon in a fit of drunkenness. He swore he never committed another crime other than the one for which he was to be punished.

Bullard was born at Mattishall and had worked on a number of farms across the county. Settling at Mr Painter's farm at Heacham, Bullard married the farmer's daughter, with whom he had five children, though only three were living at the time of his trial. Shortly after the time of his marriage, Bullard became involved with a gang of smugglers and was soon committing a variety of petty crimes and burglaries in the Heacham, Docking and Brancaster area. He became a hardened criminal, but when facing death he was concerned to record that he considered himself an accessory only. Bullard was associated with notorious smuggler William Kemble and his crew who, during a customs seizure at Hunstanton – backed up by mounted troops from the 15th Light Dragoons – on 26 September 1784, shot Dragoon William Webb (26), and Excise Officer William Green (37). Bullard was keen to point out that he saw Kemble fire the first shot and the soldier fall. He then described how Kemble obliged his men, with threats, to open fire, inflicting a mortal wound upon Green. Kemble and two of his men, Henry Gunton and Thomas Williams were captured and brought before the Norfolk Assizes in March 1785. Williams turned King's evidence but much to the surprise of many concerned, the jury found Gunton and Kemble not guilty and they walked free. It was soon after the Hunstanton smuggling incident that Bullard stole a mare from Mr Greenacre, of Ingoldesthorpe, and was caught and brought to justice. Both Loads and Bullard had dictated their confessions and signed them with an 'x.' Both admitted to their crimes, agreed with the justness of their punishment and went to the gallows on Castle Hill as penitent men.

68

FOR TABLE LINEN

William Westrupp, 13 August 1785

William Westrupp (44) was brought before the Norwich City Assizes on 18 July 1785. He was tried and found guilty of a burglary of the house of Lydia Warne, where he stole an amount of table linen. The sentence was harsh, but thanks to the attention of the clergyman who attended Westrupp in the condemned cell he revealed all the robberies he ever knew of or had been concerned in. It was soon apparent that Westrupp had been a member of a gang described as one that 'has long infested the city and have been a terror to its inhabitants.' When the day for execution came, the officials formed up at the City Gaol, and a reporter from the *Norfolk Chronicle* recorded what he witnessed:

> The Sheriffs attended in procession, which was rendered very solemn by the great attention they observed, in order to make a deep and proper impression on the minds of the spectators; the cart in which the unhappy criminal was conveyed was hung with black, a mourning coach preceded with the clergyman and the great bell of St Peter's tolled during the procession through the market, which rendered it truly striking and affecting.

Westrupp was hanged upon the City gallows on the Castle Ditches, and the paper enigmatically recorded: 'He gave several letters to be delivered after his execution.'

69

MURDER OF THE BURNHAM CARRIER

John Shilling, 25 March 1786

John Raven, a carrier from Burnham Westgate, was a man of habit who set out for Norwich at 5 a.m. every Tuesday morning. On the snowy morning of 28 February 1786, John Shilling of South Creake, a man who was well acquainted with the movements of Raven and who had stayed at the Hare at Docking the night before, armed himself with a shotgun and made his way across the fields. He spotted his quarry and followed him, keeping his head down under the hedge, until he came to a gap —where he opened fire

THE

TRIAL

OF

JOHN SHILLING,

FOR THE WILFUL MURDER OF

Mr. JOHN RAVEN,

OF

BURNHAM WESTGATE, Carrier,

AT THE LENT ASSIZES, 1786,

Holden at THETFORD, before Sir GEORGE NARES, Knt.

One of His Majesty's Justices of the Court of Common Pleas,

In the Sheriffalty of FRANCIS LONG, Esq.

———————

TAKEN IN COURT

———————

BURY ST EDMUND'S

Printed by P. GEDGE, and sold by BOOTH and SON, CHASE and Co. CROUSE and STEVENSON, BERRY and BEATNIFFE, Norwich, BARKER, Dereham, FORTIN, Swaffham, WHITTINGHAM and MARSHALL, Lynn, DUNN, Docking, POTTER, Fakenham, and by the Booksellers in Suffolk and Norfolk in General.

[PRICE SIXPENCE.]

A contemporary account of the trial of John Shilling.

without the least notice. The horse took fright; Shilling followed the cart, thinking he had killed the carrier, but when he did approach Raven, who had been wounded rather than killed, he asked him why he had fired at him. Shilling ran off to Docking, leaving Raven to nurse his wounds and raise the alarm. The tracks of Shilling's boots, studded with nails, were easily traced in the snow and a powder horn was also discovered. Mr Raven languished until the following day, when he succumbed to his injuries. John Shilling was soon under arrest and with the death of Raven was charged with his murder. Tried before Sir George Nares at Norfolk Assizes, held at Thetford, Shilling was found guilty, sentenced to death and was hanged upon the Castle Hill gallows on 17 March 1786. After hanging for the usual time, his body was cut down, prepared and, as per the sentence pronounced upon him, was hanged in chains upon a gibbet at Burnham Westgate.

70

BURGLARY AT HACKFORD

Edward Land, 8 April 1786

Edward Land was brought before the Norfolk Assizes at Thetford on 17 March 1786. He was tried and found guilty of a burglary in the dwelling house of Richard Bradford, a yeoman, at Hackford, in 1783. The stolen haul included a quantity of bacon, a pot of butter, two watches, a quantity of money, a pair of shoes and a shirt. Land was sentenced to death and hanged upon the Castle Hill gallows.

71

THREE HORSE THIEVES

Joseph Moore, Robert Sutton and Henry Cross, 26 August 1786

On 7 August 1786, three men received the full force of the law at the Norfolk Assizes for stealing horses. Joseph Moore (alias Joseph Gosden) and Robert Sutton (alias Robert Flatfoot) were charged with stealing a black gelding and a black mare, the property of John Wade and William Adams respectively. Another man, named William Waller, was also said to have been involved in the crime, but by the time Moore and Sutton were taken he was confined in Oldham Gaol. Further charges against Moore and Sutton, for stealing horses in the county of Middlesex, were also prepared in case the first cases failed. In an unrelated case, Henry Cross was tried for stealing a sorrel chestnut mare, the property of Mr Watling of Wrentham. All three were found guilty and went to the gallows on Castle Hill.

72

THE WHEATACRE
WHERRY MURDER

William Hawke and Thomas Mayhew, 30 March 1787

William Hawke and Thomas Mayhew were brought before the Norfolk Assizes, at Thetford, on 22 March 1787. They were charged with the murder of Henry Scarle, a waterman, on board a wherry lying off Wheatacre and Burgh Staithe. Simon Stannard was also brought up, accused of being an accomplice to these crimes but being admitted on evidence he was discharged. Hawke and Mayhew were found guilty, returned to Norwich and went to the gallows upon Castle Hill. After hanging for the usual time, the body of Mayhew was cut down and sent to Mr Davis, the surgeon of Thetford, for dissection, while Hawke's cadaver was conveyed to the Shire House and was publicly exposed and dissected.

73

THE FELLOWSHIP
OF CRIMINALITY

Benjamin Pearcey, John Camp, Benjamin Tungate,
and John Teasdale, 16 April 1787

Brought before the Norfolk Assizes at Thetford on 22 March 1787, Benjamin Pearcey (22) was tried and found guilty of robbing coachman John Smydies. He had relieved him of a guinea and a bad 6*d* on the highway in the parish of West Walton. Pearcey had committed the act in the company of Jonathan Booth, who had escaped from the law in Norfolk but was reported to have been hanged at Aberdeen for another offence.

John Camp (30), a weaver from North Walsham, was convicted of robbing Aaron Hubbard, who had fallen into a ditch in a drunken stupour on the King's Highway in the parish of Sculthorpe. Hubbard made off with a half crown, 1*s*, 11½*d*, a pair of buttons and a yard of cloth. Benjamin Tungate (42) – alias Littlewood or Baskins – was capitally convicted for stealing the horse of Mr Davy Windett, of Little Cressingham. Finally, John Teasdale (27) was given an appointment with the hangman for breaking open the shop of James Dawson, in Ludham, and stealing thereout a large quantity of various hosiery and drapery, including 100 yards of white lace.

Returned to Norwich Castle and held in the same cell on the morning of 12 April, the turnkeys discovered the felons had made a concerted attempt to escape. They had broken off their handcuffs and body chains, cut the rivets of their baffles and had begun to make a breach in the ceiling of the dungeon but the onset of daylight caused them to give up their attempt, having lost the cloak of darkness. All four felons were immediately handcuffed, yoked and chained and a guard was maintained in their cell until their execution upon the Castle Hill gallows.

74

NO ESCAPE FROM THE GALLOWS

John Clarke, 18 August 1787

John Clarke (alias Haynes), a native of Calthorpe, was a notorious stealer of horses who had been capitally convicted at the Norfolk Assizes in 1784. His sentence was commuted to transportation, but as he awaited the transport at the Castle Gaol, Clarke and another nine prisoners made a break for freedom. The gaoler was away from the Castle at the time, escorting prisoners to Thetford. He'd left a turnkey and two assistants in his stead, who were seized suddenly by the prisoners; their hands were tied behind them and, seizing the keys to the castle, the felons made their escape with their irons still on. Clarke soon returned to his old ways and stole a black gelding. He was retaken at Welney and committed to Norwich Castle by J. Smith Esq. Brought before the Norfolk Assizes on 30 July 1787, charged with the theft of the horse and being 'at large', Clarke was found guilty and sentenced to death. The attention of the High Sheriff had been drawn by the case and by the apparent celebrity of condemned man, and that he ordered Clarke 'should suffer as near as possible to the door of the prison in order that the felons within may be spectators of his untimely end.'

75

A HIGHWAYMAN AND SMUGGLER

John Crome, 25 August 1787

John Crome (40) was brought before Norwich City Assizes on 30 July 1787. He was charged with assaulting and robbing Robert Mendall of a silver watch and 6s (on the highway between Cringleford Bridge and St Stephen's Gate, near Eaton). Found guilty as charged, he was sentenced to death; while in the condemned cell in Norwich City Gaol he wrote this letter, dated 23 August 1787, to the *Norwich Mercury*:

I John Crome, having made no confession, beg leave, through the channel of your paper, to return my sincere thanks to Mrs Fakenham, the Governess, for the many favours I have received of her since my condemnation and also to the Sheriffs for making my situation as comfortable as might be and likewise the Revd Mr Buckle, the Chaplain, the Revd Mr Adkin and the Revd Mr Harrington, for their united exertions towards the salvation of my precious soul, which I hope, through the merits of Jesus Christ and a true repentance, I shall be enabled to receive at the throne of grace and likewise to all my friends who have been so kind as to assist me during my unhappy situation.

The *Norwich Mercury* also recorded Crome's execution:

Orders were issued by the Sheriffs that no person should be admitted to the prison on the day of execution, unless by their special permission, nor any work to be done, and that a strict fast should be observed until it was over. About nine o'clock the Sheriffs, the Revd Mr Buckle, Revd Mr Adkin and Revd Mr Harrington attended the chapel, when all the prisoners of every description were called in and an excellent sermon, suitable to the occasion, was preached... two criminals condemned at the last Assizes but pardoned by the judge before he left the city, were placed on each side of Crome, who appeared greatly distressed in mind during the service. About eleven o'clock the fetters of Crome were knocked off. He was then conducted back to the room where the prisoners under condemnation are usually kept and after the executioner had pinioned him, the felons were again called into the yard and a solemn procession was made round it. The coffin was carried by four men and followed by Crome attended by Blagbourn and Gardiner. At the jail door Crome addressed his fellow prisoners, beseeching them to pay a proper regard to the duties of the Sabbath and avoid the pernicious and lawless practice of smuggling which proved fatal to him, as being chief cause of his untimely end. Blagbourn appeared much affected at taking leave of Crome, and the silence and attention which reigned throughout the jail added to the solemnity... Having reached the place of execution on the Castle Ditches, Crome again addressed the spectators in a manner similar to what he had before done at the jail and then returned his thanks to the Sheriffs for their kindness to him... after spending nearly half an hour in prayer he was launched into eternity. We scarce ever remember a greater number of people attending on such an occasion, though the rain was very heavy both during the time and for several hours before the execution. The body after being suspended for an hour was cut down and conveyed by hearse and the next day was decently interred in the church yard of St Helen's in the city.

76

TWO MURDERERS

Joseph Wakefield and Henry Sell, 20 March 1788

The Norfolk Assizes, held before Justice Ashurst on 14 March 1788, saw the trial and capital convictions of two murderers. The first to be condemned was Joseph Wakefield, for the killing of Thomas Thwaites, of Honingham near Norwich, in November 1785; Thwaites had been gamekeeper to the Right Hon. Charles Townshend. After execution it was ordered that his body be anatomised.

The second conviction was obtained against Henry Sell (17), for the murder of Elizabeth Clark, wife of William Clark, a Walsoken farrier to whom he was apprenticed. Sell killed the unfortunate woman by putting a quantity of arsenic into the water from which she made her tea; unfortunately, this drink was partaken of by the rest of the household who were all stricken by the poison, only with the aid of a skilful surgeon were they brought back to health. Ironically, shortly after being taken into custody one of Sell's relatives died, leaving him the considerable sum of £900; it enabled Sell to employ an excellent counsel at his trial, but to no avail in the face of such damning evidence. After his execution, the body of Sell was also ordered to be dissected and anatomised. On the Castle Hill gallows both men behaved decently; Sell confessing to one of the clergymen, that attended him, that the motive for the crime was a quarrel with Mrs Clark over a broken tub. He added that having obtained the poison he had kept it for some days, even going so far as to throw it away, but to his regret he recovered it and used it to murder the unfortunate woman.

The execution of Joseph Wakefield and Henry Sell.

77

THREE FELONS

Richard Young, John Jacob and Richard Greenwood, 5 April 1788

Three more felons were tried, found guilty and sentenced to death by Justice Ashurst at the Norfolk Assizes on 14 March 1788. Richard Young was condemned for robbing Henry Larner, a carpenter from Methwold, of one guinea, 5s 6d in silver and some halfpence,on the highway at Northwold. Young's brother Abraham was also tried and condemned for aiding and abetting the crime. John Jacob was condemned for horse stealing and Richard Greenwood for a burglary at the house of Mr Peckover at Grimston; his accomplice, Daniel Cubitt, was also sentenced to death but was fortunate enough to be reprieved, as was Abraham Young. The rest kept their appointment with the hangman on Castle Hill.

78

MURDER AT THE LAMB

Timothy Hardy, 26 July 1788

Timothy Hardy had lived with his sister and brother-in-law, John Aggus (51), at The Lamb Inn on the Haymarket, until a marked fall in profits and stocks, due to petty pilfering by Hardy, led to his eviction by Aggus. A few month later, on Saturday, 5 November 1787, Hardy returned to The Lamb Inn and claimed he wished to put the quarrelling behind them and put out his hand to Aggus to settle the matter. Aggus took his brother-in-law's hand – but as he did so, Hardy pulled out a knife and ripped up Aggus's belly, causing part of his bowels to spill out. He said 'I have done for you and was my brother John Hardy of Lynn here, I would serve him the same – and now I'll stab myself, for I know I must die for it.' Hardy inflicted only a superficial wound to his body. Surgeons Denne, Norgate and Rigby were called to attend Aggus. They stitched up his wound and did what they could to relieve his pain but, despite their best efforts, poor John Aggus languished until Sunday evening, when he died. Hardy was immediately taken into custody and was soon brought before the Coroner's jury, who brought in the verdict of 'Wilful Murder' against him. Hardy was brought before the Norwich City Assize on 14 July 1788; he was tried, found guilty and sentenced to death, but it not being customary to have an execution while the judge remained in the city, the enactment of the sentence was postponed to the next Saturday. Hardy went to the gallows on the Castle Ditches (described in some accounts as Castle Meadow) attended by a dissenting minister. Resigned to his fate, Hardy acknowledged the justness of his sentence and cautioned the crowd against drunkenness, which he asserted was the cause of his dreadful fate. After hanging for the usual time, Hardy's body was delivered to the surgeons for dissection.

79

FOUR MALEFACTORS

Christopher Galloway, Ralph Dawson, Daniel Goose and James Ayers, 11 April 1789

Christopher Galloway (22) was born at King's Lynn to honest, God-fearing parents. When he reached maturity he went to sea for a short while, but did not like that life – and so he returned to land and began committing various kinds of theft, predominantly stealing horses. Galloway was finally brought to justice after committing a burglary at the house of Robert Batterham, at Terrington St Clements. Following his conviction at the Norfolk Assizes on 19 March 1789, his confession spoke of those he had injured during robberies, notably Mr Richardson, of Suffield, whom he had robbed with Ralph Dawson. Dawson (21) was brought before the same Assizes. He was tried and sentenced to death for burgling the shop of John Balls, at East Rudham. Dawson had been born at South Walsham to honest parents who had brought him up well; he had held three good positions, but when he was at Aldborough he had fallen in with a gang of smugglers and turned to a life of crime with 'manifold sins and wickedness.'

Daniel Goose (21) was born at Tasburgh. He was a weaver by trade but could not settle and began ranging around the county committing burglaries and robberies. Together with one James Ayers, he was tried, found guilty and sentenced to death for breaking into the house of Sarah Slagg, at Martham. They stole thereout some silk handkerchiefs, stockings, gloves and other items. A fellow conspirator of Ayers in a number of burglaries named John Turner was acquitted (*see* 3 September 1791). Goose also confessed from the condemned cell that he had broken into Mr Sewell's dairy, at Howe, with James Ayers and stole a quantity of butter, a hog and several joints of mutton fit for market. Executed upon the gallows on Castle Hill, it was reported 'all behaved with due penitence that indicated a due sense of their melancholy end.'

80
ROBBER BANKS

James Banks (senior), 22 August 1789

James Banks and his son, also called James, were brought before the Norfolk Assizes on 3 August 1789. Having committed a variety of robberies and burglaries, they were finally convicted of a robbery in the shop of Mr Watling at Banham. After the trial, James (junior) was respited but his father went to the gallows on Castle Hill.

81
MURDER AT WROXHAM

John Beckett, 19 March 1790

John Beckett (25) was born at Stalham. The son of a butcher, he was brought up in the same trade; on reaching maturity he worked for some years as a servant at Salhouse and latterly with a number of masters around the Wroxham area. Beckett was a troubled soul and was, in his own words, 'weary' of life and harboured 'a strong temptation to commit murder.' Beckett was acquainted with Wroxham lime burner Edward Allen, and once even discussed the way he felt with him. Both men then got very drunk together at the King's Head. The following day, Beckett kept drinking. Constantly haunted by the impulse to kill, he kept drinking heavily over several days until the evening of Monday, 8 February 1790. Beckett had seen Allen at the King's Head, where they spoke briefly, but when Allen left at about 8 p.m., Beckett followed him. About half a mile away, he attacked Allen, beating him to the ground; he proceeded to cut his throat to the degree that it almost severed the head from his body. He then robbed Allen of three guineas and a half crown and left the poor man weltering in his blood. Beckett was soon in the hands of the parish constable and was taken before the local magistrate, the Revd Daniel Collyer. Initially Beckett tried to deny the crime, saying the blood on him was from a dog that he had killed. But when he was confronted by the bloody knife found in his pocket, he could no longer deny the truth and confessed. Found guilty at the Norfolk Assizes on 12 March 1790, he was sentenced to death and was executed upon Castle Hill, Norwich.

82

IN CHAINS ON
METHWOLD COMMON

Thomas Jackson, 3 April 1790

Thomas Jackson was charged with stopping and robbing the Lynn Mail cart as it made its way between Stoke and Brandon, on 8 January 1790. He was subsequently tried and found guilty of the crime at the Norfolk Assizes, at Thetford, on 12 March 1790.

In an unrelated incident, two other felons, James Cam and Royall James King, were also sentenced to death for the violent assault and robbery of Roger Roberts, on the King's Highway at Keswick. All three were returned to Norwich Castle to await their fate and were held in the same cell. On Thursday, 1 April the keeper of the Castle discovered the three condemned men had made an attempt to escape; having forced several locks, they had managed to get into the larger rooms of the castle before they were found. All three were returned to the cell and closely restrained. Cam and King were respited for fourteen days and their sentence was eventually commuted but Jackson went to the gallows on Castle Hill an 'impenitent, morose and sullen man.'

After hanging for the usual time, his body was cut down; it was then prepared, placed in a gibbet cage and removed to Methwold Common, where it was 'hanged in chains' near the scene of his crime. The Gibbet stood on the common for many years afterwards – at least up to 1808, anyway, when it was sketched by the Revd William Newcome of Hockwold Hall. Nothing remains of the gibbet today but the area where it stood retains the name it acquired – Jackson's Hill.

83

NORWICH WIFE POISONER

Aaron Fakenham, 31 July 1790

In a case reminiscent of Henry Sell, the Walsoken poisoner just two years earlier (see 28 March 1788), Aaron Fakenham was brought before the Norwich City Assizes on 26 July 1790, charged with murdering his wife by poisoning. The dying declarations of Mrs Fakenham were presented to the court, wherein she charged her husband with being the cause of her death. A quantity of white powder was found in the teapot, but this had been imprudently thrown out before it could be examined. The surgeon reported, 'on opening the body there appeared an inflammation in the stomach and a livid spot about the size of a half crown piece.'

Fakenham had also given a voluntary confession to the Coroner in which he acknowledged he had purchased some arsenic 'near three months before, under the pretence of poisoning rats, which he put into both the teapot and kettle, of which his wife drank at breakfast.' Found guilty and sentenced to death, Aaron Fakenham met his end upon the City Gallows on the Castle Ditches.

84

THE HEN THIEF AND THE BAWBURGH ARSONIST

Robert Mullinger and Mary Adams, 9 April 1791

Robert Mullinger was a petty thief brought before the Norfolk Assizes on 18 March 1791. He was found guilty of stealing several hens, the property of Benjamin Bell.

At the same sessions, Mary Adams (alias Burgess) was capitally convicted of setting fire to the barn, stable, cow house, pigsty, cart shed and a hay stack of Thomas Burgess, tenant farmer of Mr W.C. Woodbine at Lodge Farm, Bawburgh, on 28 December 1790. The ensuing blaze destroyed not only the structures but six capital horses, several calves, as well as pigs and poultry. Adams had lived with Burgess for a number of years and had even taken his name, but when he discharged her, Mary was very bitter and was heard to declare she would have her revenge upon him at the first opportunity. Suspicion immediately fell upon Adams for the fire, and when she was apprehended a flint and steel were found in her pockets. When taken, Adams was in the company of another woman and both were taken before a magistrate. After a long examination Adams was committed to Norwich Castle. On the evidence of her companion, who had travelled with Adams to Bawburgh unaware of her intentions, she had waited as Adams went to the farm but suddenly saw the fire break out. When Adams returned, her companion enquired what she had been doing – to which she replied 'nothing that would hurt you!' She exclaimed, 'Now I am in my glory, nor did I care if I was in the middle of the flames with a shift of pitch, as I have got my mind!'

As preparations were being made for this double execution, it was announced that 'chains will be fixed across the bridge and the road on the opposite side of the hill to prevent the approach of horses during the execution.' This was following an incident at an earlier event at the Castle Hill execution site. On the day of the execution Mullinger went quietly and contritely to his end: as ever, the main focus was on a woman going to the gallows. Mary Adams did not conduct herself well on the gallows – or at least, that was the view of the press, who considered she did not choose well for the moment to make her confession, which she did 'in the presence of respectable clergymen and while in the act of receiving the sacrament.' In fact, she 'was so infatuated to say in the most positive and solemn manner her body committed the crime for which she suffered.'

85
A HORSE THIEF AND A BURGLAR

John Turner and William Bales, 3 September 1791

John Turner (25), a native of Swaffham, led a dissolute life. He had been tried at the Lent Assizes with James Ayers for various burglaries. Ayers had gone to the gallows (*see* 11 Apr 1789) and Turner was acquitted. He then went to London, where he fell in with a gang passing counterfeit money; he was caught passing the forged coins and ended up serving twelve months in the New Prison, Clerkenwell. On his discharge Turner returned to Norfolk, but found he had no money – so he decided to remedy the situation by breaking into and robbing the shop of Sarah Coates, at Great Cressingham. Turner was apprehended shortly after, tried and capitally convicted at the Norfolk Assizes on 15 August 1791. Once condemned, Turner was also keen to confess he had also been involved in the theft of a number of firkins of butter from a wagon at the St Faith's Fair.

William Bales (26) was brought before the same sessions. A native of Holme Hale, he kept bad company with two other men named Pitchford and Osborne. Bales was charged and found guilty of stealing a grey coach gelding, the property of Martin Folkes Rishton Esq., from a pasture near Lynn and selling same to Thomas Cook of Whitwell for 10*s* 6*d*. In his final confession Bales was at pains to point out he was acquainted with Pitchford and Osborne and had travelled to London with them, with horses, on a number of occasions – but swore it was his erstwhile acquaintances who had stolen the horse and not he. Irrespective of the content of his confession, Bales joined Turner on the gallows upon Castle Hill.

86
THE KETTLESTONE POISONER

William Anthony, 24 March 1792

William Anthony (33) was brought before Mr Justice Ashurst at the Norfolk Assizes, at Thetford, on 16 March 1792. The trial saw Anthony convicted of the murder of Sarah Cusher – who was carrying his child – after he had administered arsenic to her with the aim of procuring an abortion. Executed upon the Castle Hill gallows, Anthony denied to the last that he had committed the crime. After hanging for the usual hour, he was cut down, duly prepared and removed to Kettlestone Common, where his body was hanged in chains within a gibbet cage. The gibbet swung its macabre contents over the common until about 1822 when it was recorded that Charles Wright, of Dereham, picked up some of the murderer's bones from beneath it and wrote lines parodying *Mary the Maid of the Inn*:

> On Kettlestone's gloomy old common hard by,
> This gibbet was then to be seen;
> Not far from the road it engaged the eye,
> The traveller remarked it and said, with a sigh,
> What barbarous times there have been.

87

THE OLD GAME

Cook March, 6 September 1794

Cook March (24) was born at Hainford to poor but honest parents. His father was a hog-gelder and the young March followed in his father's trade for some years. However, as he did not like to 'be under any restraint', he then left home. He soon fell in with Elizabeth Garwood, described as 'a most abandoned woman.' March claimed she attempted to get him to poison her husband: she even gave him the powder to do it, but he put it in the gutter and washed it away. March tried to escape Garwood by moving to Bungay, but she followed. She came to him on the day of the fair and said if he did not take her back she would drown herself. She walked away – and fearing she might carry out her threat, March persuaded her to come back and they remained together.

It then seems they started working 'the prostitute scam', whereby Garwood would entice a man, only for March to suddenly appear and assault the 'mark', claiming to be furious that he caught him with his 'wife.' After giving the 'mark' a good beating, he would then relieve them of any valuables. Such acts would not normally be committed on main roads but in the darker, quieter lanes where prostitutes would take their clients. However, the crime was still classified as 'Highway Robbery.' March was convicted at the Norwich City Assizes, on 11 August 1794, of just such a violent assault upon Mr Eaton, who he had 'caught' with Garwood without Ber Street Gates in Eaton Hall Lane. In his confession, March admitted to violently assaulting Eaton and claimed that they both fell in the struggle:

> I got up and said 'I will make you pay dearly for being with my wife'; we fell together a second time; when Mr Eaton said, 'For God's sake spare my life.' He then gave me 6s 6d. I then let him go. I gave Sally Fox 6d to hold her tongue and gave 1s also to Garwood.

The execution of Cook March from a broadside sold after his execution.

March went on to confess to the robbery of Mr Howlett, who he beat and robbed of a guinea and a £20 note under similar circumstances. March met his end upon the City Gallows on the Castle Ditches.

88
'BLOODY WILL'

William Suffolk, 24 March 1797

William Suffolk (46) was born and bred in the village of Swafield near North Walsham. In 1797, he was a married man working his family smallholding to support his wife, four children and his long-widowed father. All seemed well in this typical country family until Will's wily eye rested on their attractive young neighbour, Mary Beck. Their relationship resulted in Mary falling pregnant. Her state was kept a secret as long as they could, but when her corsets and skirts would no longer conceal the ever-growing bump they fled to 'the grass countries', where she gave birth to the child in secret. Neither seemed to want the poor babe and Suffolk was 'confederate' in the child's murder and disposal of the body.

Whether Suffolk's wife was aware of the situation and took him back after he pleaded forgiveness, or whether Suffolk managed to concoct some story to cover his absence with young Mary is not clear – but it seems both parties returned to their respective households after their absence. Beck and Suffolk had one last fling after their return, but Mary, urged by her brother, then decided she wanted no more of their affair and told Suffolk so. The following day Suffolk caught up with Mary near Witton Heath. Mary was returning after selling three bushels of wheat, the profits of which Suffolk considered to be his. Mary

THE
LAST DYING
Speech and Confeſſion,
OF
William Suffolk,

Who was executed this Day on the CASTLE-HILL, Norwich: For the moſt cruel and barberous Murder of MARY BECK, (who is to be hung in Chains near where the Murder was done.)

I WILLIAM SUFFOLK am in the forty-ſix year of my age, was born in the pariſh of Sweael, in the County of Norfolk, of poor but honeſt parents, following the employ of huſbandry, till this unhappy thing took place. Accordingly I became acquainted with Mary Beck, and having gone up and down the graſs countries for ſome years we cohabited together as man and wife; ſhe living near to me, we ſecretly carried on the wicked correſpondence together as we had done before, during which time ſhe fell with child by me, tho' unknown to the public; after this we went into the graſs countries again, where ſhe was delivered of her infant child, which I confeſs as a dying man, that ſhe and I was both confederate in the murder of the infant, tho' unknown to the world; therefore as a dying man I confeſs the juſtice of my ſentence being guilty of the murder.

She having ſold three buſhels of wheat, upon the return, I requeſted the money which ſhe refuſed to give me, telling me it was not her property to give, for the owed it to her brother: I then aſk her why ſhe yield'd to me the night paſt, ſhe ſaid ſhe would not yield to me no more, nor be no more in my company. I then ſtroke her a blow with a cudgel I had in my hand, upon which ſhe fell to the ground; I than repeated the blows three times, and left their for dead for what I know: I then took and dragged her croſs the horſe-road, and left her head in the cart-rutt, ſuppoſing the people would think ſhe was kill'd by accident; but herein ſin and the devil deceived me, for no ſooner had I done it than I was forc'd to confeſs of the murder: But being harden'd in ſin I told the Juſtice if I got acquitted of this, I had two more to murder, and that was my Wife and the Brother of the deceaſed; but here I hope they will freely forgive me. My Mother has been dead a long time, but I have a poor aged Father now alive, a Wife and four poor little children; herein I earneſtly beg that all good people would not caſt any reflection on them for my conduct. I die in peace with all mankind. Witneſs my Hand.
William Suffolk.

The awfull reflection on the horrid crime of murder, firſt murder committed with premeditated deſign is in general the laſt ſtage of a long courſe of wickedneſs, during which the villain is hardened by conſtant practices, to ſuch a degree as to ſtop at nothing to obtain his purpoſes what ever they are, men of this diſcription tho' they perhaps may commit murder, but once in their lives, it is not from a ſence of its wickedneſs, for they are always capable of it, but from a dread of its conſequences; ſo certain is the truth of the old ſaying murder cannot be hid, that, they know that by committing this laſt and worſt of crimes, that they would ſum up their wickedneſs, and fill the meaſure of their iniquities: Secondly murder is frequantly the reſult of a ſuden impulſe of paſſion, proceeding from provocation, murder committed under ſuch circumſtances is generally conſidered as leſs wicked, and people are apt to think the murderer rather unfortunate than guilty; eſpecialy if his former conduct of life has been without reproach, men that have ſo little guard over their paſſions, ſhould for the aſſiſting grace of God; otherwiſe they may ſome time commit a ſin of the moſt henious kind, the puniſhment of which is certain and ſevere. To conclude murder is the greateſt of crimes, as it render the perpetrator of it the abhorrence of his fellow creature, brings him unpitied to a ſhameful death, and above all draws down upon his guilty head the heavy diſpleaſure of Almighty God. Let us pray therefore leaſt we fall into temptation, either from diſhoneſty or paſſion, that may lead us to ſo dreadful a ſin.

Broadside sold at the execution of 'Bloody' Will Suffolk.

indignantly said it was not hers to give because she owed her brother the money. The argument soon escalated as Suffolk made advances towards Mary and she rebuffed him. Suffolk demanded to know why she yielded to him the night before, to which she replied she would yield no more, nor did she wish to be in his company again. This was too much for Suffolk and he struck her a mighty blow with the cudgel he was carrying and felled the girl, whereupon he rained a further three massive blows upon her head with his stick cracking her skull. He then dragged her lifeless body across the cart track and left her head in the rut in the hope that those who discovered her would believe she had been killed in some tragic accident.

On his way home Suffolk was spotted by a group of locals who challenged him to why he was spattered in blood. His answers did not add up; a cry arose shortly after when Mary was discovered and the parish constable was summoned. Despite her horrific injuries, Mary still had enough life left in her to name her assailant but died soon after. When he was brought before the justice, Suffolk declared, 'I had two more to murder… my wife and Mary's brother.' Tried at the Norfolk Lent Assizes, at Thetford, he was found guilty of the murder, returned to Norwich Castle and executed upon Norwich Castle Hill before a large crowd. The notoriety of 'Bloody Will' Suffolk was confirmed with broadsheets and ballads, and was even the subject of church sermons around the county – a salutary tale to warn of the dangers of illicit passions and what they would drive people to do in their pursuit. The body of 'Bloody Will' was parboiled, tarred and placed in a gibbet cage; it was then carted back to near the scene of his crime and mounted on a tall gibbet erected on the cart track on Witton Heath, just off the North Walsham to Bacton Road. Many folks came to view the swinging remains of this notorious criminal. Eventually, his body became so unsightly – and so depleted by souvenir hunters – that it was taken down, by order of the magistrates, and buried without ceremony near the site in June 1803.

(Although nothing remains of the structure today, Gibbet Piece can still be located in Bacton Wood; OS 252 : TG 312 311).

89

ROYAL INTERVENTION

Robert Scott, 15 April 1797

Robert Scott (58) and his sons, Robert and John, were tried and convicted at the Norfolk Assizes, held at Thetford, on 17 March 1797. They had all been found guilty of stealing six heifers and one steer, the property of Messrs Fox, Page and Baker of Hindolvestone. Father and sons were all sentenced to death, but the Scott boys were fortunate to have their sentences commuted to imprisonment, leaving their father to hang alone. It was reported that HRH Prince William of Gloucester, on the solicitation of the gaoler and other persons who were present at His Highness's recent visit to the castle took an interest in the case. He attempted to save Robert Scott, but because he was thought to have dragged his sons into the life of crime, the exertions of the Prince proved abortive and Scott went to the gallows on Castle Hill.

90
MURDER OF HER ILLEGITIMATE CHILD

Rebecca Howard, 9 August 1797

Rebecca Howard (27), appeared at the Norwich Assizes, before Mr Justice Heath, in August 1797, charged with the wilful murder of her illegitimate child. According to the evidence presented in court, Howard had given the child to the care of a Mrs Margerson in July 1796 while she went to help with the harvest. On Sunday, 4 September, Howard returned and collected the child; the little one had taken to calling Mrs Margerson 'mother' and it aroused suspicion when Howard said, as she left, 'Kiss your mother, as you may never see her again.' Howard lived with Mrs Pearce and on that afternoon she returned there between 3 or 4 p.m. She then went out again and did not return until around midnight. On her return there was no baby to be seen. Mrs Pearce asked what she had done with the child, and, Howard replied, 'I hope it is happy and better care will be taken of it than I could give it.'

She added, 'I would not have come home all night if I had not been afraid of alarming you.' Pearce pointed out she was more alarmed at the loss of the child than she would have been at the prisoner's absence. Mrs Pearce was to remark that during the conversation Howard did not appear agitated in any way.

On 5 September 1796, James Pyke, a waterman, discovered the body of a male child floating amongst some weeds in the river near the malthouse, on the right-hand side of Bishop's Bridge. He recovered the body and carried it to the Adam and Eve pub in order that the Coroner might hold an inquest upon the body. The child was soon identified as that belonging to Rebecca Howard. Her behaviour during the trial was recorded as firm and collected, but while the jury were deliberating on the verdict she 'swooned away'. They were in conference for only a short while before they returned a verdict of guilty and the judge passed sentence of death.

In the lead up to her execution, Howard conducted herself with the greatest propriety. At about noon, she was conveyed from the City Gaol on St Giles to the Castle Ditches, attended by the Chaplain and a Methodist preacher. When she arrived at the gallows, after singing a psalm with peculiar emphasis, Howard addressed herself to the spectators, and exhorted them to a due observance of the Sabbath, and to place all their confidence in God; if they did which, all other things would be added to them. She then sat down. When asked if she was ready, she said, 'Stop, I want to say something else'. She then earnestly cautioned young folks of her own sex to avoid temptation and to be on their guard against deceitful men, who had brought her to an ignominious death. She acknowledged the justness of her sentence, thanked the Governor of Norwich Gaol for his humanity and attention, and expressed her forgiveness of all her enemies. Having taken leave of a young man and woman with an affectionate kiss, she exclaimed, 'Lord, have mercy on me! God bless you all!' and was immediately launched into eternity. After hanging the usual time her body was delivered to the surgeons for dissection.

91
END OF THE ESCAPERS

John Witham and Jonathan Green, 26 August 1797

John Witham and Jonathan Green were being held in Norwich Castle under sentence of transportation when they managed to escape. While they were at large, they burgled the shop of John Bloomfield, a breeches maker at Holt, stealing two pairs of leather breeches and a pair of buskins. On 11 July 1797, Mr Bloomfield had been to Norwich. On his return, when about 2 miles from the gates, he met Witham, a man he had seen before, walking with a woman on the road. Witham was wearing a pair of buskins which he suspected was the same as the very pair he had lost. Bloomfield immediately collared Witham and took him to Norwich. On that journey, Witham confessed he had escaped from the Castle and told Bloomfield if he gave him or the woman with him, whom he called his wife, a certain sum, he would inform him where the rest of his property was. Bloomfield would not entertain a deal so Witham changed his tack and gave information where his accomplice, Green, was to be found; Green was soon apprehended at Colby with a pair of breeches on that Bloomfield also recognised as his work and property.

While Green and Witham were back in Norwich Castle prison they attempted to make their escape again. They broke the stout padlocks which fastened their irons and also their body belts and were making breaches in the walls of their cells but the vigilance of the Governor and his assistants foiled their attempt and the pair were even more securely restrained. Brought before the Norfolk Assizes on 5 August 1797, they were found guilty and sentenced to death. There were to be no more escapes from Green and Witham as they kept their appointment with the executioner on Castle Hill.

92
RAPISTS

James Fleming and Samuel Windham, 3 August 1799

James Flemming and Samuel Windham, a Sergeant and a Corporal in the 34th Foot, respectively, were brought before James Mingay at the Lent Assizes for Norfolk, at

Thetford, on 18 March 1799. They were charged with having raped Rebecca Brighton (also shown as Beighton in some accounts), a girl of between eleven and twelve years of age, at Fundenhall on 29 July 1798. Evidence presented in court told of how her father, Edward Brighton, a local farmer, had gone to the King's Head at Ashwellthorpe and the girl followed. The soldiers were drinking there, as was a Private William Bynton, of the same regiment. The girl went to walk in the garden and was followed by Flemming and Windham. Bynton also followed, suspicious of their intentions. He saw all that passed but to his shame did not intervene. In the aftermath of the assault the three soldiers were taken before local magistrate Roger Kerrison Esq. Rebecca was treated as a competent witness and gave her deposition along with parents and the surgeon that examined the girl. No doubt fearing for his own skin, Private Bynton also told of all he saw. Poor Rebecca died on 4 March 1799; her case was brought before the Assizes just a few days later. Flemming and Windham were both found guilty and sentenced to death. After a legal wrangle and a question over the justness of the sentence, the execution was held in abeyance until the Twelve judges assembled to consult upon the case, on the first day of Trinity Term in 1799. They were all of the opinion that the prisoners were properly convicted and that all the points had been properly determined at the Assizes; the two rapists went to the gallows upon Castle Hill.

93

THE FORGER AND HIS TOOL

Samuel Wright, 12 April 1800

Samuel Wright (45) and William Bailey (34) were tried at the Norfolk Assizes, at Thetford, charged on two indictments, containing eight counts, for forging Bank of England notes. During the course of the trial it became very clear the main culprit was Wright, and he was found guilty and sentenced to death. Bailey was 'only an innocent tool', and was acquitted. Wright was executed on the Castle Hill and behaved with 'becoming penitence' to the end.

94
DID HE OR DIDN'T HE?

Henry Lawn, 15 August 1801

Henry Lawn (41) was found guilty of burgling the house of Mr Monsier and stealing a sorrel horse, the property of Mrs Elizabeth Utting of Wortwell; he was executed upon Castle Hill, Norwich. Despite property stolen at the time of the burglary being found in his possession, Lawn denied he was guilty to the last, swearing he had received them from a man who had subsequently absconded. Lawn left a wife and six children. After execution his body was given to his friends for interment. Curiously, Lawn had little reason to commit the crimes, for he would have inherited a considerable property in due course.

95
HANGED FOR TEN SHEEP

William Rix, 28 August 1802

William Rix (24) was born and was raised in Denton, to poor but honest parents. He was capitally convicted for stealing four sheep from Mr Whitton and six sheep from Mr Moyse, both in his home village. Rix was tried for this crime and found guilty along with his accomplice Christopher Smith (19). Smith was fortunate enough to have his sentence commuted to imprisonment, but Rix was sent to the gallows. Rix confessed to his crime, attributing his fate to 'idleness and bad company. ' After he met his end on Norwich Castle Hill, the newspapers callously commented: 'He has left a wife, but happily his only child has died since his imprisonment.'

96
FIRST ON THE 'NEW DROP'

Leeds Mays, 6 April 1805

Leeds Mays (32) was committed to the County Gaol by magistrate the Revd William Yonge in November 1804. He was charged with stealing a black gelding, the property of Fryer Richardson of Chatteris, in the Isle of Ely. He also stood charged with having stolen a brown hobby horse, the property of William Brewster of Forncett St Peter, in Norfolk. Two heifers, also found in the possession of Mays, were strongly suspected to have been stolen. These latter beasts were recognised as the property of Edward Pleasance and Daniel Hargley of Crimplesham. Mays was one of thirteen criminals tried, found guilty of their crimes and sentenced to death at Thetford Assizes, but only Mays failed to be respited and went to the gallows on Castle Hill, Norwich. His execution is significant because he was the first man to be executed upon the 'New Drop.' In the reportage of the event the *Norwich Mercury* announces the new method of execution and reflects the growing anti-execution feeling at the time:

> Leeds Mays, the unhappy convict sentenced to death at the late Assize, will be executed this day at twelve o'clock on the Castle Hill. A drop, similar to the machine in London, will be employed for the first time and, humanity hopes, for the last.

On this same day, those who took an interest in public punishments would have also seen Charles Pegg whipped in Norwich Market Place for purchasing soldier's necessaries.

97
THE SWORD OF LYNN

William Carter, 4 April 1807

William Carter (32) stole a brown mare and a man's saddle, the property of Mr Garwood, from his stable at Thurlton. Apprehended after fleeing to Colchester, he was tried and found guilty at Thetford Assizes and was executed upon Castle Hill, Norwich.

Despite being an intelligent man and a skilled cobbler, born of respectable parents from King's Lynn, Carter took to a life of crime and served aboard the prison hulks for a robbery at Lincoln. He was committed to Newgate for stealing a pair of boot legs and served his sentence in the Coldbath Fields Prison. Mr Sutor, the turnkey at Newgate, advised Carter to quit London and return to the port town of Yarmouth in Norfolk, which he did, but, sad to say, Carter left the town with a bridle in his hand and the determination to steal a horse. This act led to his arrest, trial and ultimate doom. After sentence was passed upon him, Carter formally confessed to being involved in highway robbery and two robberies at Lynn twelve years previously. He was also known to have allegiances to the revolutionary cause and it was recorded that he had confessed to a fellow prisoner that he was involved in a plot to attack the King's Lynn Custom House in November 1806. He was also involved in an attempt to seize the Sword of Lynn by which the town holds its Charter; indeed, it was to that place he had been heading when he had been taken. Carter's behaviour following his sentencing was described as 'very good' and it was claimed:

So overpowering was his sense of shame and ignominy, that he took scarcely two ounces of food from the day of his condemnation. He became so weak that his fears were great, lest he should not meet death with religious fortitude but his demeanour was exemplary and he died calling upon God for mercy.

98

THE ATTLEBOROUGH HUSBAND MURDER

Martha Alden, 31 July 1807

Samuel and Martha Alden lived in a modest cottage in Attleborough. Martha (32) considered her husband lazy and arguments between the couple became progressively worse over the period of about three years, resulting in the gruesome incident which took place on the morning of Sunday, 19 July 1807. Sam was sound asleep, tucked up in his bed after a drinking session the previous night with Edmund Draper at the White Horse pub in Attleborough. Martha could not stand his idling anymore, and seized a bill hook and leapt upon her recumbent husband. She hacked at his head, neck and throat with the tool, causing fatal wounds and hideous mutilations so severe that the head was almost severed from the body. She would later claim that she was 'seized with a sudden mania'.

Martha went to her friend, Mary Orvice, asking her to go with her to her house; when they arrived, Martha said to her, 'I have killed my husband'; taking her into the bedroom, showed her the body lying on the bed and the bill hook lying on the floor, caked with blood. Alden produced a corn sack and asked Orvice to hold it whilst she put the body into it. They then carried the body from the bedroom, through the passage and kitchen, out of the house, across the road

Martha Alden poised to deliver the first blow upon her husband.

to the dry ditch surrounding the garden and left it there, after throwing some mould over it. The following night, Alden and Orvice removed the body from the ditch in the garden and brought it to the pit on the common, near Wright's Plantation. They removed the body from the sack, which she afterwards carried away with her, and threw it down into the pit. The next morning, Orvice returned to the Alden house again and assisted in cleaning it up, taking some warm water and washing and scraping the wall next to the bed.

Subsequently, the body floated to the surface after its clumsy concealment and was discovered by Sarah Leeder as she was searching for her missing ducks; she raised the alarm and the corpse was soon identified as Sam Alden. Edward Rush, by order of the constable of Attleborough parish, searched the deceased man's residence and 'in a dark chamber', he found the bill hook, which, despite showing signs of having been washed, appeared to have blood on its handle and on the blade. Martha Alden was arrested on suspicion of murder and stood trial at the Norfolk Assizes before Mr Justice Grose on 27 July 1807. In his summing up, the judge meted out a severe warning to Mary Orvice, whom he considered most fortunate that she had not been charged with being accessory to an attempted concealment of murder. No mercy was shown to Martha Alden: found guilty of murdering her husband, she was sentenced to death, with her body to be handed to the surgeons for dissection afterwards. Her execution was recorded in *the Newgate Calendar*:

> This unhappy female was drawn on a hurdle and executed on the Castle Hill, pursuant to her sentence, in presence of an immense concourse of spectators. She behaved at the fatal tree with the decency becoming her awful situation.

99
LIKE FATHER, LIKE SON

William Fuller, John Chapman and Thomas Sutton, 9 April 1808

On 21 March 1808, at Thetford Assizes, poachers William Fuller (26), John Chapman (34) and Robert Chapman (22) were all tried for shooting at William Bussey, a gamekeeper of Lord Cholmondeley, who lived in a lodge at Great Bircham belonging to the Houghton Park estate. On the night of 28 January, Bussey was watching for poachers with five assistants when, near a plantation called the triangles, he heard the report of guns and went to investigate. The gamekeepers heard men coming down a pathway and concealed themselves. As the men approached, Bussey and his colleagues rose from their concealment and challenged them. The men raised a shout and fired two guns, wounding Bussey in the face, chest and arms. Despite his wounds, Bussey closed on the men but being weak through loss of blood, he was thrown down by John Chapman, who remained standing over him until moments later, when another gamekeeper arrived and came to his rescue. All three poachers were found guilty and condemned to death under the 'Black Act.' Robert Chapman was reprieved but the rest of the gang went to the gallows on Castle Hill, Norwich.

At the same Assize, and sharing the gallows with Chapman and Fuller was a Trowse man, Thomas Sutton. Sutton had already served a sentence of seven years' hard labour on a prison hulk for the theft of a pony from General Money of Trowse. On his first appearance before the Thetford Assizes, Sutton had been lucky to escape the gallows; his own father, Robert Sutton, had been executed for horse stealing (*see* 26 August 1786), while his elder brother was transported for seven years for the same offence. Sutton wanted to join his brother, so he stole a silver spoon expecting to receive a sentence of transportation for the crime; he was tried but the case was dismissed through lack of evidence. Sutton then resolved to steal a pony from General Money and was apprehended a few miles from the city, riding on the animal. This time, Sutton was sentenced to death but was reprieved on account of his youth and sent to the hulks at Woolwich. Upon his return, the General took an interest in the young man and tried to set him back on the straight and narrow, but the woman Sutton had intended to make his wife left him, his brother died during the time of his transportation and memories of the ignominious loss of his father haunted Sutton. He became depressed and decided to commit a crime that would lead to the termination of his life. The product of this desire saw Sutton return to General Money's estate and fire a cart lodge, barn and stack of barley on 4 November 1807. Sutton surrendered himself the same day and confessed his crime. At his trial, Sutton was said to have behaved in an 'audacious manner,'; another source recorded he 'betrayed strong symptoms of such depravity, as is hoped may be attributed to an insane mind.' When the death sentence was passed he requested to be taken back to Norwich so that he might 'be hanged among his friends' – and so he was.

100
ROBBERY AT BARNEY

Charles Harper and Edmund Impson, 10 April 1813

Charles Harper (26) and Edmund Impson (21) broke into John Butler's shop and dwelling house, at Barney, using two boys named Richard Webb (16) and Henry Tuck, who they had co-opted to keep watch. Escaping with goods to the value of £300, the robbers exchanged their old hats and clothes for the new ones they found in Butler's store, but foolishly left their old clothes behind. Subsequently, these clothes were identified and led directly to the perpetrators. All four were captured at the house of Mr Robert and Mrs Sarah Gore, where the robbers had been before the raid, and to which they returned with the stolen goods afterwards. The stolen goods were found hidden in the house, and confronted by such evidence the gang confessed to their guilt. Tuck was admitted as evidence for the Crown, while the three remaining felons were tried and found guilty at the Norfolk Assizes, held at Thetford. The Gores were tried at the same Assize and sentenced to fourteen years transportation. Harper, Impson and Webb were all sentenced to death, but Webb was reprieved, leaving Harper and Impson for the gallows. Both men freely confessed to their crime and recorded their gratitude to their friends who had petitioned to save them from their ignominious death. On the morning of their execution both men took the sacrament, took an affecting leave of their fellow prisoners and proceeded with a firm step and an unaltered countenance to the place of execution. On the scaffold they fervently joined in prayers and submitted to their sentence 'with the fortitude of men and the resignation of Christians.' After hanging for the usual hour, the bodies were delivered to their afflicted relatives and conveyed home by them for interment.

101
UTTERING A NOTE

Edward Lea, 6 April 1816

Edward Lea (33), alias Armstrong, was a Lincolnshire man from a good family; he was big boned and very strong, hence his appellation of 'Armstrong.' Lea was well known at Boston as the 'ganger' of the embankers, who worked on the river near the town. Lea was indicted by the Governors and Company of the Bank of England for uttering a £2 note, knowing the same to be forged. Upon arraignment, Lea pleaded guilty but at the recommendation of the court withdrew his first plea and entered one of not guilty. Unfortunately for Lea, a chain of collateral evidence demonstrated he had other forged notes and base coin in his possession and had been directly and indirectly involved on a number of occasions in attempts to pass them off as the real thing. Lea was found guilty and sentenced to death. Upon securing this conviction, the counsel for the prosecutors stated that it was not the intention of the Governors of the Bank of England to push the capital part of these charges to a greater extent than was necessary for the public safety. Having pursued Lea, as an example to others, they would not prosecute against the other prisoners, the minor charges of 'having notes in their possession, knowing them to be forged' being only a transportable offence.

Lea's behaviour, both before and after his trial, had been exemplary; he left no confession but was very much resigned to his fate. A contemporary account of his execution on Castle Hill concluded: 'He appeared deeply affected by the awful situation in which his unlawful conduct had placed him and the tears that rolled over his countenance, bespoke the anguish of his mind.'

DOWNHAM RIOTERS AND A FARMER TURNED THIEF

Daniel Harwood, Thomas Thody and Thomas Moy, 31 August 1816

When Downham Market agricultural labourers demanded wages of 2s per day, to be paid every Monday and Thursday, their employers refused. The situation rapidly escalated, culminating in a riot in the town on 20 May 1816. Armed with clubs and other weapons, the rioters smashed windows and raided shops and stores. The situation was only quelled after Upwell Cavalry were called out and the Riot Act read.

On 24 May, another disturbance took place when two women and several men, accused of being rioters, were removed from the town to Norwich Castle. Brought before Lord Chief Justice Gibbs at the Norfolk Assizes, nine men and six women were found guilty and sentenced to death for their role in the riots; no true bills were found against one man, seven people were bound over to keep the peace and John Stearn was transported for seven years. Stearn was joined by many of the other rioters who had been sentenced to death but had their sentences commuted, until eventually only Daniel Harwood (22) and Thomas Thody (25) were left for execution. Harwood was a native of Gooderstone and lived near Downham. He was unmarried, but worked hard with his wagon and team, in jobs for farmers in his locality. Thody was born at St Neots in Huntingdonshire and had resided for several years with his wife and two small children at Necton, where his father worked was coachman for local gentleman Mr Mason.

Petitions were raised in an attempt to save these men, one of them from the people of Downham Market, signed by four of the prosecutors, three overseers, two church wardens and over seventy townspeople. They argued that the pair were led astray by the fatal example of the people of Southery, notably 'the bad women of the place', who came with many others into Downham. Sadly, these were not successful.

Harwood and Thody were joined on the gallows by Thomas Moy (32). Born at Guestwick, he was a tenant farmer with 100 acres at Binham, a wife and seven young children to support. Times were hard and he had been caught stealing sheep at Elmham. John Knowles, his farm employee and accomplice in the crime, gave evidence against him, saving his own life but sending his master to the gallows.

The execution attracted great interest and a huge crowd attended. It was recorded in the *Norwich Mercury* by a reporter who was present:

> Having taken a last farewell of their relatives and friends and an affecting leave of their fellow prisoners, and after being indulged in waiting till the last moment, in the forlorn hope of reprieve, they proceeded to the place of execution. When the prayers appropriated to the

solemn occasion were concluded, they submitted, with manly resignation, to the awful preparations for death. Harwood was fixed first to the fatal tree. Thody was the next sufferer, and he suffered indeed, as far as related to mental suffering; he had hitherto conducted himself with patient fortitude and with a steady step had ascended the scaffold but when the rope was placed on his neck, the remembrance of his wife and children, who he loudly called upon and deplored, overwhelmed his mind and with agonizing screams he would have fallen in a fit, [had] he not been supported by the exhortations of the Ordinary and his fellow-sufferers and by the soothing attentions of those around him. He recovered soon from his fainting state and stood up firmly while the executioner performed his office upon him and Moy who was the last tied up. The raised part of the platform immediately fell and they died with some convulsive struggles, in which Moy appeared to be the longest sufferer.

The final comment was very telling: 'No malefactors ever expired with greater sympathy from the immense multitude, which covered the whole surface of the hill adjoining the place of execution.'

103
MURDER OF THE WELLS GLOVE MAKER

James Johnson, 23 March 1818

On Saturday, 11 October 1817, Robert Baker, a Wells glove and breeches maker, was making his rounds collecting money from the neighbouring villages – a round trip of about seven miles. When he did not return on Saturday evening, his family were not unduly worried, as they knew a number of people had outstanding debts with him and may have taken some finding. When he did not return by sundown on Sunday, his family were alarmed and his two sons began a search for him on Monday morning. The body of Robert Baker was found near the corner where Black's Lane joined Market Lane, a few hundred yards from the town. He had been victim of a horrific and violent robbery. It appeared an attempt had been made to cut his throat and the back of his skull had been 'beaten in' with such force that several portions of the skull had been driven into the brain. Two sticks were found near the spot, one broken in two by the force of a blow, and, the other, the property of Mr Baker, found 'covered with clots of blood, brains and hair;' further fragments of another stick, broken and bloodied in the attack were found nearby. County Magistrates ordered the printing of 3,000 handbills giving notice of the murder, which were distributed by constables among every coach, fish cart and other transports leaving the city. An appeal for information, with a reward of £100 upon conviction of the perpetrators, was also published in the *Norfolk Chronicle*.

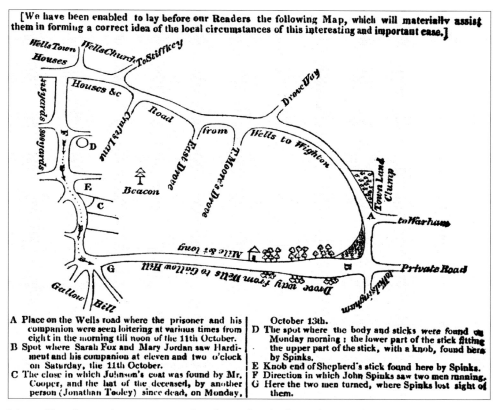

[We have been enabled to lay before our Readers the following Map, which will materially assist them in forming a correct idea of the local circumstances of this interesting and important case.]

A Place on the Wells road where the prisoner and his companion were seen loitering at various times from eight in the morning till noon of the 11th October.
B Spot where Sarah Fox and Mary Jordan saw Hardiment and his companion at eleven and two o'clock on Saturday, the 11th October.
C The close in which Johnson's coat was found by Mr. Cooper, and the hat of the deceased, by another person (Jonathan Tooley) since dead, on Monday,

October 13th.
D The spot where the body and sticks were found on Monday morning: the lower part of the stick fitting the upper part of the stick, with a knob, found here by Spinks.
E Knob end of Shepherd's stick found here by Spinks.
F Direction in which John Spinks saw two men running.
G Here the two men turned, where Spinks lost sight of them.

Map and key charting the events surrounding the murder of Robert Baker at Wells.

Suspicions had been aroused when two men had walked into a Fakenham clothes shop run by William Waller. The pair bought complete changes of clothes, paid for them in cash, put them on in the shop and then left their old clothes in bundles on the counter. Subsequent examinations revealed these clothes to be bloodstained and they were identified as the property of James Johnson (30) and William Hardiment (27). The pair had been seen loitering in the area where the murder was committed and a pair of men, matching their description, had also been seen running away from the scene of the crime towards Gallow Hill and Fakenham.

During that same evening, the pair was also seen at the Duke of York public house in Fakenham. More than one witness later recalled seeing Johnson in possession of a distinctive pocket book that answered the description of the one carried by Mr Baker. The landlord also confirmed that Johnson and Hardiment had been in the pub; they stayed there overnight and had left on Sunday morning. Johnson then went to the Wymondham area and was apprehended at the King's Head Inn at Hethersett. Hardiment, who remained at large, and another man, named Benjamin Neal, were charged with being accessories (*see* 1 April 1822). Tried at the Norfolk Assizes before Mr Justice Dallas, Johnson was found guilty, sentenced to death and his body was ordered to be delivered to the surgeons to be anatomised. The execution was carried out on Castle Hill, Norwich, before a crowd of between 3-5,000 people.

After hanging the usual time, the body was cut down and duly delivered to the surgeons. Mr Wilson, a gentleman from London, and Mr Austen, a pupil of Mr Dalrymple's, performed the dissection and prepared the subject for lectures delivered by Mr Crosse.

104

'CAPTAIN' BELCHAM OF CASTLE ACRE

James Belcham, 10 April 1819

On 12 February 1819, James Belcham (31) and William Thurrold (38) were brought before the Norfolk Assizes charged with breaking and entering the Ostrich pub at Castle Acre and stealing 500 yards of hempen cloth, worth £70, the property of Thomas Smith of Bressingham. Their defence was that they had found the stolen cloth in a hay stack: they claimed they were only guilty of attempting to sell that cloth. Both men were found guilty of theft and sentenced to death, but Thurrold was reprieved. Great interest was shown in this case, especially in his local area: Belcham was a Castle Acre man and his parents were of 'reputable character.' A curious twist may have determined the fate of Belcham. He was the head of a gang of lighters and had obtained the appellation 'Captain', which was thought by some at the time to have given the court the notion that he commanded a gang of depredators in the neighbourhood. Because of this misunderstanding he was made an example of, by being sent to the gallows on Castle Hill. Belcham left a wife, two young children and a wife near her confinement. He was buried in Castle Acre churchyard, on the Sunday following his execution. His funeral sermon was heard by a 1,000 strong congregation and was published as a chap-book.

105

PYCRAFT THE POISONER

John Pycraft, 16 August 1819

John Pycraft (35), a gardener at Westwick, had taken a dislike to his wife and had tried to cause her death by mixing poison with a meal of pork and potatoes, washed down with tea. In the event, his infant daughter consumed the majority and died, whereas Mrs Pycraft, although made very ill, recovered. John Pycraft was brought before Mr Justice Burrough, at the Norfolk Assizes, charged with administering arsenic to his infant child.

Broadside sold
after the execution
of John Pycraft.

The Trial and Execution,
Life, Parentage, & Education,
OF
JOHN PYCRAFT,
AGED 35,
Who was Executed on the Castle Hill, Norwich, on Monday, Aug. 16th, 1819
for the wilful Murder of John Pycraft his infant child.

The above unhappy Criminal is a remarkable and awful instance of the Depravity of human nature, and the fatal effects of not reflecting upon the consequences of giving way to vicious and sinful temptations.—It appears that this miserable man has passed the greatest part of his life in the humble occupation of a Gardener, and was in the employ of Squire Peters of Westwick, where acting as under Gardener he received the small sum of Six Shillings per week, with which however he was enabled by his extreme frugality (being a particular near living man) to obtain a moderate subsistence and has lately purchased half an Acre of land at North Walsham, on which he has built a House; he has been married about two years, during which it seems he has frequently indicated his unhappy disposition in an unnatural dislike to his wife, a quiet and inoffensive woman, with whom he led a very uncomfortable life in consequence. Of a secret attachment which existed betwixt him and another woman of a bad character. It appears that the object of his diabolical design was not his child, as his intention was evidently to be the death of his wife, and for which purpose, he in company with another man, procured at the Shop of Mr. Purland, Chemist, St. Simon's, an ounce of white Arsenic and afterwards administered the same to his wife, by mixing it with the food which he expected his wife only would partake of, but unfortunately the child became the innocent victim of the fatal drug; but being immediately interred, the cause of its death was not discovered till fourteen days afterwards, when a suspicion arose in the neighbourhood, and on examining the Corpse, (after it had been taken up) the child was found to have been poisoned, and in consequence of certain words which dropped from the father, it was strongly suspected that he was its murderer—the Coroner's Jury which sit on the body, accordingly brought in their Verdict of Wilful Murder against John Pycraft.

His Trial which came on on Friday last hours, during which time twenty six witnesses appeared against him, and the circumstances of the murder being clearly made out, the Jury found him GUILTY!—The awful sentence of the Law was immediately passed that he should be hung by the neck till he was dead, and his body afterwards delivered to the Surgeons for dissection.

He was a man of a very diminutive statue, and an uncommon singular appearance; the length of his body being so disproportioned, and his legs unusually short; still however, his countenance exhibited no marks of that ferocious disposition which could stipulate him to the atrocious deed; neither does it appear from what we have been able to collect concerning him, that his conduct previous to this murder was ever known to be remarkably bad; nor was he a man by any means addicted to drunkenness, but on the contrary, of a particular sober habit, owing in some measure to his penurious disposition. However, he appears to have had a dislike to his wife without any provocation on her part, which so completely divested his mind of every feeling of humanity; that he had for some time thirsted for her blood, in order as it is supposed that he might the more easily follow his vicious inclinations by a connexion with a dissolute woman, in preference of whom he would have made no scruple in sacrificing the life of his lawful wife, and which finally induced him to take away the life of his innocent and unoffending infant, who with its mother look'd to him as their only protection, and who were naturally the objects which ought to have been most dear to him.—What must have been the feelings of such a father when viewing the lifeless corpse of his innocent child murdered by the parent whose delight ought to have been to have cherished it in his bosom! The father who could look without remorse at such an unnatural deed was unworthy to live, and was justly punished by an ignominious death.

He was accordingly Executed pursuant to his sentence amidst a vast concourse of spectators who assembled on the Castle Hill at an early hour to witness the awful retribution of Justice; and though amongst them were numbers who lived in the neighbourhood of the culprit and consequently were personally acquainted with him, yet such was the feeling of horror excited by his Guilt, that few were seen to be affected with pity towards him; for disgust at his unnatural conduct took place of the commiseration which otherwise would have been bestowed upon him, and he was launched into eternity an awful and striking example of the dispensation of Providence in bringing to light the deeds of darkness committed by a murderer, which though perhaps impenetrable to human eye, can never be concealed from that Omnipotent Being who " searcheth the hearts of men."

DEATH! 'tis a melancholy day
To those that have no God,
When the poor soul is forc'd away
To seek her last abode.

In vain to heaven she lifts her eyes,
But guilt, a heavy chain,
Still drags her downward from the skies,
To darkness, fire, and pain.

Awake, and mourn, ye heirs of hell,
Let stubborn sinners fear;
You must be driv'n from earth, and dwell,
A long for ever there.

What shall the wretch, the sinner do,
He once defied the Lord;
But he shall dread the Thund'rer now,
And sink beneath his word.

Tempests of angry fire shall roll,
To blast the rebel worm,
And beat upon his naked soul
In one eternal storm.

Prepare me, Lord, for thy right hand,
Then come the joyful day;
Come, death, and some celestial band,
To bear my soul away.

[R. LANE, PRINTER, BRIDEWELL-ALLEY, NORWICH.]

Pycraft made no defence and after a trial of six hours was found guilty and sentenced to death. At his execution Pycraft cut a diminutive form and a decrepit figure. It was recorded that after the fall of the gallows' trap, almost ten minutes passed before the visible signs of life left his body, even though, as accounts of the time pointed out: 'every precaution was taken to shorten his sufferings by the addition of some heavy appendages.' After hanging for the appointed time, Pycraft's body was handed over to the surgeons and, after the dissection was performed, his body was exposed for public view for one hour at the Shire House.

106

THE BRESSINGHAM STABBING

Edward Fisher, 28 August 1819

On 18 July 1819, William Harrison, a linen weaver, was walking home from Bressingham at about 9 p.m. when Edward Fisher came up to him and stabbed him just below the navel. Fisher also said something about his wife that Harrison did not distinctly hear. He then said, 'I'll have you taken up,' turned and went down Fen Street. Harrison was lucky to survive the attack and swore he had no quarrel with Fisher; he freely admitted he knew Fisher's wife but insisted he had not been intimate with her. Fisher was arrested by Constable John Branch; he said he did not care and wished he had done it before, 'for Harrison had caused more dispute between him and his wife than any man he knew.' Tried and found guilty at the Norfolk Assizes, William Harrison was described as having 'a reserved, sullen and gloomy temper, in his religious profession a Methodist and to a certain degree of unsound mind.'

Executed on Castle Hill, Norwich, he left a wife and seven children.

107

FINAL JUSTICE FOR THE WELLS GLOVE MAKER

William Hardiment, 1 April 1822

William Hardiment (32) and Benjamin Neale (44) were brought before the Norfolk Assizes, at Thetford, on 28 March 1822. They were being tried for their part in the murder of Robert Baker at Wells on 11 October 1817. Their fellow accomplice, James Johnson, had already gone to the gallows (*see* 23 March 1818). The bill against Neale stated he 'did counsel and procure Hardiment to commit the murder.' This case was based on the statements of fellow prisoners, foremost among them Thomas Robinson, held at Aylsham Bridewell in an adjoining cell, who claimed to have overheard Neale and Hardiment plotting the crime. However, it was believed that Robinson held a grudge against Neale after a planned escape attempt went awry; he was left so aggrieved that he was heard to say he would 'glory in getting Neale hanged'. Thus the Grand Jury threw out the charges against Neale and he was acquitted. The case against Hardiment proceeded; indeed it was upon information given

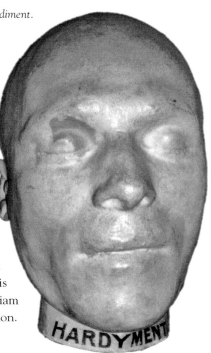

Death mask of William Hardiment.

to the authorities by the same Thomas Robinson. Robinson had met Hardiment in Beverley, in Yorkshire, in December 1821. Robinson passed this information on to the relevant authorities and as a result Hardiment was traced and arrested. Witnesses from the trial of James Johnson gave their testimony again, confirming they had seen Johnson and Hardiment together at the time of the murder and how they were connected to the bloody clothes and some of the goods stolen from Mr Baker. Found guilty of his involvement in the murder, Hardiment was sentenced to death and was returned to Norwich for execution on Castle Hill. Just like Johnson, his accomplice who swung before him, the body of William Hardiment was delivered to the surgeons for dissection.

108
STACK FIRING AT DISS

Noah Peak and George Fortis, 13 April 1822

Noah Peak (40), of Shelfanger, and George Fortis (29), of North Lopham, were both ex-soldiers who had served in the Peninsula War and were both present on the field of Waterloo. Implicated in the confessions of two accomplices, both men were charged on the oath of Diss farmer John Kent, who identified them as accessories to the firing of three of his hay stacks on 25 February 1822. Accomplice William Baker turned King's evidence and told the damning story of how Peak had invited him to come and have some food and how he then accompanied Peak and Fortis as they fired the stacks that same evening. Having been found guilty, both Peak and Fortis made their confessions from the condemned cell; Peak confessed to the Chaplain that it was he who had entered the stack yard with the 'live tarf' and placed it in the straw to start the fire. Asked for his motive, he said he wanted to send a 'flash and a scare' to alarm the local farmers and to frighten them into making a more generous allowance to the poor.

Peak and Fortis were sent to the gallows on Castle Hill. Both men were permitted to address the crowd. Fortis gave an eloquent address urging others to learn from his errors, while Peak urged all to take note of what Fortis had said, and then went on to declare that

A COPY OF THE
Dying Words
SPOKEN ON THE GALLOWS,
BY GEORGE FORTIS,

The youngest of the two men who were Executed on Saturday, on the Castle Hill, taken down in writing by a genleman whose veracity may be depended upon.

" My dear friends, I am now on the point of execution, and I confess being on the premises at the time of the stacks being burnt—but I did not burn them, but still I am as bad as the others. My dear friends, I hope you will refrain from sin and resist the devil, and he will fly from you. Pray my friends do pray for me now ; for it is no use when I am no more. I hope that the Lord will forgive me ; and I pray that the Lord will receive my soul into heaven. I do not speak to justify myself ; but I well know that nothing but the blood of Christ can save me.——God bless you all.

O Lord ! receive my sinful soul,
Have mercy on my guilt ;
The blood of Christ have made me whole,
For me, that blood was spilt !

All you that now around me stand,
A warning take from me ;
Unto the word of God attend,
And shun bad company.

You see me here a wretched man ;
But short will be my stay ;
Yet on my Saviour I'll depend,
To wash my sins away.

Pray for my soul, good people all,
And pity my sad fate ;
A moment hence the drop will fall ;
I have not long to wait.

And may the blood of Jesus Christ
Atonement for me make ;
On his dear name my comfort rest,
He died for sinners sake.

Whilst the unfortunate young man was thus praying and making intercession at the throne of Grace, through the merits of our Redeemer, Noah Peak was also earnestly engaged in silently offering up petitions for divine mercy, and praying for blessings on the family he had left behind ; and in this state of devotion the drop fell, and they were both launched into eternity.——The words which were uttered by the young man, seem to have made such an impression on those who stood near enough to hear them, that for some minutes after the fall of the platform the most awful stillness prevailed, interrupted only by the sighs and tears of compassion for the fate of the unhappy sufferers.

(WALKER, PRINTER, NORWICH.)

A copy of the speech delivered from the gallows by George Fortis. (NLIS)

some of the witnesses against them had 'sworn wrongfully.' After a prompting from the Chaplain, both men acknowledged the justice of their sentence. It was reported that, after being 'tied up and the caps drawn over their faces, while they were distinctly and audibly repeating after the Chaplain, a short prayer, the platform fell and they died, almost without a struggle.' The execution was recorded as 'skilfully performed by the executioner from the Old Bailey.' After hanging for the usual hour, the bodies of Peak and Fortis were taken down and given over to their friends for burial in their respective native places. In an ironic postscript, it was noted that it was not three years since Peak had come to Norwich to collect and convey home for burial the body of Edward Fisher, his fellow parishioner, who was executed on Castle Hill for stabbing William Harrison (*see* 28 August 1819).

109

A CITY HANGING

James Smith and Henry Carter, 24 August 1822

In January 1822, the home of William Balls, at The Half Moon, Stone Hills, Norwich, was robbed of 16 gallons of liquor in bottles and a purse containing £8 in notes and copper coins. The perpetrators were an infamous gang of night thieves, known as the 'Cossey Gang'. Only one gang member was made answerable for this theft; his name was James Smith.

Tiring of foot depredations, the gang found stables belonging to those who had retired to bed by 10 p.m. and stole their horses in order to steal game, poultry or sheep, returning

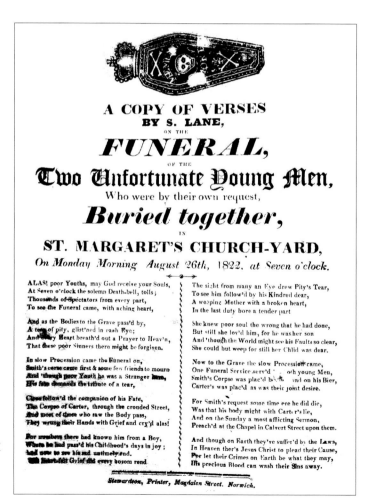

Unusual broadside produced after the execution of James Smith and Henry Carter. (NLIS)

the horses 'almost jaded and harassed to death' in the early morning. Standing before Mr Justice Best, at the Norfolk Assizes, Smith was found guilty of being involved in the robbery at the Half Moon. Due to the pernicious nature of the gang, an example had to be made and so Smith was sent to the gallows.

In a separate case, Henry Carter (17) and William Crisp (20), alias Arburn, were tried for entering the dwelling house of John Clarke in the Parish of St Paul, Norwich and stealing several articles. Their plunder included five silver teaspoons, a silver pepper box, one metal tea shovel, silver mounted spectacles and one optic glass. Of the pair, Carter was sent to the gallows.

Both these offences were committed in Norwich and thus both felons were held in Norwich City Prison and were taken to their place of execution in a procession from St Giles Street. Headed by the Under Sheriffs on horseback, the Sheriffs were accompanied by the Chaplain, and the minister came next in a mourning coach, followed by a cart 'covered by black cloth on which sat the two malefactors, each with arms pinioned, neck bare and head uncovered, and each sitting on the coffin destined to receive his lifeless body.' It was noted that Smith was well behaved but Carter acted with great levity during the progress of the procession through the Market Place to the scaffold erected near the weighing machine on Castle Meadow. Smith went to his death penitent but Carter seemed to evince 'perfect indifference to the fate which waited him.' After hanging for an hour, the bodies were taken down and carried by twelve bearers to the house of Carter's parents. Both men were buried in St Margaret's churchyard on 26 August.

110

IN A LONELY COTTAGE AT SHOULDHAM

William Bray, 5 April 1823

William Bray (20), Edward Turvey (19) and Matthew Craven (19) were charged with burglary in the house of Mrs Ann Bird of Shouldham. These three men were at a meeting of the Ranters religious group and plotted the robbery during the sermon. Mrs Bird was an elderly lady who lived in a lonely cottage; on the night of 27 February 1823, the men broke in through a shutter with a mattock and forced the terrified lady to give up her money, which came to £18 16s 6d. Bray then attempted 'to violate her person and used her with great brutality.' It was he who went to the gallows.

While in the condemned cell he cried out to God almost continually, in a lamentable manner. Bray, a native of Tottenhill near Lynn, was visited by his own pastor, a respectable Wesleyan Methodist preacher who travelled 40 miles to minister to him. On the morning of his execution, Bray was steady until he reached the scaffold where:

Trial and Execution
OF
WILLIAM BRAY,
AGED 20,

Who was Executed in pursuance of his Sentence between the two Lodges in front of the Castle and County Goal, Norwich, for forcibly entering the house in the night of the 27th February, 1823, of Mrs. ANN BIRD, of Shouldham in Norfolk, and compelling her to give him her money, and in attempting to violate her person.

This unfortunate young man was tried with two others for a burglary in the house of Ann Bird, of Shouldham, Norfolk, at the last Thetford assizes.

Ann Bird, the Prosecutrix, a woman far advanced in years, deposed as follows : I live at Shouldham ; my house is two hundred yards from any other persons ; it was broken open on the night of the 27th of February last ; on that night I went to bed at ten o'clock, and previous to doing so secured all the doors and windows myself. About half-past ten I thought I heard some one at the shutter, and a little time after thinking I heard the same noise again I got up and looked through the chamber window. but could not see any one ; soon after I heard a report, which seemed like that of a gun, and in a little time heard the same noise again ; when I went to the back window, opened it and shrieked out murder ; I heard the sash below put up and some one bustling as if breaking into the kitchen ; in a short time I saw some men coming up stairs ; did not know how many until they came into my sleeping room ; where I had run to on seeing them approach, having shut myself up and held the door until overcome with fear, when three men rushed in ; one of them, I do not know which asked me for my money, I told them I had none several times. he threatened to kill me if I did not comply ; and the threat appeared to be uttered by more voices than one, they still persisted in knowing where it was, and on my still refusing to inform them, they broke open a chest standing in the bed room, with something they brought with them, what I cannot tell ; one of the persons held a cudgel up to me and told me to get my money and give it them, which I did out of the box ; it was a large size box where I laid my clothes ; the money was in a canvass bag amongst them at the bottom of it.---The value of property stolen amounted to 2l. 17s. I dont know the exact sum that was in the bag ; part of such sum they took out of my pockets under my pillow. They pulled the clothes about which were in the box, took a black silk cloak, two black silk handkerchiefs from thence, and a small knife out of my pockets.---They then broke open another box in the room, when two of them went down stairs, saying they would look about while the remaining one finished up stairs, he proved to be the unfortunate Bray. Having completed his search, he was guilty of the most disgraceful conduct towards the prosecutrix ; which she proceeded with the utmost pain to herself to give an account of ; but most fortunately for her he did not succeed in his diabolical intentions.

The witness then proceeded to add, Bray remained up stairs full half an hour, when one of his companions came up stairs and wished him to leave the house I did not see much of the prisoners' features that night. [The witness was here directed to turn and look at the prisoners.] I think Bray was the person who treated me so ill. I saw them before the magistrate, but had no recollection of any but Bray---I think it was Bray who took my pockets from under the pillow and the knife.

It appears that this wretched person has been brought up by poor though honest parents, whose instructions he too late bewailed not following ; for from the time of his trial to the period of his leaving his prison for execution, the consciousness of his guilt, the misery of his deplorable situation, and the dreadful fate attending him, so deeply affected his mind, that his sighs and groans were sufficient to penetrate the hardest heart, and draw tears of pity from the most abandoned.

He was brought forth before many hundred spectators ; old and young, of both sexes, who to behold his youth, seemed most deeply concerned for him, that he should by his wickedness be thus cut off by an ignominious death in the flower of his youth. He spent the usual time in fervent prayer ; at length the fatal moment arrived, and he was launched into —a dreadful eternity,—trusting his example would be a warning to thousands to shun all evil temptations.

Broadside sold after the execution of William Bray.

…it required the utmost attention of his Minister and all around him to prevent the return of the paroxysms of grief and terror, the effects of which were strongly marked upon his countenance as he left the prison for the scaffold. The customary devotion being ended, he was tied up, suffering with trembling submission, and while repeating a portion of the Lord's Prayer, the drop fell and after a few short struggles he passed into eternity.

Once executed, his parents were too poor to send for his remains and so they were interred in the churchyard of St Michael-at-Thorn, Ber Street, Norwich.

111

FOR A SHEEP...

John Wood, Thomas Butler and Richard Everitt, 18 April 1829

John Wood (41) and Thomas Butler (29) were charged with killing a sheep, the property of Thomas Wootton of Walsoken, with intent to steal the carcass. Mr Wootton noticed his sheep missing and found the skin and some of the entrails in a nearby dyke. Two bundles of mutton were also found on Mr Jolly's grounds and when taken to John Harrison, the butcher, they were found to fit the skin. Earlier that evening Wood and Butler had been seen acting suspiciously with two bundles, like those containing the mutton, and had violently assaulted Henry Terrington when he challenged them near Mr Jolly's gate. Tried, found guilty and sentenced to death, it was recorded that, as the dread sentence was passed, Wood and Butler 'appeared very little affected by it.'

Richard Everitt (28), alias Robert Wilson, and his brother Edward (21) were charged with stealing a bay mare, the property of Thomas White of Wretton. They were acquitted but a further case was immediately brought against Richard for the theft of a chestnut filly belonging to William Parker, a farmer of Fincham. A third case was then heard of how Everitt had stolen a chestnut mare from fishmonger Rowing Pond, of Wretton; he was also found guilty of this offence. A further two indictments, on similar charges, were not pressed against him; the judge donned the black cap and Everitt was sentenced to the gallows. The execution was conducted by the 'Metropolitan finisher of the law' William Calcraft, who had recently been appointed as the executioner for the City of London and Middlesex on 4 April 1829 (a post he was to hold until 1874). A crowd conservatively estimated to be in excess of 10,000 had come to see the execution. The masses covered the extensive area between the bridge and the opposite houses, increasing in density up to the entrance gates, over which some persons had climbed to take up their positions at the foot of the drop, in contravention of the strict orders of the Prison Governor. Clearly these rogues attracted the ladies to the degree, as it was commented that the women present at their execution outnumbered the men two to one. A contemporary report stated:

At about 12 noon on the appointed day the prison door opened and Butler was the first to be led out, accompanied by Mr Johnson and his assistant. They walked down the bridge with a firm step and ascended the ladder on the scaffold with equal steadiness. Being placed on the platform to the right looking towards the Castle, the rope was instantly adjusted to his neck, the cap drawn over his face and during the dreadful trial of suspense which ensued to him, his tall athletic figure remained erect and unmoved. The Chaplain had by this time left the goal and reached the scaffold in readiness to perform the sequel of his sacred but painful office for the penitent offenders. The convict Woods was now brought down. His step was slow yet firm and on reaching the top of the platform he turned sideways for a moment as if to take a glance at the vast multitude but the executioner, proceeding to fix the rope, he turned as Butler had done, with his back to the populace and continued steadfast. Everitt comfortably to his own express wish, was last led forth; his visage wore a hue of deathlike paleness, betraying the anguish and restless agitation of his mind. But his deportment was decorous and the few occasional exclamations to which he gave vent as he approached the gallows were those of repentant sorrow... The poor fellow trembled every limb and seemed to need support, which was afforded him by the Governor with all that worthy individual's characteristic humanity.

Everitt ascended the scaffold, bowed respectfully to the multitude and as the executioner adjusted the rope he turned to his fellow sufferer Wood and bade him farewell. The crowd then spontaneously took off their hats. The Chaplain, Revd James Brown, read the appropriate service and upon a signal from the Governor the executioner caused the drop to fall and the three unfortunate men were launched to eternity. Butler and Woods appear to have had nearly instantaneous deaths but Everitt died hard, his extremities showing life was not extinct until after the lapse of several seconds. The execution was completed by 12.15 p.m. After hanging for an hour, the bodies were untied and conveyed back to the gaol, where they were placed in the coffins prepared for them and buried at the expense of the county. None of the remains of these executed felons were claimed by relatives or friends.

112

THE NORWICH DUMPLING POISONER

John Stratford, 17 August 1829

John Stratford (42) was a hard-working and athletic man, with a wife and six children, who worked a respectable trade as a whitesmith in the City of Norwich. Indeed, much of the iron work for the new Norwich City Gaol, including parts for the gallows, had been forged at his shop on King Street. Stratford and his wife had been friends with Thomas and Jane Briggs for about seven years when John became intimate with Jane. She became pregnant as a result of her liaison with Stratford and when she told him of her situation he said he hoped 'she would not go her time' and gave her 'something to take', but she did not take it. She carried the child to term and gave birth in June 1828.

Jane's husband, Thomas, was subsequently taken into the Norwich Workhouse infirmary after he had become bedridden with cancer of the face. Jane had regularly bought flour for his diet of 'thick milk' mixed with flour, a meal which had to be fed to him through a feeding pot. Jane complained she could not always get enough flour, a problem she repeated in front of the Stratfords.

The confession of John Stratford published as a broadside.

CONFESSION

OF JOHN STRATFORD,

Sunday, Aug. 16, 1829,—This day the Sheriff of the City, S. W. Stevenson, Esq. gave the following verbal particulars.

The prisoner admitted that he took the flour, as stated by the girl Hook in her evidence, which he said was mainly correct ; but there were some parts of the testimony against him very imperfect, and he wished them to be corrected ; but they related to minor points, and were therefore unnecessary to be refuted He said, his object was to destroy the life of Briggs, and it would seem that he was anxious he would quit the world before the birth of the child, in order that he (Stratford) might be exempted from the maintenance of the infant, in consequence of affiliation. He further says, that after he had left the bag of flour he was, upon reflection, conscience smitten at the heinousness of his crime, and he would have given worlds to have got the parcel back, but his effort to do so was paralized, and he dared not make a disclosure to his paramour. This part of the confession goes entirely to exculpate the wife from suspicion of being *particips criminis.*   He adds, that the burden upon his mind increased day by day, as he continually apprehended the intelligence of the completion of his diabolical scheme ; and when he found that the scheme was frusterated, and another person had fallen a victim to his hellish stratagem (as he terms it), he was worked up to a pitch of madness. He very much laments that he should have made the asseveration of innocence in Court, and earnestly prays to God to pardon him. He is almost constantly attended by the Rev. Mr. Millard, the chaplain of the jail, to whose pious exhortations and instructions he is remarkably attentive. He is a man who has read much, and possesses an intelligent mind, but unfortunately he has converted that which might have been a blessing into a destruction. With tears he exclaimed, " I attribute my downfall primarily to reading the AGE of REASON, and the recent work of Charlile ; and the secondary cause is my illicit connection with that abandoned woman Briggs."

Yesterday his wife and six children went to the prison to bid him farewell, and we are told by a spectator that the interview was heart-rending, the prisoner evinced the least ebullition of feeling of the whole, being a man of remarkable strong nerve. The youngest child said—" When will you come home to tea ?" His fortitude forsook him, and he wept aloud.

The prisoner was born at Postwick, four miles from this city, and in the village of his father, who is 90 years old, and lives to lament him. He is a smith by trade, and supposed to be the most ingenious machanic in Norwich.

Twelve o'clock having nearly arrived, the Sheriffs and the officers of justice proceeded to the room where the prisoner was engaged with his spiritual adviser. The executioner bound his arms and wrists. During this ceremony he behaved with uncommon firmness, frequently declared his sentence was just. The melancholly procession then passed through the court-yard The prisoner walked with a firm step, when he reached the foot of the drop, he knelt down on the steps; the chaplain read a prayer which he had composed for the occassion. The prisoner at intervals exclaimed, " Lord pardon my iniquity, for it is great! He then approached the Sheriffs, and thanked them for their kind attention to him. He then shook hands with every person within his reach, and having ascended the platform he resigned himself to his fate with becoming fortitude.

His body was afterwards laid in the Guildhall for public inspection, and then removed to the Hospital to be anotomized

R. LANE, PRINTER, ST. GEORGE'S, NORWICH.

In January 1829, John Stratford bought two ounces of arsenic from Richard Cross at his chemist shop, claiming it was to kill rats. Cross knew Stratford and thought nothing suspicious of his purchase; his apprentice, William Dawson, recalled he put each ounce in a paper marking it with the word 'poison'. On 11 February, Stratford turned up at the workhouse with a sack of flour marked 'To Thomas Briggs, sick in the workhouse', which he left at the kitchen window and it was put in a cupboard ready for future feeds. On 2 March, John Burgess, husband of Rhoda, one of the nurses used some of Brigg's flour to make some dumplings. When they were cooked John asked his wife to have her share, she carried two pieces to her son, came back and ate some of what was left with Mary Moss and Ann Piller. Rhoda rapidly and violently fell sick, as did the others who had partaken of the dumplings. John Burgess had eaten heartily and was soon taken to his bed saying 'I am a dying man.' City Surgeon, Mr John Coleman, was sent for, but he found Burgess in a dying state. He was suffering excruciating pains in his stomach and was vomiting constantly. Burgess died at about 6.15 p.m., that same day. His post-mortem examination, by Mr Dalrymple, revealed evidence of arsenic poisoning, a finding confirmed by poisons expert William Stark. Stark also examined the flour that the dumplings were made from, this was also found to have arsenic mixed in it. The writing on the bag the flour came in was also matched to a sample of Stratford's handwriting.

John Stratford was investigated and when his King Street premises were searched, the papers containing arsenic from Cross's chemist were discovered, now only containing one ounce. Stratford was brought before the Assizes and when called upon for his defence, he said, in the most emphatic manner, 'My Lord, I am perfectly innocent of what is laid to my charge. Moreover, I never was within the gates of the Workhouse, either before or at the time it has been sworn I was there.' Witnesses, such as the son of Alderman Herring and the Revd R. F. Elvin, also spoke favourably of his character, but after due deliberation the jury returned a guilty verdict and Stratford was sentenced to death.

Stratford dictated a condemned cell confession in which he disputed that he used the arsenic from Cross the chemist. He used a third of an ounce of arsenic, which he had received in the course of his work, which he powdered, sifted and added to the flour. Stratford went on to confirm he had taken the flour to the Workhouse confessing '...my object was to destroy Briggs, from the fear that exposure of my intimacy with the woman Briggs would break the peace between my wife and me.'

Broadside sold after the execution of John Stratford. (NLIS)

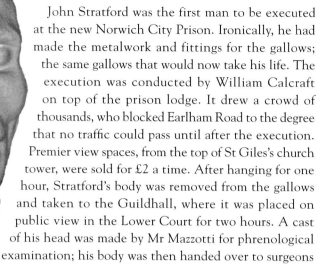

Death mask of John Stratford.

John Stratford was the first man to be executed at the new Norwich City Prison. Ironically, he had made the metalwork and fittings for the gallows; the same gallows that would now take his life. The execution was conducted by William Calcraft on top of the prison lodge. It drew a crowd of thousands, who blocked Earlham Road to the degree that no traffic could pass until after the execution. Premier view spaces, from the top of St Giles's church tower, were sold for £2 a time. After hanging for one hour, Stratford's body was removed from the gallows and taken to the Guildhall, where it was placed on public view in the Lower Court for two hours. A cast of his head was made by Mr Mazzotti for phrenological examination; his body was then handed over to surgeons for dissection under the supervision of Mr Dalrymple at the Norfolk and Norwich Hospital. After being wired together, it was used for years afterwards as a skeleton for the instruction of anatomy. A chap book entitled *Some Account of John Stratford who was Executed after the Last Assizes for the City of Norwich* was published shortly after Stratford's execution by Joseph John Gurney, brother of prison reformer Elizabeth Fry, under the pseudonym of 'One of his Fellow Citizens.'

113
THE THORPE ROBBERIES

William Lovet and John Simmons, 10 April 1830

William Reynolds was sitting with his wife and family at their home in Thorpe, at 8.30 p.m. on 6 March 1830, when three men burst in and began to beat him and his wife with a club and thick sticks. Mrs Reynolds was attacked by William Lovet (20); the other, recognised as John Loveday, threw Mr Reynolds to the floor and demanded money. Reynolds passed over his purse, containing 8s. This was not enough and Reynolds was ordered upstairs where he was dealt a severe blow to the head that bled profusely. On reaching his room Reynolds struck at the other man, William Lovet, with his shotgun. He missed but the robbers fled. Constable Brooks apprehended Lovet at the Chequers Inn with another man named Tubby. Loveday was also brought into custody, but the case against him and Tubby did not hold. However, the case against Lovet was proved and he was sentenced to death.

John Simmons (31) was found guilty of burglariously entering the house of David Harvey of Thorpe, with two others, on 2 January 1830. Harvey bolted his door but it was forced open; he then grabbed his sword and thrust it at the intruders but he was knocked down by a bludgeon and was severely beaten. One of the thieves then threatened to cut Mr Harvey's throat unless he gave them money. Hardly able to move after the beating, the robbers lifted him up and he gave them his watch and another purse, which contained about 25s. Mr Harvey recognised the voice of one of his assailants as that of John Simmons, a man with whom he had worked, as did his wife and lodger. Simmons was found guilty and was warned by the judge, as he passed the sentence of death, that he had 'no hope of mercy'.

Simmons and Lovet were executed by William Calcraft. Their bodies were taken down after the execution and laid in the mill-yard of the Castle Prison, where the different classes of prisoners were marched past.

The Trial and Execution of W. LOVET, and J. SIMMONS.

WHO WERE

EXECUTED

BETWEEN THE

Two Lodges

ON THE

Castle Hill

NORWICH,

ON

SATURDAY

April the 10th,

1830.

The above two unfortunate young men were executed for crimes of a similar nature, viz. stealing in dwelling-houses, with the aggravated circumstance of having wantonly and cruelly, beat and misused the persons whom they robb'd, the Eldest of the two John Simmons, aged 31, was after the most patient investigation found Guilty of having broken into the dwelling-house, of a man named Harvey of Thorpe, and besides robbing him of his Watch & Money, &c. most violently beating him in the most cruel and barbarous manner, so that he was left nearly for dead!—and the Judge in passing Sentence upon him expatiated on the enormity of his Guilt, and held out not the least hopes of mercy for him in this world!—

Wm. Lovet, was after the most clear & satisfactory evidence convicted the dwelling-house at Wm. Reynolds situated in a lonely part of Mousehold Heath, and in company with two other persons did feloniously steal from his person eight shillings, besides striking him the said William Reynolds several times with a bludgeon with which the Robbers were armed, and the Wife of Reynolds also received several Blows from the Ruffians, in endeavouring to protect her husband from their violence—a circumstance which most very much against them in the opinion of the learned Judge, who expressed his indignation of their conduct in the strongest terms,—and on passing the sentence of Death! on Lovet, exhorted him by all means to prepare for death, for that the cruelty that they displayed in treating even the Female, for whom most Men would have shown some remorse, proved that the Criminals were the most depraved of Characters and totally unworthy that mercy should be extended to any of them, and he being the only one that there was sufficient evidence to convict, he would most assuredly suffer the full penalty of the Law! which was accordingly put in Execution, although the greatest interest and intercession was made by the Friends of the two unhappy young Men to obtain a mitigation of the severity of their Sentence! and till the last, hopes were entertained of mercy for one, if not both, but alas! their days were numbered—and they suffered pursuant to their Sentence, amidst a vast concourse of Spectators, to numbers of whom the two culprits were well known, whose fate excited the commiseration of the beholders on account of their Youth and connexions!!

In taking a view of the untimely end of these two unfortunate young Men, it is impossible to refrain from trembling at the course of life that have brought them to this fate. Young Lovet, especially whose Parents were in decent circumstances and who had therefore an opportunity of becoming a creditable Member of Society, had it not been for the pernicious example of Bad Company,—which was also the ruin of the unfortunate Man Simmons, whose Sabbaths instead of being spent according to the commandments of God, were passed in debauchery and vice—in houses were infamy was the only thing to be learned, and vice the only pursuit encouraged,—how dearly have they now paid for the few moments of false enjoyment that have tempted them to their destruction! what miserable reflections must those poor young fellows have felt since their condemnation! at the thoughts of the scenes that 'have' step by step led them to the commission of the Crimes, for which they have now so severely suffered. What Pangs of Remorse must have shaken their Souls on ascending the Fatal Drop? In view the thousands assembled to witness their dying agonies! when they behold for the last time numbers of their former acquaintances—and some perhaps who first drew them into the vicious courses which have brought them to destruction! Where now is the comfort to be derived from their counsel; those companions of their Guilt may now view perhaps with unconcern their sufferings, and turn themselves to the same courses that they have then seen terminate so fatally!—What would these two poor young Fellows have now given could they but call back the time that they have spent in the Alehouse in corrupting each other with evil examples, and hardening each other in a contempt for every thing that was Righteous! how glad are they now to cling to the only hope that is left them, the merits of a Blessed Redeemer! through whose intercession alone they can hope for the final remission of their sins in the life hereafter. That Blessed Saviour! whose precepts they have so long neglected, and whose doctrines they so greatly despised! whose arms are still open, to receive those who truly repent, and whose love for us can wipe away our Guilt, although our crimes were as the Sand upon the Sea Shore!—Whose Blood was spilt on Mount Calvery that we might to ... and who left the Kingdom of his Father to suffer scorn, derision, and crucifixion for our Sins! who meekly and lowly suffered the taunts and revilings of his Persecutors, to work out our Salvation! who died that we might live! and gave his blood for our Redemption!—Than than is the best, the only hope of there two poor sufferers, Christ is their only mediator! he alone can sooth their Repentant Souls with his divine Grace! he will take the burthen of their Sins upon him, and cry—'' Come unto me all ye that are weary, and heavy laden and I will give you rest.'' And we in beholding the awful spectacle of their Deaths! fervently pray: that they may have had this comfort in their Dying Hours, to know that grace have found them in their lonely cells, and the blood of Jesus was their Cordial that sooth'd their afflicted Souls in the last moments of Anguish; and that through him they have only chang'd a life of Sin and Wickedness, to receive through Repentance a Life Everlasting!!!

COPY OF VERSES.

O Lord receive our sinful souls,
Have mercy on our guilt;
The blood of Christ have made us whole,
For on that blood was spilt.

All you that now around us stand,
May this a warning be;
Unto the word of God attend,
And shun bad company.

You see us here two wretched men,
But short will be our day;

Yet on our saviour we'll depend,
To wash our sins away.

Pray for our Souls, good people all,
And pity our sad fate;
A moment hence the drop will fall,
We have not long to wait.

And may the blood of Jesus Christ
Atonement for us make;
On his dear name our comfort rest,
He died for sinners sake.

(Walker, Printer, St. Lawrence, Norwich.)

Broadside sold after the execution of William Lovet and John Simmons.

114

THE VITRIOLIC REVOLUTIONARY

Richard Nockolds, 9 April 1831

Richard Nockolds (also spelt Knockells) was one of the leading activists during the Norwich weaver's riots in January 1830. The riots were put down by city officials and to keep it quiet, mounted troops patrolled the streets. Frustrated by the officials' indifference to the needs of the weavers, Nockolds' fury festered, finally manifesting itself in a vicious attack upon John Wright, one of the principal master manufacturers of Norwich. Leaping out of the shadows on St Faith's Lane, Nockolds threw vitriol (Sulphuric Acid) in Wright's face. Dreadfully injured and partially blinded by the corrosive liquid, Mr Wright discharged his pistol at his assailant but Nockolds escaped. The attack drew a great deal of publicity,

A CORRECT ACCOUNT OF THE
Trial, Execution, Life, Character & Behaviour,
Of the unfortunate Man who suffered on the Castle Hill, at Norwich, on Saturday the 9th of April, 1831, with an interesting detail of the manner in which the unhappy Culprit have conducted himself, from the time of his Condemnation, with the affecting separation betwixt Knockolds and his family which will long be remembered as the most heart-rending scene ever witnessed within the walls of a Prison !

The greatest degree of interest amongst all classes of people both in City and County was excited on the trial of RICHARD KNOCKOLDS, Thirty-four years of age, who was indicted for maliciously setting fire to the premises of Mr. Ducker, Swanton Abbot, and destroying property to a great amount !—The trial of the prisoner lasted for an unusual length of time, and the Court was crouded to excess.—The crime being of a nature the trial should bereave them of him for ever !—For it seems with all his crimes the attachment of this man's wife and family of little ones to the unhappy father, and husband, was great in the extreme. And the meeting that took place betwixt them in the Prison was of such an affecting description, that the heart must be hard indeed that could have witnessed it without tears—how heart-rending ! to behold five blooming children, taken their last long farewell of a

The execution of Richard Nockolds drew a lot of public interest and sympathy.

but despite a reward of £100 being offered to anyone who could identify Wright's assailant, Nockolds was not given up.

In November 1830, the voices of disquiet rose again, but this time from farm labourers, after so many of them had been rendered superfluous by the new harvesting machinery. Activists like Nockolds mustered labourers into rioting mobs, who set about machine breaking; they also set fire to hay stacks in a number of locations across the county. At the 1831 Lent Assizes, Richard Nockolds and three alleged accomplices were accused of setting fire to stacks which were the property of farmer William Blake, of Swanton Abbott. They were found not guilty of this crime but were immediately charged with the same offence on Richard Ducker's farm. Nockolds was proved to have left notes at the scene; his handwriting matched and the notebooks showing the indentations of the messages written were presented in court. In the face of this evidence, Nockolds stood little chance of evading the charge and he alone was found guilty and sentenced to death. Nockolds was penitent; he confessed to throwing vitriol in the face of Mr Wright and pleaded forgiveness for his wife and young family. Nockolds was executed in front of Norwich Castle on 9 April 1831. After hanging for the usual hour his family were allowed to take his body away. They exhibited it at his cottage by the Cavalry Barracks gates in Pockthorpe. A small charge was made to view his body and a contemporary report concluded 'a considerable sum of money was in this way raised for his widow.'

115

TRIPLE ON THE DROP

William Thirkettle, William Pye and Gilpin Reynolds, 12 April 1834

William Thirkettle (27) had been born at Beeston and left home aged seventeen. In 1833, he was a common labourer, living at Woodbastwick, and working on a farm occupied by Mr Burroughes at Panxworth, where he earned a few extra coins as an occasional watch over the land. On the night of 7 October 1833, he returned home to Maria, his wife of six years. They retired to bed between 8 and 9 p.m. After being in bed for over an hour, Mr Thirkettle got up with a bad disorder of his bowels. When he returned, he found his wife nursing their six-month-old baby. She then went to sleep again, only to be awoken by a heavy blow on her forehead, delivered by her husband with his watching stick. He then continued to beat his wife until she fled, bleeding, to the kitchen, where she lost consciousness. Thirkettle attempted to blame the attack on four poachers who, he claimed, had intruded into the cottage. Even though she was beaten and bruised, Maria was convinced her husband had carried out the attack upon her. When Adam Dunn, the Blofield constable, arrived, he found Thirkettle's stick still covered in blood and Maria Thirkettle still lucid enough to accuse her husband with the words, 'You are the rogue.'

Title page of the pamphlet reproducing the sermon preached by Revd C. N. Wodehouse after the execution of Thirkettle, Pye and Reynolds.

A SERMON

PREACHED

AT THE CHURCH OF ST. MARY COSLANY,

On Sunday, April 13th,

BEING THE DAY AFTER

THE EXECUTION

OF

THIRKETTLE, PYE, AND REYNOLDS,

ON THE

Castle Hill at Norwich.

BY

THE REV. C. N. WODEHOUSE,

Prebendary of Norwich and Curate of St. Mary's.

FOURTH EDITION,

WITH ADDITIONAL PARTICULARS

BY

THE REV. JAMES BROWN,

Chaplain to the Castle.

Norwich:

PRINTED BY BACON AND KINNEBROOK.

PRICE SIX-PENCE.

William Thirkettle was brought before Mr Baron Vaughan at the Norfolk Assizes. Mr Reeve, the Blofield surgeon, who had attended Maria, stated 'she had received many blows struck with great violence' and candidly said he 'did not expect her to recover.' Hospital surgeon Mr Norgate, described the extent of Mrs Thirkettle's injuries: 'six wounds on her head, two of her teeth knocked out and a very extensive wound over the right eye, some two and a half inches in length, leaving the bone bared.' Mr Norgate was convinced it was three or four days before they stabilised Mrs Thirkettle and she was confined to hospital for nearly a month. Once the case had been heard, his Lordship asked Thirkettle if he had anything to say in answer to the charges. He despondently replied 'I have nothing to say of any use.' The jury retired for but a few minutes before stating they were of the opinion that Thirkettle had intended to kill his wife. They found him guilty and passed the sentence of death upon him. Thirkettle remained unmoved and unremorseful but once he encountered the prison chaplain, the initial shock cleared and he became aware of full horror of the dread sentence that had been passed upon him and he frequently burst into floods of tears.

Gilpin Reynolds (24), an agricultural labourer, was strongly suspected of being the culprit responsible for about twenty fires in the neighbourhood of Corpusty. Finally a case was found against him: he was accused of setting fire to a rick of straw, the property of Mr Hase of Corpusty, on 4 November 1833. The evidence presented in court revealed Reynolds had been the first to raise the alarm of fire and turned the cattle out of the yard where the fire had started; he also rendered considerable service in the attempts to extinguish it, remaining in a pond of water, up to his knees, filling pails for the bucket chain until the fire was brought under control. Several footprints were found near the scene of the fire, one of which was carefully cut out of the ground to be preserved in a box as evidence, nine days after the fire. Once Reynolds was in custody, his highlows (a type of agricultural boot) were compared with the footprint taken at the scene. Both were presented in court. As the prosecutor was convinced the print matched the sole of the boot, they were handed to the jury for inspection. Witness William Eke testified he had seen Reynolds pass his house in the direction of the Mr Hase's stack about half an hour before the alarm of fire was raised. Reynolds also gave a conflicting account of how he came to be there when he and some of the other villagers retired to the Wheat Sheaf pub after extinguishing the fire. The jury were convinced enough to return a verdict of guilty and Reynolds was sent to the gallows. Initially, he continued to proclaim his innocence of the crime for which he was to face death, but acknowledged that he deserved his sentence for many other offences. A short while before his execution Reynolds finally confessed to setting fire to Mr Hase's stack.

William Pye (32) and James Watts (25) were tried for setting fire to an outhouse at Coltishall; an act they had carried out when they were worse for drink, after a night at Willis' beer shop. There was some doubt over Watt's involvement and he was found not guilty, but Pye, who had changed his story a number of times, was found guilty and sentenced to death. By the time of the execution, it was strongly believed that Watts had in fact set the fire and then run off, while it was Pye who had taken a horse and ridden to raise the alarm. There was no re-trial and Pye went to the gallows. Watts came to watch the execution, but when he was recognised in the crowd he was obliged to make his escape to avoid their wrath.

116

'A RECKLESS LOVE OF MISCHIEF'

James Clarke, 18 April 1835

On the night of 20 January 1835, in the rural village of Buxton, James Clarke (20) went to his neighbour, Ben Dawson, looking for an ember to start a fire for his mother. He said he had just returned from the Lion public house, where he had seen his mother, who had been washing; she was tired after a long day and she had asked him to go home and light a fire for her. The neighbour's fire was nearly burnt out, but there was enough to get a light. Moments later, Robert Page and Gideon Fitt were passing along the road near John Bambridge's wheatstack, on Bartram's Meadow, when they observed a glint of light through the hedge. Curious about what the light could be doing there, the men went to investigate and saw a man, who they firmly believed to be Clarke, with a flame between his legs. They then observed him take a sheaf from the stack, put a light in its place, put the sheaves down on the fire – and the stack burst into flames. Clarke then retreated along the side of a hedge. Despite both witnesses deciding to 'go after' the incendiary, he disappeared. Soon after, the alarm was raised for help to extinguish the fire. Many people came to assist, with James Clarke among them but the stack was consumed by the flames. Curiously, it was only some time later, when Clarke, having failed to secure regular employment in Buxton, had gone to King's Lynn to follow his long-term intention of going to sea, that Page and Fitt told their story. Upon receipt of this statement, George Rayson, the constable of Buxton, set off in pursuit of Clarke who had, by that time, sailed up to Sunderland and found a position on a vessel which was waiting to sail. The constable traced Clarke's lodging house and took him at night, from his bed, and conveyed him with due speed over a distance of 300 miles to Norwich Castle.

Clarke was brought before Norfolk Assizes for trial. He admitted the stack was situated about 100 yards from his own house but he declared his innocence, claiming he had gone to the area to gather kindling for his mother's fire, saw the light near the stack and ran there to help extinguish the resulting fire. Clarke's defence made much of Page and Fitt's failure to reveal what they knew until quite some time after the event, but to no avail: the jury were convinced of his guilt and Clarke was sent to the gallows. After his condemnation, Clarke was left to reflect in his cell for half an hour; when the Chaplain entered he found the man in tears. Clarke did not deny his guilt; indeed, he confessed to the crime but he vehemently denied any part in any of the other seven similar offences that had occurred around the area of his village. He then took pains to point out that he bore no grudge against Mr Bainbridge, admitting he had always treated him with kindness but committed the offence on a whim, partly under the influence of drink but mostly 'from a reckless love of mischief.'

On the day of the execution a vast crowd was drawn to watch but they were concerned to see Clarke's nerves fail; despite being a naturally tall and powerful man, he had to be supported by a warder on the drop. Once the drop fell, it was noted: 'convulsive movements of the frame for several seconds indicated a painful death.'

A curious event occurred at this execution when a pensioner named Mr Wyer, who was well known for his eccentricities as a cake seller, publicly declared on Castle Hill that he would 'take the sufferer's place for 5s.' There was no switch of the condemned but nonetheless Wyer went home and hanged himself.

117
THE BURNHAM POISONERS

Frances Billings and Catherine Frarey, 10 August 1835

In a short row of cottages, standing adjacent to North Street in Burnham Market, lived the Billings, Frarey and Taylor families. Nearest the road, living in cramped rooms above Thomas Lake's carpenter's shop were Robert and Catherine Frarey with their three children. Next to them were Peter and Mary Taylor. Finally, James and Frances 'Fanny' Billings lived on this row with several of their children. She had given birth to fourteen children but only nine were living at the time of the trial.

Two sudden deaths, initially blamed on a mystery 'sickness', occurred in quick succession within the Frarey household in early March 1835, leaving poor Catherine Frarey (40) mourning as a widow and for the loss of a child staying with her. Two weeks later, neighbour Mary Taylor,

3 Dreadful Murders
BY POISON.

A full and true account of the dreadful and shocking Murder committed last week at BURNHAM MARKET, in the County of Norfolk on Mary, the wife of PETER TAYLOR, a journeyman shoemaker of that place; showing how she met with a painful but very sudden death by ARSENIC BEING MIXED WITH HER FOOD, as is suspected by her husband and two women of loose character with whom he was connected; and containing also a further account of the death of Mr. FRARY and a child who died in the same place as is suspected by the same treacherous means.

Some of the most distressing and harrowing murders ever remembered in the County of Norfolk, not even excepting the case of MARY WRIGHT, have just been perpetrated at Burnham Market, and have produced a surprising degree of excitement in that town and neighbourhood. On Thursday morning the 12th day of the present month, MARY TAYLOR, a married woman between 40 and 50 years of age, was taken very ill, and on Mr. Cremer the the surgeon being sent for he at once saw and said she was poisoned; and although all was done that could be done to save her life the poor women died the same night in the greatest agony. An Inquest was held on the following day before F. T. Quarles, Gent. Coroner for the Duchy of Lancaster; but there being then no proof of how the deceased came by the poison, although it was evident that her death had been caused by taking it, the Jury found a verdict to the effect that she died from the effects of arsenic, but by what means administered was unknown. It being remembered, however, in the neighbourhood, that there had been an intimacy between the husband of the deceased and Fanny Billing, a married woman living at the next door, and she being of a loose character, other inquiries were made It was then found that this Fanny Billing had a short time previous purchased some arsenic of a neighbouring druggist, saying at the time that she wanted it for a Mrs. Webster of Creake to poison some vermin with it. These rumours increased so much that two Magistrates in the neighbourhood (Frederick Hare and Henry Blyth, Esqrs.) thought proper to hold a special Meeting at the Hoste Arms, on the following Wednesday and summon the parties concerned before them. Mrs. Webster of Creake, denied ever having employed Billing to purchase poison;—a quantity of arsenic was found in Taylor's house mixed with some flour in a poke from which the deceased had

eaten, and it seemed surprising that if the husband knew nothing of, he should not be poisoned too, but he, it seems, was not effected. Taylor and Billing were at once taken into close custody, and several examinations have succeeded, which have caused, we understand, their being both fully committed to Walsingham Bridewell to take their trials for the murder next week at the assizes. As Billing was about to be removed by the Constables, a woman by the name of Frary, who had also been living near them, was over-heard to say to her "Mor hold your own, and they cannot hurt us." This led to other suspicions, especially as Frary's husband, and a child which had lived with them, had died 2 or three weeks before very suddenly. Frary was then also taken into custody, & the bodies of the husband and child disinterred & examined as to whether they died by poison. Their stomachs were brought to Norwich to be analized, and although we have not yet learned the result there is hardly any doubt but their lives were taken by the same treacherous means. Taylor, whose family we believe live at Whissonset, has been married near 20 years, and although there is no family, always appeared to live very comfortably with his wife: he has, too, always borne a steady moral character, and was a singer in the Dissenters' Meeting House in that Town for many years. The wife was a most steady and industrious woman, frequently maintaining both her husband, and herself by her industry he being frequently incapable of working from ill health, and this she has done entirely since last Whitsuntide.

Well might SOLOMON say of a loose woman—" he that goeth after her is as an Ox going to the slaughter, or a fool to the correction of the stocks: he goeth after her straitway 'til a dart strike through his liver,— as a bird hasteth to the snare, and knoweth not that it is for his life."

[WALKER, PRINTER, ORFORD-HILL.]

Broadside produced at the time of the trial of the 'Burnham Poisoners'.

wife of Peter Taylor (45), a journeyman cobbler, was taken violently ill. She died in the course of the afternoon and evening of 12 March. Mr Cremer, the local surgeon, had been summoned but could do nothing for Mary – and his suspicions were aroused. At the inquest, it was suggested that Peter Taylor had been 'associated' with Frances 'Fanny' Billings (46), who was described as 'a woman of loose character,' but this dalliance was not considered relevant to the death. The contents of Mary Taylor's stomach were analysed and found to contain arsenic, but by whom or how it had been administered remained unknown. Suspicion within Burnham fell upon Mary's slothful and unfaithful husband Peter Taylor.

Enquiries revealed Fanny Billings had recently bought arsenic from Henry Nash, the local chemist. When questioned, Billings claimed she was buying it to poison rats and mice for Mrs Webster of Creake; a statement Mrs Webster flatly denied. A poke of flour from the Taylor house was tested and traces of arsenic were found; this was enough for magistrates to

Broadside sold after the execution of Billings and Frarey, the last women to hang in Norfolk.

remand Peter Taylor and Fanny Billings to Walsingham Bridewell for further questioning. As Billings was being removed by constables onto the cart to go to the bridewell, Frarey was quoted as calling out, 'Mor, hold your own and they cannot hurt us.' Frarey was soon in custody too. As the weight of evidence against her was revealed, Catherine Frarey buckled under the pressure and went into rapid physical and mental decline.

By the time of the Summer Assizes the bill against Peter Taylor had been ignored by the Grand Jury. Concerns over Frarey's deteriorating health raised questions of her ability to stand trial but, nonetheless, Billings and Frarey appeared at the Norfolk Assizes on 7 August 1835. Investigations revealed the women had plotted to bring about the removal of each other's 'human obstacles' – *quid pro quo*. Frarey was charged with administering poison to Mary Taylor, with Billings as an accessory before the fact. The

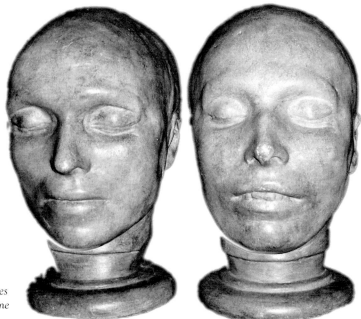

The death masks of Frances Billings (left) and Catherine Frarey (right).

second indictment charged them both with murdering Robert Frarey. The death of the child was not mentioned in the charges.

It was proved both women had purchased poison and their motives were suggested. Neither prisoner said a word in their defence, nor called any witnesses. After a short deliberation the jury found both the women guilty. Frances Billings and Catherine Frarey dictated their confessions to the crime in their condemned cells, adding that they had not only mixed arsenic with Mr Frarey's porter and gruel, but with his pills too, and that it took four doses of the poison to kill him. The execution scaffold was usually erected at the lower end of the bridge, near the porter's lodges for Norwich Castle Prison. But 'out of proper consideration for the exhausted condemned, whose bodily powers would prove inadequate to sustain them in walking the distance', the scaffold was erected at the upper end, nearer the door to the prison. This also made the proceedings visible to most of the vast crowd who assembled to watch the execution. It was particularly noted that the crowd, which numbered several thousand, consisted of an extraordinary number of women.

Shortly before the hour of twelve, the executioner suspended two ropes from the gallows' beam. Billings wore her 'coloured clothes' and walked with what appeared to be a firm step; Frarey, wearing widow's weeds, was near collapse and had to be carried up the steps of the scaffold. Placed upon the gallows' trapdoor, ropes around their necks, the women held hands; the fatal bolt was drawn, the trap fell and they were plunged to eternity. The hanging of Frances Billings and Catherine Frarey proved to be the last public double execution conducted in the county, and they remain the last women to be hanged in Norfolk.

118
HANGED FOR BAD MORALS?

Peter Taylor, 23 April 1836

Peter Taylor remained in Norwich after the trial of Frarey and Billings and even went to observe their execution. When the eyes had fallen away from the main spectacle, many people who had travelled down from Burnham for the event recognised Taylor and felt aggrieved at his temerity in being there, causing him to beat a hasty retreat. Taylor attempted to return to his brother's house, but the people of Burnham wanted him out of the village. A mob of villagers attacked the house, smashing windows and breaking down the doors. Gaining entry, they demanded that Taylor be handed over to them. They were told he was not there; in fact, he was hidden in the closet. Once the mob had left, Taylor fled to his father's house, only to be re-arrested upon new evidence coming to light, showing him to be more complicit with the murders than was previously believed.

He was brought before the magistrates and was re-committed for trial at the next Assizes. In all, Taylor would serve twelve months in prison before he would eventually stand trial. Witnesses claimed they had seen Billings pass Taylor a small paper packet and heard her say, 'here is enough for her.' Edward Sparks testified that he overheard a conversation when, on the morning before the death of Mary Taylor, her husband clapped his hand on Billings' shoulder and said, 'Never mind, she will soon be done away with, and it will soon be all right with us.' Despite brave attempts by the defence counsel to score points against the character and credibility of the witnesses, the jury found Taylor guilty of being an accessory before the fact and he was sentenced to death. Hanged before a large crowd, Taylor protested his innocence to the last.

NORWICH.

SUPERIOR SURGICAL INSTRUMENTS, COLLECTION OF RARE SKULLS, SKELETON, VALUABLE MEDICAL BOOKS, LECTURE DIAGRAMS, PREPARATION GLASSES, AND SURGERY FURNITURE.

CLOWES AND FLOWERDEW are favoured with directions from DONALD DALRYMPLE, Esq., who is retiring from Surgical Practice, to *Sell by Auction*, in the Large Room, at the Norfolk Hotel, Norwich, on *Thursday next, March 31st*, 1859, at Twelve o'clock, his numerous and very superior Instruments, which were particularized in last week's papers, and in catalogues, to be obtained or posted free on application at the Auctioneer's Offices, Bank Chambers, Norwich.

Notice for the sale of Mr Dalrymple's effects, including the skeleton of Peter Taylor.

Broadside sold after the execution of Peter Taylor.

Taylor's body was acquired by eminent Norfolk and Norwich Hospital surgeon Mr Donald Dalrymple, who made it into a skeleton and used it for the instruction of anatomy. Dalrymple inherited a considerable fortune on the death of his father-in-law and retired from surgical practice; his effects were sold at auction by Messrs Clowes and Flowerdew, at the Norfolk Hotel on St Giles Street, Norwich on 31 March 1859. The skeleton realised £2 10s and was bought by a Norwich Hospital medical student, Shephard T. Taylor. He later recorded, in his diary, that his manservant, Fox, and the surgery boy 'conveyed my skeleton to the carrier's, where it caused some excitement by the accidental protrusion of one of its feet through the straw.'

119

THE DENVER FORTUNE TELLER MURDER

George Timms and John Smith, 29 April 1837

Hannah Mansfield (50) was described as a woman of 'eccentric habits' who lived on Denver Common. It was also a popular belief she had hidden money and valuables in her home – where she was found murdered with her throat cut on 3 January 1837. A considerable amount of plate and £20 in cash had also been stolen. Three unknown males had been seen in the area, claiming to be embankers, shortly before the murder. Lynn police officer Mr Wright tracked the men to Doncaster where he arrested John Smith (25), alias Day, John Varnham (23) and George Timms (22). He returned them to Norfolk, where they were held at Swaffham. They were tried at the Norfolk Assizes on 6 April 1837. All three were found guilty and sentenced to death, but Varnham was commuted to imprisonment

after full confessions were received from Smith and Timms. The execution was attended by a crowd of thousands, who were shocked to see Smith was in the last stage of rapid decline. He had to be assisted to the scaffold. An eye witness recorded: 'After the bolt was drawn and the bodies swung round, a piercing cry rose from the dense mass of people of both sexes.' After hanging for the usual time, the bodies were taken down and carried into the interior of Norwich Castle Prison. All the prisoners were brought forward to view them in the place where they lay, as a warning that, if they did not mend their ways, the same thing could happen to them.

Broadside produced before the trial of the alleged murderers of Hannah Mansfield.

THE HEMPNALL POISONER

Charles Daines, 27 April 1839

On 11 March 1839, Mrs Hannah Daines stumbled to the doorstep of her neighbour, Mary Alexander, bent double with excruciating stomach pains and vomiting. Mrs Alexander sent word to Hannah's carpenter husband, Charles Daines (51), and assisted her friend back to her home where she also discovered two young children and another neighbour, Elizabeth Mills, sitting in a chair; all were racked with similar symptoms. Soon more concerned neighbours came to the house. When Charles returned home he was met at the door by Mrs Alexander. He appeared surprised at the situation and asked if Hannah was ill. Mr Utting, the surgeon, had been sent for and Mr Daines enquired what she had been taking, Mary said it had only been tea. He replied, 'Surely there is nothing in the water.'

When Surgeon Utting arrived, he soon diagnosed poisoning and took possession of the sop and remnants of tea. Three-year-old Elizabeth Daines died at 4 p.m. and when Mrs Mills died a short while later, Charles Daines was arrested on suspicion of murder. Dr Firth of Norwich analysed the stomachs of both victims, along with the sop and tea, and found arsenic present in all of them; a broken basin filled with 'pink powder' from the Daines residence was found to contain *nux vomica* and arsenic.

Daines was first indicted at Norfolk Assizes on 11 April for the murder of his daughter, but after half an hour's deliberation, the jury believed there was reasonable doubt and acquitted him. The following morning Daines was charged with the attempted poisoning of his wife; a sordid tale then emerged. Daines

Broadside sold after the execution of Charles Daines, 'The Hempnall Poisoner'. (NLIS)

THE LIFE, TRIAL, CONFESSION, & EXECUTION OF

CHARLES DAINES, AGED FIFTY,

Who was Executed on Saturday, April 27th, 1839, for poisoning ELIZABETH DAINES, his Daughter, 3 years old, and ELIZABETH MILLS, his Neighbour, at HEMPNALL.

CHARLES DAINES, was a Carpenter, and resided at Hempnall, in Norfolk, was married, and had three children; he was considered a steady industrious man, and appeared affectionate to his children, for which several persons subscribed for counsel to defend him on his trial, as he was respected previous to his imbibing those horrid ideas, the perpetration of which has brought him to his untimely end.

On the evidence which was given on the 11th of March, after sending for her husband, I found her very sick outside the door, she vomited very much, I led her home, Elizabeth Mills was sitting in a chair very sick and ill: there was on the table some sop in a basin, and tea in a copy, there was a tea kettle on the fire place. When the Prisoner came home he asked what was the matter, he said is Elizabeth ill? I said yes, he asked me what they had been taking; I answered some tea; he said surely there is nothing in the water; he reached hold of the kettle and went out with it; on his return he said he had emptied the kettle and rinsed it out and filled it with fresh water; he pointed to the sop and asked if that was any thing they had been taking of, and said he would take that and throw it away; I answered we had sent for Mr. Utting, and I thought it ought to be there when Mr. Utting came: The Prisoner went to the pantry and brought out some powder in a broken basin, he said it was some powder he had bought to kill mice; he said he did not know how it should come into the kettle, except the mice had been in the broken basin and then into the pint pot with which he had filled the kettle; the women (Fryer and Rackham) said, a Doctor ought to be sent for; he said he thought it better to get some medicine quicker than he could get a Doctor; Prisoner went for some, it was unknown wine and castor oil.—The Child died about four o'clock.

John Daines aged 18, son to the prisoner stated, he came home about nine o'clock on Sunday Evening, the 10th March, my mother was upstairs, not in bed, my father in bed; when I came in, the two children, my father and mother were the only persons in the house; I locked the door after me; a pail of water stood in the back house; I drank out of it with a pint mug; I went to bed; I got up about six o'clock next morning; my father was up; my mother came down as I was fit to go out; my father went out before me; before I went out I drank some more water from the same pail, with the same mug; I went to work with my father; the kettle produced is the same; when I took the mug from off the stool, several things were on it; the kettle usually had the lid on.

Sarah Friar stated, I heard Prisoner say he never had any Poison in his house until he got two-pennyworth of Figs, to destroy the mice, he would not have any, as he must have a witness.

J. Utting, Surgeon, Long Stratton, was sent for to Hempnall; I found the little girl, the son, and Mrs. Mills very ill; I went to Mrs. Daines, she had symptoms of poison (arsenic) in her stomach; I took possession of the sop and tea.

Mr. Firth, Surgeon, Norwich, analysed the stomachs of the victims, together with the sop and tea, he found them to contain arsenic; he also analysed the powder in the basin which was nux vomica and arsenic; he washed the kettle three times and found arsenic each time.

The Judge proceeded to comment on the evidence, leaving the Jury to decide of the cause of their deaths arose from poison and whether administered by the Prisoner, if so, they would find him guilty, and if in case of any doubt, they would acquit him.—The Jury retired he found an hour, and on returning, acquitted the prisoner!

On the following morning he was again placed at the Bar on a charge with having attempted to poison his wife. Mr. Evans stated the case for the prosecution, who said he was the last person to complain of the verdict of the Jury on the former trial. He could not then call the witness before them, but in this instance where the injury was personal to the wife she would be made an evidence. Another circumstance was, that, unfortunately, the prisoner during the last two years had formed a criminal connexion with a woman named Lloyd who proved the Prisoner said to her: his wife was so ailing a person, and he wished her to keep single that he might marry her if his wife died.

Hannah Daines the wife of the prisoner was sworn. I drank tea on the 10th March, I used a copper tea-kettle; my husband drank tea with me; I felt no bad effects; I put the kettle in the back house, against the boiler, under the shoe shelf; the lid of the kettle was off. My husband got up rather before six next morning; I got up soon after six, and came down stairs; my husband was just leaving the house as I came down; my son left almost directly after; I found the fire lighted; my husband usually lights the fire when he gets up first; the kettle was filled and on the fire; my husband usually fills it if he gets up first; no one was in the house till I got my children up; I dressed them and gave them their breakfast, it consisted of sop made with some water from the kettle, I then made tea for myself, I drank one cup, about 5 minutes after I felt bad in the stomach, there was a sort of heat in my throat; the children kept throwing up very much; I sent for Mrs. Mills, she came directly, she took a cup of tea, she seemed struck very bad; I went to Mrs. Alexander and she sent for my husband; I know Ann Lloyd, she is a widow, my husband has been acquainted with her about a year and a half: I have had words with my husband about her because he did not behave so kind to me as he used to do.

The evidence of all the witnesses were similar to those on the Thursday, and the case for the prosecution being closed, his Lordship summed up the evidence. The Jury retired, and after an absence of an hour returned a verdict of GUILTY! The learned Judge in a most impressive manner proceeded to pass on the prisoner the awful sentence of the law, earnestly imploring him to repent of his crime and to make his peace with God.—The prisoner almost immediately after being taken to his cell, made an entire CONFESSION of his guilt to the Chaplain of the Gaol. He also acknowledged he had made the attempt on two former occasions—one by putting a small quantity of arsenic on some fried potatoes, and the other by mixing a portion in some peasoup. After his condemnation he became quite resigned to his fate, acknowledging the justice of his sentence, and endeavoured with the assistance of the Chaplain to prepare himself for the awful change.

On the morning of EXECUTION, the throngs of persons from the villages for miles round kept entering into the city till the hour approached, and up till 12 o'clock numbers were seen thronging up every entrance to the Castle hill. At the usual time the mournful procession commenced moving from the Castle to the foot of the Scaffold, which after a few minutes the wretched man ascended, he appeared resigned, the executioner having adjusted the rope, the necessary preparations being completed, the bolt was drawn and he was launched into eternity!

had been having an affair with local widow, Ann Lloyd, for the past two years. Daines had told Lloyd his wife was 'an ailing person, not long for this world, and that he desired Mrs Lloyd to keep single until his wife died.'

The jury were convinced of Daines' guilt and after passing the death sentence, the judge implored that Daines repent and make his peace with God. Upon his return to his cell, Daines made a full confession to the prison chaplain and also admitted attempting the poisoning on two other occasions. Daines' execution drew a large crowd and it was recorded, 'He appeared to die an extremely hard death.' The body of Charles Daines was buried in the churchyard of St Michael-at-Thorn, on Ber Street. He was the last executed felon to be buried without prison walls in Norfolk.

121
'I'M INNOCENT OF THIS HERE JOB'

John Randalsome, 22 August 1840

John Randalsome had lived as a servant for eleven years, during which time he had formed a relationship with Elizabeth Punchard, who he had promised to marry in 1838. They were living apart, but she heard that Randalsome had got married; when she asked him about this, he lied, saying, 'you may make yourself comfortable, I am no more married than you are.' Two weeks later, Randalsome asked his wife Mary to meet him at her father's farm at Thwaite. He attacked her, severely wounding her about the head and face with a wooden hedge stake before throwing her into the pond where she drowned. The crime was investigated by the Superintendent of Police, Henry Hubbersty. When questioned about the crime, Randalsome replied, 'God strike me dead but I'm innocent of this here job.'

He was found guilty at the Assizes on 3 August and was executed on Castle Hill,

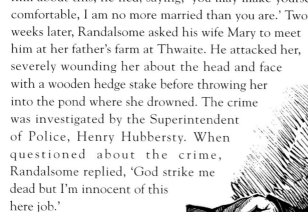

John Randalsome in the dock at the Assizes.

protesting his innocence to the end. After hanging for an hour, he was cut down and buried in the precincts of Norwich Castle Prison.

122

TWICE IN THE POND, ONCE ON THE GALLOWS

John Self, 14 August 1841

John Self (20) was an agricultural labourer living in a cottage with his father's family near Wymondham. About 2 miles from his home lived a young girl named Jemima Stimpson (15); neither knew the other well, let alone had any relationship. On 17 July 1841, Jemima was working for Mr Rush, cutting thistles in a turnip field about a mile distant from the homes of Self and Stimpson. Self was at work on a drift way, called 'the Loke', adjacent to the turnip field. He went over to Stimpson and they struck up an acquaintance during their meal break. They then returned to their labours until about 4 p.m., when Stimpson left her field and was seen walking to a barley field known as Gaire's Close, where Self had just arrived from his work, carrying a spade over his shoulder. The pair then walked on and disappeared from view behind a tall hedge.

By 4.30 p.m. Self was back home, and decided to finish braiding a straw hat for his brother until it was time for him to retire to bed at his usual hour. Jemima Stimpson did not return home, however, and her family had great concern for the whereabouts of the girl and so a search was organised. Searchers, near the gap at Gaire's Close, found a large spot of blood and trampled grass. Following a track, forced through the barley, they came to a pond where they found Jemima's body. Self was the last person seen with her and police constables were soon at his house. Self was out, but their search uncovered bloodstained trousers, a knife known to belong to Jemima in the pocket of his coat, a bloody cloth, wet stockings and a spade spattered with blood. When Self was asked to account for the blood on his trousers, he claimed he had been working with Jem Wright,

John Self, the cruel murderer of Jemima Stimpson.

Broadside sold at the execution of John Self. (NLIS)

who had cut his finger 'with some stubbs'. However, when questioned about this, Wright denied this was the case and Self was brought before the Norwich Assizes on 28 July. After a deliberation of just a quarter of an hour, the jury returned a verdict of guilty and Mr Justice Williams pronounced the sentence of death.

When all hopes of reprieve were gone, Self wrote his confession. He had killed Jemima after he had 'played with her' and she threatened to tell her mother of it and expose him. Self threw her down and struck her with his spade a number of times, until he believed he had killed her; he then took her by the heels, and dragged her to the pond and threw her in. Returning to the place of the murder, Self attempted to cover his tracks before returning for his spade by the pond. When he arrived, he found Jemima sitting about two yards from the edge of the pond with blood running from her wounds. Her eyes appeared to 'fix' upon him, but she neither cried nor spoke. Self threw her back in the pond and pressed his spade upon her neck until she drowned. Self was executed in front of a large crowd upon Castle Hill by executioner William Calcraft. After hanging for about an hour, the body was taken down and buried within the precincts of the prison.

THE YARMOUTH SHOP MURDER

Samuel Yarham, 11 April 1846

On 18 November 1844, Harriet Candler was found murdered at her shop on the corner of Row 152 fronting Howard Street, Great Yarmouth; her head had been battered with a hammer and her throat had been cut with a knife. The suspects, James Hall, James Mapes and Robert Royal, were brought before the Norfolk Spring Assizes in 1845; Samuel Yarham, another member of the gang, the chief witness for the prosecution, having turned Queen's Evidence also appeared.

Trial, Execution, & Confession OF **SAMUEL YARHAM**

For the **WILFUL MURDER of HARRIET CANDLER**, of Great Yarmouth, who was executed on the Castle Hill, on Saturday April 11th, 1846.

SAMUEL YARHAM was placed at the bar at the Norwich Assizes, for the Murder of Mrs. Candler, at Yarmouth, on the 18th of November, 1844. It will be recollected, that Mrs. Candler occupied the lower part of a house at Yarmouth, the upper part being held by an attorney named Catchpole. Yarham's wife was servant to him, and Yarham himself was allowed to pursue his business of a shoemaker on the premises. At the time of the murder, Yarham, and three men, named Royal, Mapes, and Hall, were apprehended, and Yarham made a confession, implicating the three men in the murder. They were tried for the offence; each, however, succeeded in proving an alibi, and acquittal followed. So insensed were the public against Yarham, that he was obliged to quit Yarmouth. Subsequently Yarham made a confession to Mrs. Dick, (the individual who found the money that was stolen,) that he was the party who cut the old lady's throat; he was, in consequence, apprehended in Gloucestershire, and now appeared to take his trial. In a measure the testimony was substantiated by Mrs. Dick's daughter, who swore that Yarham was the identical individual who was observed, after the stolen property was found, poking in the sand for the treasure. Mr. Dasent made a powerful address to the jury in favour of the prisoner, arguing that the fact of Mrs. Dick having withheld this important evidence so long, was sufficient to throw distrust upon her testimony. The judge having recapitulated the evidence, the jury returned a verdict of Guilty, and the prisoner was sentenced to be hanged. The wretched man, who had listened to the trial with close attention and to the awful sentence of the Learned Judge without evincing any emotion, save a slight and occasional quivering of the lips and eyes, was then removed from the dock, while the shouts of the populace on the "hill" resounded in his ears.

My hour is come, my glass is run, now by the law's decree,
On Saturday next condemn'd to die upon a fatal tree;
All for a cruel murder as all do understand,
Which has caused great sensation and horror thro' the land.
In vain I sought to cloak my crime, and steadfastly deny'd,
That I had been her murderer, and many schemes I try'd;
Thinking thereby to save my life, but vain was every plan,
For in the minds of all mankind I stood a guilty man.
When I review my wicked life, I shudder with dismay,
No consolation cheers me—a wretched cast-a-way;
No ray of hope revives my soul, to look beyond the sky,
While every moment seems to say," To-morrow you must die.

CONFESSION

On the 19th of November Yarham stated to Mrs. Dick that he was the murderer, three weeks after that he met her in the market, and said, he let them (Mapes, &c.) in at the back door, he told them that she kept her money in her bedroom. While there were Mrs. Candler came in sooner then they expected, on hearing her come in they put out the light, and sit upon the bed, Royal went in & asked for half-an-ounce of tobacco, and as she was getting it, Hall knocked her down with a pair of pincers, they thought she was dead. Mapes then ran to the Feathers' tap. As he was going along the Market Gates he saw a person turn a light on him, who afterwards appeared to be Layton. He then ran home telling the others to bury the money and give him a signal. When he went home he cut her throat with the lard knife. Royal gave the signal and he opened the window and saw Royal going down the street, a man came up and they both went away together.

THE EXECUTION.

This morning the above unhappy malefactor paid the forfeit of his life to the offended laws of his country. No execution of late years has attracted so large an assemblage of spectators, some thousands being present. About nine o'clock he took some refreshment, and shortly afterwards the sheriff arrived at the castle, and immediately proceeded to the condemned cell. The usual melancholy preparations having been completed, Yarham was brought to the room where he was to be pinioned. He appeared quite calm & collected, and walked with a firm step. The melancholy procession then proceeded towards the scaffold, which he mounted without any assistance, and in less than a minute the drop fell, and the wretched culprit was launched into eternity.

The sacred laws of GOD and man I spurned with disdain,
Left no dishonest means untried, my purposes to gain;
But now my crimes have found me out, the blood my hands have
Now cries aloud for vengeance on my devoted head. (shed,)
O could I for one moment a last'ning world address,
If in this world or that to come, the hope for happiness;
The ranks of factious traitors, as from destruction run.
Flee from those hellish counsels, which thousands has undone
For had I been by timely wise, and kept the honest way,
I might have been a prosperous and happy man this day;
But mask the sad alternative— I die by law's decree,
A wretched malefactor upon a fatal tree.

Walker and Co. Printers, Church Street, St. Mile's, Norwich.

Broadside sold after the execution of Samuel Yarham.

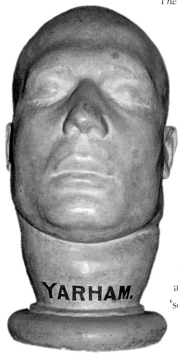

The death mask of Samuel Yarham.

The three were acquitted, but Yarham seems to have been under the misapprehension that, having informed against his fellow gang members, he could not now be accused of murder himself. He even went so far as to boldly claim that he had dealt the fatal wounds inflicted upon Mrs Candler. Yarham was tried and found guilty at the Norfolk Assizes on 27 March 1846. His execution fell on Tombland Fair day and was conducted in the presence of 30,000 spectators. Festivities were suspended for the duration of the execution, but once it had been carried out 'gongs, drums and other instruments commenced their uproar and the mountebanks and clown their antics while the whirl-gigs and ups-and-downs were soon in full swing.' Owing to the 'scandalous character' of the proceedings, a public meeting was held at St Andrew's Hall on 17 April, under the presidency of the Mayor, and it was decided to petition Parliament for the abolition of capital punishment.

124
THE STANFIELD HALL MURDERS

James Blomfield Rush, 21 April 1849

The Stanfield Hall murders were one of the most infamous crimes of the nineteenth century and remain the most notorious case in the history of crime in Norfolk. Books and broadsides recounting every dramatic and lurid detail of the murder sold in unprecedented numbers; the 'Sorrowful Lamentations' of the murderer sold an incredible 2½ million copies across the country. Columns, pages and whole supplements were given over to the murders, in both local and national papers. Queen Victoria was recorded as taking a personal interest and even one of the greatest authors of his day, Charles Dickens, visited the scene and recorded his impression that it had 'a murderous look that seemed to invite such a crime.' Simply naming the location would stimulate talk of the crime and the dastardly deeds connected with it – Stanfield Hall. James Blomfield Rush, the perpetrator of the murders, fitted the bill of a classic Victorian melodrama villain perfectly, not only

Stanfield Hall, c. 1849.

in physical appearance, in both his build and dress, but in his behaviour, manners, morals and sinister schemes that were exposed at his trial. His wax image 'taken from life at Norwich' by Madame Tussaud was displayed in her Chamber of Horrors for over 120 years.

Rush was a farmer with pretensions of being a country squire, but he had a long record of dubious deals and financial problems; he was always trying to find legal loopholes to get himself out of debt or bad financial commitments. He also failed to defend suits brought against him for seduction and bastardy, by more than one complainant. Rush was to meet his match in Isaac Jermy, the Recorder of Norwich, who knew the law and finance and was not afraid to use it to his advantage.

The mortgage from Isaac Jermy to Rush for his home, Potash Farm, was due for settlement on 30 November 1848, but Rush had no way of paying it. On the night of 28 November 1848, Rush walked the short distance from Potash Farm to Stanfield Hall, where he disguised himself with a mask, wig and whiskers and hid in the shrubbery. When Isaac Jermy stepped out from the hall after dinner, to take in the evening air, Rush shot him at almost point blank range. The masked assassin then strode into the hall, where he shot dead Jermy's son. A further shot caught Mrs Jermy's upper arm, while a second wounded Eliza Chastney in the groin and thigh as they attempted to flee upstairs. The murderer then made his exit by the side door. After medical examination, it was thought Eliza had received 'a whole charge', causing a compound fracture of the bone. The wound to Mrs Jermy's arm eventually resulted in amputation. Despite wearing a disguise, the bulk and gait of Rush were quite unmistakable and he was soon under arrest.

THE EXECUTION OF
JAMES BLOOMFIELD RUSH

AT

NORWICH CASTLE, APRIL 23rd., 1849,

For the murder of Isaac Jermy, Esq., the Recorder of Norwich, and his son, I. Jermy Jermy, Esq.,

AT

STANFIELD HALL.

Between 11 and 12 o'clock the bell of St Peter's, Mancroft, tolled the death knell of the criminal. When conducted to the turnkey's room to be pinioned he met Calcraft, whereupon he said to Mr Pinson " Is this the man that is to do the business ?" The reply was " Yes." When he was pinioned he shrugged up his shoulders, saying " This don't go easy ; it's too tight."

Within two or three minutes after 12 o'clock the mournful cavalcade proceeded from the interior of the Castle to the spot on which the gibbet was erected. The chaplain, who headed the procession, read, as he passed along, part of the burial service.

When the procession left the Castle gate to proceed to the gibbet, Rush presented a most melancholy and dejected appearance. He was dressed in a plain suit of black, wearing no neck-hankerchief. His shirt collar was turned down. For about twenty yards he walked with a firm unwavering step, but in a moment afterwards he raised his pinioned hands to his face and trembled violently. He then removed his hands from his face, and turning up his eyes to heaven, assumed the attitude of penitence and prayer. On reaching the gallows the rev. chaplain offered up a prayer. While this prayer was being read the condemned convict seemed to be deeply impressed with the awful character of his situation. Immediately on the close of the prayer he beckoned to Mr Pinson, the governor of the Castle, when the following brief conversation ensued :

Rush : Mr Pinson, I have a last request to make to you. It is that the bolt may be withdrawn while the chaplain is reading the benediction—" The grace of our Lord Jesus Christ, and the love of God, and the fellowship of the Holy Ghost, be with us all, evermore."

Mr Pinson : I will communicate your wish to the chaplain, and I have no doubt it will be attended to.

The hangman then placed the unhappy convict under the beam on which he was to hang, and affixed the fatal rope around his neck. Rush said, " For God's sake give me rope enough. Don't be in a hurry ; take your time." Then moving his head about, he said " Put the knot a little higher up, don't hurry." The rev. chaplain proceeded with the prayer, and on arriving at the words " The grace of our Lord Jesus Christ," &c., Calcraft withdrew the bolt, the platform went down, and all was over. His death was greeted with loud applause by an immense crowd who had assembled to witness the execution.

Good people listen unto my song,
And girls to whom honest hearts belong,
Pay great attention to what I say,
And by the wicked be not led astray.

Poor Emily Sandford was learned well,
Yet mark what to her fatal lot befel,
The serpent's tongue caused the tears to gush,
For she was betrayed by James Bloomfield Rush.

She begged most pleadingly to be his wife,
And lived with him a most unhappy life,
And though the hot tears down her cheeks did flow
The monster heeded not Miss Sandford's woe.

But seeing that she now was ruined quite,
She stood upon her feet in female might,
And with her pale hand stretched towards his face
Said, " God will curse thee for my deep disgrace."

Forboding were the words Miss Sandford said,
For murderous thoughts were in the wretch's head.
He set to work, and speedily did plan,
The death of servants, husband, wife, and son.

A five barrelled pistol he soon did buy,
And then a mask upon his face did try,
Put on his hat and cloak and pistols drew,
Within its fold a bloody deed to do.

For Stanfield Hall he quick did start,
And old Squire Jermy he shot through the heart !
And while the grey-hair'd man lay bleeding there,
He shot his son and lovely wife so fair.

Eliza Chestney to her Mistress ran,
Saying, " dearest mistress, who is this man ?"
And, while she pressed her mistress to her heart,
A bullet pierced in a dangerous part.

James Bloomfield Rush was then to prison sent,
Miss Sandford against him a witness went,
She was well avenged—for on the gallows high,
The base seducer was condemned to die!

The Judge soon told him that his race was run,—
That he must die for murderous deeds he'd done,
To use the time that yet on earth was given,
In making peace with his God in heaven.

O had you witness'd the parting hour,
Of this wretched man and his nine children dear,
Your hearts would break to think that they might see,
Their father hung upon a gallows tree.

One of many variations of the broadsides sold at and after the execution of James Rush, the infamous 'Stanfield Hall Murderer'.

Rush's trial opened on 29 March 1849 at the Norfolk Assizes before Baron Rolfe. Rush had arrogantly turned down offers of legal counsel, opting to conduct his own defence; he was often belligerent and attempted to intimidate the prosecution witnesses. When Rush presented his defence he spoke for a marathon fourteen hours. His five witnesses were hardly worthwhile, and some were even damning; amongst them was Maria Blanchflower, a nurse at Stanfield Hall. She stated she had seen the disguised murderer but did not recognise the figure as Rush, despite having passed within a few feet of him. Rush asked, 'Did you pass me quickly?'– an unfortunate slip of the tongue, especially in open court. After a deliberation of just ten minutes, the jury returned a verdict of guilty and Rush was sentenced to death. The behaviour of Rush in Norwich Castle Prison was very much the same before, during and after trial and sentence. He adopted the airs and phraseology of a devoutly religious man, but his act fooled no one. Rush was executed in front of Norwich Castle by William Calcraft on 21 April 1849. His execution drew a crowd of thousands, some of whom came on special trains from London and other parts of East Anglia. An eye witness recorded the scene:

James B. Rush drawn from life in the dock at Norfolk Assizes.

The wretched creature looked for an instant on the vast mass of spectators, whose earnest gaze was upon him and on every movement he made, and then turned himself round and faced the castle – his back being towards the populace.

Clearly Rush could not resist one last defiant gesture. He shook hands with the Governor; Calcraft then drew the white hood over Rush's head and, having fastened the rope to the beam, set about adjusting the noose around Rush's neck. Unable to resist a last whinge, Rush snapped at the executioner from under the hood, 'This does not go easy! Put the thing a little higher – take your time – don't be in a hurry!' These were to be Rush's last words. As the Chaplain read the section requested by Rush, 'The Grace of our Lord Jesus Christ…,' the signal was given and the bolt was drawn, releasing the gallows' trapdoor, 'and the scene of life closed upon this malefactor, almost without a struggle.' The crowd maintained an eerie silence, excepting a few faint shrieks as the trap fell; the sound of the falling trap and the tightening rope was audible over some considerable distance.

After hanging the usual hour, Rush's body was taken down and removed to the prison on a wheeled litter. In the afternoon, Rush's head was shaved and a cast was taken for phrenological study by Mr Bianchi of St George's Middle-Street, in Norwich. The remains of James Rush were then buried within the precincts of the prison.

125

MURDER ON THE ESTATE

Henry Groom, 16 August 1851

On the afternoon of 4 July 1851, the body of John Ayton, the Earl of Leicester's Superintendent of the brick and tile works at Burnham Overy, was found shot dead in a pit at a plantation on the Holkham Estate. Henry 'George' Groom had made himself conspicuous by his obvious loitering near the entrance to the pit, being recognised by Dr Young as he drove by. A shepherd also came forward who had noticed Groom running

A naive illustration from a broadside recounting the murder of John Ayton by Henry Groom.

near the plantation and stooping as if he wished to avoid being seen. After the shots were heard Groom was spotted again, this time running away; he even brushed past the shepherd, keeping his head hanging down as if he didn't wish to be recognised.

Wells constable George Lumley arrested Groom (32) at his house. Groom swore he knew nothing about the murder, but upon being searched a £5 note from Messrs Gurney Bank and a watch belonging to the murdered man – containing watch papers with Ayton's name written thereon – were found about his person. When the police searched Groom's house, they discovered a large pistol that appeared to have been recently discharged. A further fifteen sovereigns and twelve half sovereigns, the latter wrapped up in a piece of paper, on which was written a memorandum in Ayton's writing, were also discovered. Indicted on the 28 July, the evidence against Groom was damning and his motives were clear. Groom had worked at the brick yard for some time, but proving 'unsuitable' for the work was moved to less lucrative employment on the estate. Groom blamed Ayton personally for this and let his animosity be well known about the estate. Knowing Ayton's routine, he thought he could kill and rob him without detection.

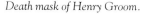

Death mask of Henry Groom.

Tried at the Norfolk Assizes, Groom had no counsel; being very deaf, he used a hearing trumpet throughout the trial. Groom agreed he was around the scene at the time of the murder, but denied killing Ayton; he accounted for the money found under his bed by saying he had found it on the road and insisting 'nobody has ever seen me kill a man.' The jury returned a unanimous verdict of guilty for the murder and theft; the judge, Mr Justice Cresswell, had no option but to don the black cap and pronounce the sentence of death by hanging.

126
THE TITTLESHALL MURDER

William Thompson, 8 April 1854

On 18 November 1853, a pool of blood was discovered on the road at Tittleshall. Following the trail of blood through a gap in the hedge into a wood, the blood spattered body of Norwich jeweller and watch dealer Lorenz Beha was discovered in a ditch. Horrific wounds on the poor man's head and face had been inflicted by a woodman's axe found close by the body. Investigations led to William Thompson (21), who had bought a watch from Beha and still owed £6 5s for it. It transpired that Thompson was not 'in funds' to meet his debt, so he murdered and robbed his creditor. Tried before Lord Chief Baron Parke at the Norfolk Assizes, Thompson was found guilty and sentenced to death. Of his execution upon Castle Hill, it was recorded that, 'the criminal's struggles continued five minutes', but criticism was reserved for the crowd:

The lowest and most degraded classes in the city and county assembled on the hill... and more scenes of drunkenness and immorality were exhibited than had been seen for a long time previously in Norwich.

Death mask of William Thompson.

Broadside sold after the execution of William Thompson. (NLIS)

THE TRIAL, SENTENCE CONFESSION, AND EXECUTION OF

William Thompson,

Aged 21, who was Executed at Norwich, on Saturday April 8th, 1854, for the Wilful MURDER of LORENZ BEHA at TITTLESHALL, NORFOLK.

William Thompson, 21 was charged with wilful murdering Lorenz Beha at Tittleshall on the 18th of November last and stealing from his person two 5£5 bank notes five sovereigns four half-sovereigns twenty shillings a sixpence, a four penny piece 3 silver watches of the value of £18 twelve watch keys sixteen box keys of the value of 3s and one purse value 6d. his property.

Mr. Evans and Mr. Bulver appeared for the prosecution, and Mr. Cooper for the defence.

The prisoner appeared on the whole to be careless and indifferent as to the result of the proceedings against him.

The following evidence was then adduced.

Harriet Ewing said—I am the wife of Robert Ewing, and live at Wellingham On November 18th I saw Lorenz Beha he had a carpet bag with him. He was in the habit of coming to my house once a month. He generally came at noon on Friday's He stay at at my house about five minutes on leaving my house he went on the Tittleshall road that road lead him past Mr. Norton's plantation.

John Roberson—I live at Tittleshall and am a butcher by trade Tittleshall is about a mile from Wellingham, On the 18th Nov. I was going from Tittleshall to Wellingham, when near Mr Norton's Plantation I observe some blood in the road This was about 3 o'clock in the afternoon I was the right side of the road In the ditch I observed a body and some more blood. I procured the assistance of four persons and soon after this the clergyman Mr. Digby came up. We examined the body, the face was very much cut The trousers pockets were turned inside out There was a box lying by and a bag, the box was pickled, A stick laid on the right side of the body, and also an umbrella we also found by it the ditch, there was a great deal of blood it the body was the body of Mr. Lorenz Beha, it was removed to the Griffin Inn at Tittleshall.

COPY OF VERSES.

In now they drack from far and near
this wretched sight to see
A youth scarce twenty years of age
Suspended on a tree,
My time is come my race is run
No longer I can stay
I see grim Death approaching me
To summons me away,
What a dismal sight to see
Exposed on Norwich fatal tree.

I Lorenz Beha did way-lay
There I in ambush stood
I with a hatchet did him slay
And robbed him of his goods
I took from him his property
And beat his body sore
Then dragged him to a lonesome spot
And left him in his gore

Mr. J. Jump, Surgeon, said—I am a surgeon, and live at Litcham. I was shown a body on the evening of the murder. It was shown me as the body of Beha. On the following Monday I examined it minutely.

William Webster,—I am a butcher, residing a Tittleshall, I left my home about half-past eleven on the morning of the day of the murder I passed the place about a quarter to twelve, I saw Thompson near the plantation, He had a stop and a cap on

Mr, Cooper, counsel for the prisoner, then made a very able defence.

The jury, after a very brief deliberation, returned a verdict of GUILTY.

The Clerk of the Arraigns—w Thompson you have been found guilty of the wilful murder of Lorenz Beha what have you to say why sentence of death should not be passed upon you—

THE PRISONERS DEFENCE

I left my father's house, Tittleshall, on Friday, November the 18th, at about half-past eleven o'clock in the forenoon, and went for a walk up the Wellingham road, When I had got up to Mr. Riches' plantation. it was about twelve. I saw a man get up from the bushes in the plantation. He asked me if I knew what time it was I told him that I thought about twelve. I then walked on and saw him either lying or sitting down in the same place. When I got round the corner to Mr. Norton's plantation, which was about eighty or one hundred yards from the place where I first saw the man, I got over the fence to ease myself, While I was doing so, Wm. Webster, the butcher, came past, There was a man standing in the ditch by the side of the dead body he was bent over it, I saw his hands was wet and daubed with blood I asked him what he was after he immediately got out of the ditch and got hold of me round my legs and daubed my trousers with blood he begged of me not to tell any one he said if I did he would chop me down I see him take out the purse some money he then put his hands into his waist coat pocket he pulled 3 watches 3 he gave me I said I would not have them he said I should he, in a dark person, I never saw him no more till I got to Roper, that is all I can say about it.

Now I am cast and doomed to die
On Norwich Castle tree
And of the multitude around
No one does pity me
I see the hangman me approach
I see the awful spot
And as I feel the hangmans grasp
I tremble on the Drop.

Near Tittleshall I did reside
And happy might have been
And such a dead as I have done
Was scarcely ever seen
Farewell my friends a last farewell
No power can me save—
I now must go, in grief and woo
Unto the silent grave

The Judges Address

The Chief Baron then assumed the black cap, and proceeded to pass sentence of death Prisoner at the bar you have been found guilty of wilful murder, upon evidence as clear as conclusive, and as decisive as I ever heard in a court of justice—It is now my painful duty to pass the sentence of the court upon you, that you be taken to the place from whence you came , and from thence to the place of execution that you be hanged by the neck until you be dead. and that your body shall be buried in precincts of the prison.

EXECUTION

At an early hour, the space before the Prison was crowded to excess by persons of both sexes anxious to witness the execution of the wretched prisoner, which increased to such a degree, that a number of people suffered from the pressure, The Sheriffs with their attendants arrived at the prison they then proceeded to the condemned cel, where they found the Rev. Ordinary engaged in prayer with the wretched culprit. After the usual formalities had been observed of demanding the delivery of the body of the prisoner into their custody, he was conducted to the press room where the executioner with his assistants then commenced pinioning his arms. During these awful preparations the unhappy man appeared mentally to suffer severely. All the arrangements having been completed, the prisoner, who, then trembled violently walked with the melancholy procession, preceded by the Rev. Ordinary who read aloud and in a distinct tone, the burial service for the dead. Whilst the executioner was adjusting the fatal apparatus of death, the prisoner was deeply absorbed in prayer, the executioner having drawn the cap over his face, retired from the scaffold and the signal having been given, the bolt was withdrawn, and the unhappy man was launched into eternity. After which he struggle for a few moments, after which he ceased to exist.

William Thompson made a full Confession while lying under sentence of Death.

O God receive my wretched soul
Look on me from on high
And as I on the platform stand
Give me fortitude to die
And may my fate a warning be
To people old and young
I tremble when I think upon
The dreadful deed I done

Cursed Satan tempted me
Upon that fatal day
To meet my innocent victim
And barbarously him slay
I now must go for on this earth
I am not fit to live
Oh God above look down on me
And all my sins Forgive.

Gifford, Printer, Norwich

127

THE LAST PUBLIC EXECUTION IN NORFOLK

Hubbard Lingley, 26 August 1867

Benjamin Black served all his life on Sir Hanson Berney's estate at Barton Bendish, as had his father before him. At about 4 a.m. on Friday, 17 May 1867, Black went to investigate the shots he had heard coming from the estate woods. His dead body was discovered by a labourer near the entrance to the wood at about 6 a.m. Black was peppered with shot from the top of his forehead to the top of his left breast; he had been robbed of what little money he had about him and an attempt had been made to rip his watch from him, but his pocket had proved too tight (the chain had broken and the assailant had fled without it).

Superintendent Watson of Downham Market led the investigation. After initial enquiries, suspicion fell upon Benjamin's nephew, Hubbard Lingley (24), who was employed as under-woodman. He had been working in the wood on the morning of his Uncle's murder. Summoned to the scene, tears ran down his face at the sight and he wrung his hands sorrowfully intoning, 'Oh, My uncle, my uncle!' Lingley drew suspicion to himself after he was first to notice his uncle's purse had gone. Then when he prevaricated over the location of his shotgun, he was taken into custody. Afterwards he showed the police where his gun was hidden; it showed signs of being recently discharged and the remnant of a percussion cap was still evident. Paper with which the gun had been loaded was picked up near the body. There were even footprints found in the region of the body that matched those of Lingley.

Brought before the Norwich Assizes on 8 August, before Mr Justice Byles, the evidence was compelling. Lingley's relationship with his uncle, it transpired, had been less than

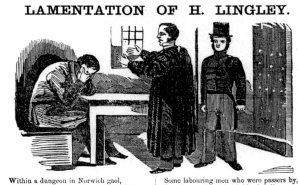

The Lamentation of Hubbard Lingley, sold at his execution.

harmonious. Lingley had abused his position and pushed his family favours too far. Labourer John Spinks testified to an incident two months before the murder: when Black had reprimanded Lingley because he had left his work too soon. Lingley had threatened he would 'do for him.' On the Saturday before the murder, Lingley had been heard to say of Black that he would 'finish him off one day, – him, I hate him.' The jury returned a verdict of guilty in less than twenty minutes. His Lordship then passed sentence of death.

Lingley's demeanour while in gaol was recorded as 'quiet and decorous' and when all hopes of a reprieve were finally exhausted, he paid close attention to the advice and consolation of the Chaplain, Revd James Brown; he wrote his confession while in the condemned cell. Lingley claimed he had gone poaching with two others but had been caught out by his uncle and shot him down before he could raise the alarm. Lingley concluded: 'I am the real murderer; it was my shot, my gun and my hand which pulled the trigger and caused the death – no one else.'

The execution was carried out by William Calcraft. Executions were normally carried out on a Saturday, Market Day. In Lingley's case, the event was moved to a Monday and was conducted at 8 a.m., hence the lesser, but not inconsiderable, number of 12,000 people who gathered to watch the execution of Hubbard Lingley. They probably did not realise it was to be the last public execution in Norfolk.

128
EIGHTEEN YEARS LATER...

William Sheward, 20 April 1869

On 21 June 1851, the first of a number of female body parts were found at a variety of locations around Norwich and its suburbs; they were uncovered as far apart as Hellesdon Road, in a field off Hangman's Lane (now Heigham Road) and on Alder Carr at Trowse Eye. John Walter Sales, the cocky cleaner of Bull Close, found some suspicious sludge around 300 yards from Tabernacle Street, opposite the 'Old Lady's Hospital' [sic]. He was startled as it appeared to be filled with blood. Only when he had heard about the body parts being found around the city did he alert the police and a PC Sturgess came to inspect the sludge, now in the dung heap on Bull Close Road. Human entrails, more grisly flesh and part of a breast with a nipple still attached were discovered.

Within the four weeks of searching, the police had two hands, two feet, a thigh-bone, lower leg bones, parts of a pelvis, some vertebrae and a grisly selection of flesh, strips of skin and muscle. The portions of flesh were preserved in wine and examined with the bones by a team of three local surgeons, Mr Nichols, Mr Dalrymple and Mr Norgate, who concluded the remains were those of an adult female. Unfortunately, their opinion of her age, which they pronounced as being about twenty-five years, proved very inaccurate. The method of dissection of the body parts did not evince an experienced medical hand or even

CITY of NORWICH

SUPPOSED MURDER

Several parts of a human body belonging to a person supposed to have been recently murdered, and to be that of a young female between the ages of sixteen and twenty-six years having been, within the last few days found in the environs of the city of Norwich.

Information is requested to be given to the Chief Constable at the Police Office, Guildhall, Norwich, of all females who may have been recently missing together with any particulars which may lead to the detecting of the person or persons who committed such supposed murder.

The portions of the body already found comprise the right hand and foot and several bones, with numerous pieces of skin and flesh. Further search is making for the head and remaining parts of the body.

H. WOODCOCK,
Mayor.

Poster circulated after the discovery of dismembered remains in Norwich.

a butcher. A thought was promulgated that the body parts had been distributed about the city as a sick prank by medical students. About a month after the last body part was discovered, Police Sergeant Peck was instructed to bury the remains in two vessels, and to throw lime on top, in a vault under the Guildhall. For all intents and purposes, the mystery of the body parts was consigned to history.

That was, until 1 January 1869, when William Sheward (57) walked into the South London suburban police station on Carter Street, Walworth. Sheward could no longer live with the guilt of the murder of his wife, Martha and – having failed to take his own life on the doorstep where he had met her – he handed himself over to the police and confessed. Sheward had argued with his wife over money while he was shaving and ran the razor into her throat, killing her almost instantly at their home on Tabernacle Street, Norwich. He then disposed of her body by dismembering it and distributing the parts around Norwich. Martha was not instantly missed, her closest family were in Wymondham. She was much older (54) than the age ascribed to the body parts by the surgeons. The murder, however, weighed heavily upon Sheward's mind; he took to drinking to calm his nerves and had become an alcoholic by the end of 1868.

Sheward was returned to Norwich to face trial. When news got out of his impending arrival, a massive crowd gathered on Thorpe Station, so Sheward was handed over to Norwich City Police at Trowse and transported directly to the Norwich police station in a shuttered and anonymous cab. He was brought before Norfolk Lent Assizes on 29 March 1869. Sheward was shorter than average, and insubstantially built; he had aged before his time and was weakened, almost totally crippled by the acute rheumatism he suffered in both ankles. The crowd who packed out the public gallery could hardly believe this little old man could have

The execution of William Sheward as depicted in the Illustrated Police News.

143

committed such an abominable crime. The case was presented over two days and after over an hour of deliberation, the jury returned a verdict of guilty. Once the sentence of death was pronounced Sheward was removed to Norwich City Gaol. He spent his remaining days in the infirmary, on account of his rheumatism, and wrote his final confession there. The combination of fear and agonising rheumatism caused Sheward's legs to give way and Chief Warder Hall and Warder Base had to link hands and carry him to the pinioning room. Sheward was then carried to the scaffold, where executioner Calcraft carried out his duty. Around 2,000 people waited in front of the prison gates to see the black flag raised in signal of the completion of the execution. Sheward has the distinction to be the first person to be executed behind closed doors in Norfolk and proved to be the last person executed at Norwich City Gaol. Sheward was buried a short distance from the scaffold, his only grave marker being his initials carved on a stone and set in the wall of the prison by Mr Hibbert, the stonemason of Chapel Field.

129

'YOU SHAN'T STAY WITH NO ONE ELSE'

Henry Webster, 1 May 1876

Labourer Henry Webster (61) was a man of quiet and respectable appearance who lived with his wife Sarah (53), known in the village as 'Sairey', at Cranworth. He was known in the village as 'King' Webster as he tried to 'lord' himself over others: one chap book went so far as to state, 'Everyone disliked and yet feared him. He was the best labourer for miles around, first in work, first in bullying and first in fighting.' The Websters had been married for thirty-seven years, but rather than the passage of time mellowing the man, his quarrels became more frequent and violent.

Sarah was described as a strong, powerful and good-looking woman, who could regularly find good situations working in nursing positions, but Henry was a jealous man; he accused her of infidelities she did not commit and they frequently argued over her long absences when she took up work placements. On 15 September, Webster had gone to his wife's

Henry Webster.

144

Sarah Webster.

place of employment and asked her to come home for a while. On their return journey they called in at their son Jimmy's house, who brought up the matter of some violent language Webster had recently used about the absence of his wife. Sairey became angry, upon which Henry Webster called his son 'a bad bastard' for mentioning the incident and exited the building, making a mark upon the doorpost and saying he would never enter his son's door till the mark wore out. On the morning of 17 September 1875, another row erupted between the Websters when Sairey wished to return to her employer at Hingham. Henry Webster wanted her to stay and bake pies, to which she replied, 'If I bake my pies, I will put some poison in, you old villain.' and reiterated she wished to return to her employer that day. Webster issued the ultimatum, 'Will you stay with me or not?' She refused and Webster replied, 'Then you shan't stay with no one else' and stabbed her with his knife. Sarah pleaded with him but Webster said, 'It is too late now'; he went to the foot of the bed, pulled her down by her hair and slashed his knife across her throat. At his trial, before Mr Baron Cleasby, Webster pleaded provocation and claimed that the deed was one committed in a fit of resentment. The jury found Webster Guilty of murder and the sentence of death was pronounced upon him. Webster maintained a callous air of total indifference to his fate throughout. While in the condemned cell he refused all visitors, even his family, and refused the ministrations of the prison chaplain. His reply was the same to all 'the job would soon come off and the sooner the better.' Webster's execution was to be the first private execution to be conducted at Norwich Castle. It would still draw a large crowd outside and a flagstaff was erected atop the battlements in preparation for a black flag to be flown, to indicate that the sentence had been carried out. The scaffold was erected on the north side of the keep but was not too far from the condemned cell: Webster commented upon the noise of their work, spread over two days, by asking, 'What's all that hustling and jostling?' The execution itself was conducted by William Marwood; one reporter who was permitted to attend recorded Webster's final moments:

The poor old man limped to the foot of the scaffold, his bald head fanned in the breeze of the bright May morning and looked his last upon his fellows. Arrived under the fatal beam, Marwood quickly slipped the white cap over the culprit's face – there was a moment of suspense – and then a dull thud and the body of Henry Webster swung a lifeless corpse.

130

FURY OF THE BLACKSMITH

Henry March, 20 November 1877

Henry 'Harry' March (59) and Henry Bidewell (56) had both worked for decades in the blacksmith's shop owned by veterinarian Thomas Mays (76), in Wymondham. Mays had already retired from veterinary practice and was looking to sell up and retire completely when he informed both March and Bidewell that they should start looking for new employment. March was an irascible man who had been heard raise his voice to Bidewell on a number of occasions over the years, and he soon leapt to the conclusion, albeit an erroneous one, that Mays was going to pass the business over to Bidewell, his longest serving employee (Bidewell had served Mays for nearly forty years, whereas March had been in his employ for just thirty years). From that time the arguments between March and Bidewell increased in frequency, until, around around noon on Saturday 20 October 1877, Henry March could contain his anger no longer. Bidewell was sweeping up in the shop and got in the way of March, who pushed him out of the way. Bidewell took exception to this and they began arguing after about a quarter of an hour of exchanges, Bidwell jeered at him for losing his job and declared that he was now above March. March snapped, grabbed a square iron bar and struck Bidewell with it about the head, knocking him into the coal pit. Their employer, Thomas Mays, was alerted by Sarah Bailey, his servant girl, who had heard

Dramatic coverage of the murders of Henry Bidewell and Thomas Mays by Henry March from the Illustrated Police News.

The death warrant for Henry March. (NRO)

At the Delivery of the Gaols of Our Lady The Queen of the Winter Assize County Number 8

holden at Ipswich —

in and for the said Winter Assize County — on the 29th day of October — in the 41st Year of the Reign of Our Sovereign Lady Queen Victoria, and in the Year of Our Lord 1877 Before The Honourable Sir Robert Lush, Knight, The Honourable Sir Henry Hawkins, Knight, Judges of the High Court of Justice, John Napott Maule, Esqr, One of Her Majesty's Counsel learned in the Law

and others their Fellows, Justices of Our said Lady The Queen, assigned to deliver the aforesaid Gaols of the prisoners therein being.

Henry March is convicted of Murder and it is ordered and adjudged that he be taken hence to the place from whence he came and hence to the County gaol at the Castle of Norwich in the County of Norfolk and thence to a lawful place of execution and that he be there hanged by the neck until he be dead and that his body be afterwards buried within the precincts of the Prison in which he shall have been last confined after this conviction And it is ordered that this Court Note the Sheriff of the County of Norfolk be charged with the execution of this Sentence

To the High Sheriff of the County of Norfolk.

Charles Platt.
Clerk of Assize

Letter from executioner William Marwood to the Governor of Norwich Castle regarding the execution of Henry March. (Courtesy of Stewart P. Evans)

To The Governor of the Castle Norwich

WILLIAM MARWOOD
EXECUTIONER
CHURCH LANE,
HORNCASTLE,
Lincolnshire, England

Nov 13th 1877

Dear Sir

Pleas acording to Promise in my Last Letter to you conserining the Time of my Arival at Norwich For the Execution of the Prisoner all well i shall arive by the Express Train from London about 9 aClock at Night Monday night the 19 day you may Depend on the Time all well

Pleas Set Som Won meet me at the Staishon in Plain Dress i shall have a umbrela in my hand and a carpit Bagg Pleas i Remain your Humble Servant

To The Governor of the Castle Norwich

Wm Marwood
Church Lane
Horncastle
Lincolnshire

147

EXECUTION OF H. MARCH,

THE

Wymondham Murderer.

Henry March was executed for the murder of Thomas Mayes, and Henry Bidewell, at Wymondham, by beating them to death with a bar of iron.

Broadside sold at the execution of Henry March.

the quarrelling; looking through an open window, she had seen March strike Bidewell. Mays came out to investigate and saw Bidewell's feet protruding from the coal pit. He cried 'Oh, March, what have you done?' and rushed over to attend to Bidewell. March later confessed that he thought he 'might as well be hung for two as for one' and as Mays leaned over Bidwell, March turned his anger on his master with the same weapon. Both Mays and Bidewell suffered repeated blows and died soon afterwards from their horrific injuries.

March then went home, removed his work apron and strolled over to the Three Feathers pub for a pint. He then returned to his home on Pople Street to await the arrival of the police. Apprehended at his home and removed from his tearful wife and daughter, March was brought before the Wymondham Divisional Petty Sessions the following Monday, where he claimed he was intoxicated and remembered little of what had occurred. He was tried before the Ipswich Winter Assizes on 1 November 1877, before Mr Justice Hawkins; after hearing the case, the jury retired for fifteen minutes and returned a verdict of guilty against March. As the sentence of death was passed, it was noted March stood impassively, despite the gravity of the sentence. When all hope of a reprieve was lost, March earnestly regretted his crimes; he wrote a full confession and expressed his thanks to the Governor and warders of Norwich Castle Gaol for their kindness to him. The scaffold was erected in a paved courtyard behind the north face of the keep, a short distance from the pinioning room. The execution itself was carried out by William Marwood. The newspaper representative present recorded the final moments:

When on the platform, after Marwood had strapped his legs, the unhappy man heaved a great sigh, with his head upturned, appeared to silently engage in prayer but before the rope was adjusted and the cap drawn, he made a profoundly respectful bow to those present.

When all the preliminaries had been completed, Marwood disappeared from the platform leaving on it the Governor and the head warder, one on each side of the culprit, who, however, from first to last, maintained the greatest coolness and firmness. In another instant the bolt was drawn and the culprit fell such a distance that death was instantaneous; the fact the sentence of law had been duly carried into effect being publicly notified by the hoisting of a black flag from the top of the keep.

131
THE CATTON HORROR

William George Abigail, 22 May 1882

Maidservant Jane 'Jennie' Plunkett (23) met and formed a relationship with hotel 'boots' William George Abigail (22) when they worked together at the Star Hotel on the Haymarket, Norwich, in 1881. A change of management later that same year saw both of them lose their jobs. Jennie and William continued their association but found new situations with separate employers. Jennie fell pregnant and to cover any shame the couple claimed they had been married by special license and continued from thereon as husband and wife. When Jennie's pregnancy became advanced she lost her job and the couple arranged a short-term lodging with William's half brother, John Shepherd, and his wife Eliza, at Mill Hill, Catton, moving in on Friday, 21 April 1882.

It was a bit of a full house; William had been living there for a while, sharing a room with Mrs Shepherd's younger brother, George Peachman (8), but he had claimed he had arranged a new home and would be taking up residence there, with his new wife, the following week, so young George was moved out temporarily to sleep downstairs. Curiously and for a reason still unexplained, William handed his notice in to his employer the following day. On the night of Monday 24 April, the young couple went out and appeared happy and carefree. At about 6.30 a.m. on the morning of Tuesday 25 April, young George was suddenly woken

Grave marker stone for William George Abigail, let into the wall of the exercise yard at Norwich Castle Gaol.

by a gunshot; he ran to the bottom of the stairs and called for Eliza. She came down and settled her little brother back into his temporary bed. About quarter of an hour later the boy was disturbed again by heavy boots coming down the stairs. He heard them exit the back door and disappear into the distance.

The Shepherds had apparently not heard the shot or dismissed it as something away from their house. Nor did they suspect anything out of the ordinary until Jennie failed to come down for breakfast. At around 8 a.m., Mrs Shepherd went to see if she had overslept and found Jennie laying face down. with the bedclothes up to her ears and one arm trailing outside the bed. Taking her hand and feeling it was cold, and then noticing blood on the pillow, Eliza ran out from the room, crying, 'Jennie has killed herself!' John Shepherd went to investigate for himself; he ran to summon the police. Police Surgeon, Dr Robert Mills was soon sent to the scene, and found two wounds: one in the neck, just below the left ear, and the other between the fourth and fifth ribs. This shot had penetrated the heart. Dr Mills was convinced both wounds were fatal – and thus Jennie could not have inflicted shots herself.

Abigail was apprehended when coming out of Dove Street onto Guildhall Hill, Norwich, that same evening. He was tried before Baron Pollock at the Norfolk and Suffolk Assizes, at Ipswich, on 6 May. The jury retired for about fifteen minutes before they returned a guilty verdict, but with a strong recommendation for mercy on account of the youth of Abigail. As the death sentence was passed, Abigail became 'almost prostrate with grief.' Despite the jury's recommendation and a petition supported by many respectable and worthy people, the appeal for commutation failed. While in prison, Abigail remained composed and refused to confess. Finally, however, while he was in the prison chapel for the Sunday service before his execution, when singing the hymn 'I am not worthy, Holy Lord,' he broke down and after hearing the Chaplain's sermon on the subject of 'Thou shalt not kill' confessed his guilt. William Abigail was executed in due form by William Marwood at 8 a.m. the following morning.

132
THE GOODALE MESS

Robert Goodale, 30 November 1885

Robert Goodale (45) was a market gardener at Walsoken, just over the border in Cambridgeshire, where he worked the land with his wife Bathsheba and their sons. Sadly, Goodale regularly drank to excess and had been seen arguing with his wife on more than one occasion; he had even been seen chasing her with a hedge hook.

On 15 September 1885, Goodale started another argument with his wife – but this time he picked up a piece of iron and struck her so hard that he thought he had killed her. He then attempted to hide her body in their covered well but it would not sink, so he

used a ladder to push her under the water. When Bathsheba's body was discovered and the post-mortem examination had been performed, it showed she had not died from the wounds: she had drowned. Tried at the Norfolk Assizes, before Mr Justice Stephen, Goodale was found guilty and sentenced to death.

Executioner James Berry was engaged to perform the execution. He was informed that Goodale was a big man and that he weighed 15 stone and stood 5ft 11ins in height. He was the second largest man Berry had executed, and according to the 'table of drops' Goodale would require a drop of 7ft 8ins. Berry, however, was not happy with this length; he had observed Goodale and it was plain the man had become a physical wreck: despite his size, Benny noticed that his neck was not very muscular and so Berry shortened the drop to 5ft 9in.

The officials for the execution, Under Sheriff J.B.T. Hales, Mr Haynes S. Robinson, the gaol surgeon, Governor Dent and an invited number of local press men gathered at the prison from an early hour on 30 November 1885. At 7.30 a.m., Berry conducted his final tests on the gallows. At 7.55 a.m. the great bell of St Peter Mancroft church began to toll and the officials gathered by the condemned cell to make their procession to the prison bathroom, where Goodale was pinioned. Berry later recalled:

> When I went forward to pinion him he was crying like a little child. Approaching him from behind I slipped the strap around his body. He wriggled to prevent me buckling it, and I had to tell him in a firm tone to be a man.

Pinions secured, it was time to move off on the final walk to the gallows. However, Goodale refused to move and had to be dragged along, screaming and shouting. The gathered officials and Berry had all been somewhat unnerved by Goodale's display.

As Goodale got closer to the gallows he was seen to physically and mentally break down and while passing between a state of collapse and terror he repeated, 'Oh, God, receive my soul.' When in position on the gallows, Goodale's legs would no longer support him, so two warders were deployed to hold him up while Berry put the final pinion strap around his legs, the white bag over his head and adjusted the noose around his neck. Berry, with lever in hand, asked Goodale, 'Do you wish to say anything?' Goodale replied in the negative and before the church bells of Norwich struck the final chime of eight, Berry pushed the lever, the traps fell open and Goodale dropped through. Berry recorded what happened next in his memoirs: 'We were horrified, however, to see the rope jerked upwards and for an instant

An imaginative rendition of the execution of Robert Goodale by the Illustrated Police News.

I thought the noose had slipped from the culprit's head or that the rope had broken.'

As the black flag was hoisted on a flagstaff erected over the right hand entrance to the Gaol, to let the crowd outside know that execution had been carried out, the Governor, Surgeon and Berry looked into the pit below. A horrible sight awaited them:

> …it was worse than that, for the jerk had severed the head entirely from the body and both had fallen into the bottom of the pit. Of course death was instantaneous so that the poor fellow had not suffered in any way; but it was terrible to think such a revolting thing should have occurred. We were all unnerved and shocked. The Governor, whose efforts to prevent any accident had kept his nerves at full strain, fairly broke down and wept.

When the onlookers had recovered their composure, as per Home Office regulations, an inquest was held on the body of Robert Goodale under the Coroner E. S. Bignold Esq. in the magistrate's room at the castle. The witnesses all spoke favourably and fairly of the thoroughness of Berry, pointing out that the executioner was sober. The head of Goodale had been severed from the body as cleanly as if done by a knife. The jury considered the evidence and their views were clear: 'Robert Goodale came to his death by hanging according to judgement of law, and in answer to the Coroner, the jury did not consider anyone was to blame for what had occurred.'

Although acquitted of any blame, the 'Goodale Mess' haunted Berry for the rest of his career and probably for the rest of his life. In 1892 he retired, and after a brief lecture tour he found religion and toured evangelical churches as a respectable preacher who declared he 'gave himself to Jesus.' Charles Mackie, the author of the Norfolk historian's essential two volumes of *Norfolk Annals*, had been present at the execution as a press representative, when he was a reporter on the *Norfolk Chronicle*, and recalled the execution when he looked back on his career many years later. With quite some pride he declared he had been present at what could quite justifiably be called 'the last judicial beheading in England.'

THE HINGHAM MURDER

John Thurston, 10 February 1886

John Thurston (30), an ex-soldier working as a labourer at Hingham, had been drinking with fellow labourer Henry Springall on the evening of 5 December 1885. Thurston had been working in a gang with five or six men, including Henry Springall, who was seen, by Thurston, to change a sovereign. Thurston commented to a workmate named Scase, 'It is a long time since I had a sovereign but I won't be long before I have another. It won't be a bad thing to put a coat over his head.' A short while later, Springall left the pub to go home, and Thurston decided he would follow him and relieve him of a few shillings. By the time Springall reached Ringer's Lane, Thurston had armed himself with a large flint stone; he smashed it into Springall's skull and battered him to death. A group of men spotted Thurston just as he finished the attack and had begun to rifle the dead man's pockets. Thurston spotted them too: he sprung over a fence into a field and fled. He was soon traced and a cursory examination of the clothes and footwear he had been wearing revealed fresh blood and dirt. One of his boots was also compared to a print left near the scene of the crime and proved a match. Brought to the Wymondham lock-up, Thurston was charged with wilful murder and brought before Mr Justice Hawkins at the Norfolk Assizes, where he was found guilty and sentenced to death. Thurston was very penitent for his deed and made a full confession. Executed by James Berry, Thurston went through the gallows trap uttering a prayer; death was recorded as 'instantaneous'.

(Author's note: John Thurston was the nephew of Henry Webster, who had been hanged at Norwich Castle for the murder of his wife. *See* 1 May 1876)

Letter from executioner James Berry confirming his arrival time at Norwich for the execution of John Thurston.

134

LAST TO HANG AT THE CASTLE

George Harmer, 13 December 1886

George Harmer (26) was released from Norwich Prison on Saturday 14 August 1886, after serving one month's imprisonment for an assault on his wife. Returning to his home in Wilde's Yard, Scoles Green in Norwich, he was greeted by a note from his wife stating she had left him. Neighbour Sarah Kemp saw Harmer and invited him in for breakfast. He was much distressed and was crying at the loss of his wife. After breakfast, he asked Mrs Kemp for a razor to have a shave. She said she did not have one, but gave him 3*d* to go and get a shave. Harmer said he would go to his mother-in-law to try and discover the whereabouts of his wife, and added that he was going to get some money and would pay her back; she replied that she did not want it. Harmer then called in on neighbour Mrs Mary Savage and stayed about an hour, talking mostly about his wife.

Harmer turned up next at the house of his friend Ted Nelson, a saw-maker living on Lower Westwick Street and a man known to the police, with convictions for felony and poaching against him. Harmer told Nelson he would do no more work until he had found his wife and stated, 'I've made up my mind to get some money and mean to rob old Last so I can go and see my wife.' Nelson advised him 'not to get such nonsense in his head' but Harmer could not be dissuaded and concocted an idea: he would make a rough wooden pattern and use it to rob Last. Harmer asked Nelson for a pencil and a piece of board but Nelson refused. After failing to purloin Mrs Nelson's washboard for the same purpose, Harmer went away. He returned a while later with a piece of wood and asked Nelson for a pencil, but, again, Nelson refused. Harmer then picked up a file and set about marking the panel. Nelson asked what he wanted it for and Harmer replied, 'I want to attract the old man's attention.' Harmer then produced a plasterer's hammer and explained while Last was distracted he would 'hit the old — over the head and daze him.' Harmer finished marking the board and left.

Master carpenter Henry Last (64) was a bachelor, who lived in a cottage that stood in Post Office Tavern Yard on the corner of School Lane, off Bedford Street and a narrow passageway leading to Old Post Office Street (now known as Exchange Street). Fatally, he was rumoured to have hoarded money. When Harmer turned up at Last's door he received no answer, so he spoke through the window to neighbour Mrs Catherine Richmond, asking if Last was at home, but she said she did not know where Mr Last was. Harmer said he would call again and walked off. An hour later, Last returned and Mrs Richmond informed him of his visitor and he thanked her. A short while later, she saw Harmer with a board approaching Last's door again. About twenty minutes to half an hour later, she heard Last's door bang and someone walk out of the yard very quickly.

Mr Last was not seen for the rest of the afternoon; neighbours became worried when they saw his door was ajar, and by 8 p.m. were so concerned that neighbour Henry Chilvers fetched Last's friend Peter Hoydahl, the proprietor of the Livingstone Hotel. They obtained a light and entered the house to investigate. Inside, on the ground floor, within an area screened off from the main living room, they were suspicious to see what appeared to be a pile of sacks lying on the floor. Lifting them, they discovered the body of Henry Last with his head battered in by a blunt instrument. Later, medical examination was to identify the weapon as a plasterer's hammer.

Mr Last had been robbed of what little money and portable valuables he had. After news of the murder broke, Norwich City Police were tipped off by Nelson on Tuesday 17 August, 'because innocent people were being taken', but more likely because he was worried the trail would somehow lead to him. By the time police arrived at Harmer's home, he had sold up and fled to London. Harmer was traced via his luggage which he had forwarded to his new address, and he was arrested on 19 August. A hammer, of the type used to murder Henry Last was found in his possession. Brought before Mr Justice Field, at the Norfolk Assizes, on 22 November, Harmer was found guilty and sentenced to death. When all hope of reprieve was lost, Harmer was contrite and wrote a full confession of his crime. On the Friday and Saturday preceding his execution, Harmer, who was under the ministrations of the Chaplain, the Revd H. Tompson, became very penitent and was visited by his wife, his parents and other relatives; he was much affected by these final meetings and farewells. On the morning of his execution, Harmer rose shortly after 6 a.m. after passing a quiet night. After partaking of a scant breakfast of toast, Harmer was visited by the Chaplain at 6.30 a.m., who stayed with him until about three minutes to the hour of eight. Then executioner James Berry, attended by the acting Under Sheriff, surgeon to the gaol, the Governor and the chief warder, entered the condemned cell. Harmer submitted to pinioning, a procession was formed and the group proceeded the distance of about 8 or 9 yards to the scaffold. Harmer walked firmly to the drop and joined fervently in the responses with the Chaplain. A reporter who was present recorded the final moments:

> Berry rapidly placed the cap over Harmer's head and adjusted the noose, the last words of the criminal being 'Lord have mercy upon me.' Exactly after eight o'clock Berry pulled the lever, giving a drop of 4ft 6in. Death was almost instantaneous.

The inquest returned the usual formal verdict and thus on Monday 13 December 1886, George Harmer was the last person to be hanged at Norwich Castle Gaol.

135
THE SPROWSTON SLAYING

George Watt, 12 July 1898

George and Sophia Watt had been married for twenty years. Over the years, it seems, their relationship had declined into persistent cruelty and drink-fuelled violence, until Mrs Watt applied for a separation order, which was granted in February 1898. In an attempt to get away from Watt, Sophia went to stay with Miss Paston on Northcote Road. George Watt (44), a Norwich shoemaker and labourer, tracked her down and burst into the house exclaiming, 'Now I have found you.' Miss Paston screamed 'Murder!' but Watt closed on Sophia, threatening, 'I shall kill you; remember your days are my days. I shall kill you, Sophy; some day I shall kill you.' He then left.

Mrs Watt moved into Campling's Yard, and despite the order standing against him, Watt again found her and threatened to stab her with a formidable knife. Fortunately their son James was visiting his mother at the time and managed to wrestle the knife from his father, sustaining a number of cuts in the process. He then proceeded to give his father a severe punishing with his fists. George Watt was summoned for the assault, but it appears the beating he had received gained him lenience from the court and he was only fined 5s. Watt went back to his lodgings in Fishgate Street and his wife moved again, this time to No. 25, Denmark Terrace, Sprowston, taking their children with her. Mrs Watt had brought in the lion's share of the family income and the unemployed Mr Watt was soon suffering the privations caused by lack of money.

Not being very literate, Watt got friends to write letters on his behalf imploring his wife to take him back and promising to give up the drink. Sophia was determined to keep her husband at a distance. Watt was desperate and bought a revolver from gun-maker John Henry Emms on Orford Hill for 8s. Later, Watt claimed he bought the gun with the intention of killing himself, but instead he went around to No. 25 Denmark Terrace to see his wife, on the afternoon of Thursday, 14 April. He arrived at the back gate at about 2.30 p.m. and found his wife hanging out the washing; their children were also in the garden, but frightened by the approach of their father, ran inside. Last to leave was their little daughter. Sophia said, 'I expect she is afraid of you.' Watt replied he would not hurt her. Sophia took a few steps to go inside but Watt followed her; he wanted them to be reconciled. Sophia said 'I will not have anything more to do with you. I have heard your promises so often.' Sophia then walked towards the house; George Watt did not move, so she attempted to pass him – but he then raised his hand, now containing the revolver, levelled it at her head and pulled the trigger. Sophia slumped to the ground. He fired again

George Watt.

and again, and then set about beating her about the head with the butt of the weapon. Neighbour George Drake cried 'Murder!' and chased Watt up the road but was threatened; then Watt made his escape through the Norfolk & Norwich Arms. He was at large for about three hours, but news spreads fast and having been recognised as the wanted man by a number of people on Magdalen Street, and as a mob was beginning to form, the policeman arrived and placed Harmer under arrest.

Brought before Mr Justice Hawkins at the Norfolk Assizes, Watt was found guilty and sentenced to death; there was no attempt to obtain a reprieve. George Watt was the first person to be hanged at HM Prison Norwich on Prison Road; he was executed by father and son James and Thomas Billington. Reporters were still allowed to be present at the invitation or discretion of the Governor; two were present at the execution of Watt and the following is the published account of what they saw:

At a few minutes to nine Billington and his son entered the convict's cell and speedily adjusted the necessary straps. A procession was then formed and marched to the coach house. The Chaplain, the Rev. S. Cox, wearing his surplice, led the way, reciting sentences from a special form of service which has recently been issued by authority for use at executions. Immediately behind him came Watt, walking with a firm tread and upright bearing between two warders. He moved with a military step [Watt had been a soldier] and but for a twitching of the muscles of the face might have been on parade.

The executioners were close in attendance, and then followed the Governor (Captain Frederick Bell), the prison surgeon (Mr H. S. Robinson), the Under Sheriff (Mr Peter Hansell), Chief Warder R. Broom, a number of warders and then the reporters. The prison bell during this time was tolling, as it had been doing for quarter of an hour. As soon as the coach house was reached Watt stepped upon the trapdoors. One of the Billingtons adjusted the noose round his neck and the white cap over his head, while the other fastened his legs. But a few moments were thus occupied and then the lever was pulled and Watt dropped into the pit as the Chaplain was saying, 'Good Lord deliver us.' The whole business was carried out with the utmost expedition. Death was evidently instantaneous. There was not the slightest movement on the part of the convict. Dr. Robinson, after a few moments interval, descended the pit and pronounced life extinct.

Small knots of people had gathered opposite the entrance to the gaol and at various points in the vicinity, from whence a view could be obtained of the flag staff, on which the black flag was displayed, announcing that the sentence of death had been carried out. A certificate was posted outside the prison confirming Watt's demise. The black flag was flown for one hour and was lowered at the same moment Watt's body was removed from the rope and placed fully dressed upon a bier by the side of the gallows. It remained there until the conclusion of the inquest, when it was duly coffined and interred in the south-west corner of the prison yard, in a grave some 8ft deep. The Revd S. Cox read a shortened form of burial service, adapted for the occasion, and then the grave was filled in, first with quicklime to speed decomposition then levelled to the surface with earth.

136

THE YARMOUTH BEACH MURDER

Herbert Bennett, 21 March 1901

Early on the morning of Sunday 23 September 1900, the body of a woman was discovered among the dunes on Great Yarmouth's South Beach; she had been strangled with a mohair bootlace from one of her own boots. The first police officer on the scene was PC Manship. Manship had been to sea for seven years and carefully noted the type of knots tied in the lace; there were three in total, a reef knot at the back of the neck, at which another section of lace had been joined (a mend to the old lace) and to the left front, tied with two reef knots with a 'grannie' knot on top to stop slipping.

The murdered woman was initially identified as a Mrs Hood, who had been staying with her daughter Rose (about two years old) at the boarding house of Mrs Eliza Rudrum at No. 3 Row 104. The unfortunate little girl was of little help to the investigation; the only tangible clues were a photograph of 'Mrs Hood' and her daughter on the beach, taken during their short stay in the town. This was copied and despatched on twelve routes to circulate from town to town across the country. The only other clue was a laundry mark found on her underclothes, bearing the number 599, which was also circulated. Police investigations moved slowly, despite the growing national media attention in the search for the true identity of 'Mrs Hood'. A final verdict of wilful murder against 'a man unknown' was made, but no real leads were forthcoming. During the second week in October, Yarmouth's Chief Constable, William Parker, made the decision he was not making enough headway with his local team and called in Scotland Yard, who assigned Chief Inspector Alfred Leach of the CID to the case. Eventually, in early November, the break they were all hoping for came, when the laundry mark was finally traced to the Bexley Heath Laundry. It revealed that 'Mrs Hood' was in fact Mrs Mary Jane Bennett of No. 1 Glencoe Villa, Bexley Heath

Mary Bennett and daughter Ruby on Yarmouth Beach.

and after further investigations, it emerged that she had been involved in a number of confidence tricks with her husband, Herbert John Bennett. When he was traced, Bennett claimed he was estranged from his wife and had not seen her for some time and had taken up with another woman. When Bennett's lodgings were searched, police discovered a revolver and curious items such as male and female wigs, a false moustache and, most significantly, a long gold necklace with a silver watch, of a type very similar to one worn by 'Mrs Hood' in Great Yarmouth; police believed the chain was even discernable on the beach photograph found among Mrs Bennett's effects.

Herbert Bennett swore he had not been to Yarmouth at the time of the murder and knew nothing of the matter. The chain found in his possession (and seen in the photograph) was considered as the vital link. Fears over being unable to find an unbiased jury in Norfolk saw Herbert Bennett brought to London and the trial, before Lord Chief Justice Alverstone, opened on 25 February 1900. It obtained him the dubious honour of being the first man to stand on a capital charge at the Old Bailey in the twentieth century. Bennett was fortunate to obtain the services of one of the most brilliant defence counsels of his age, Edward Marshall Hall. Marshall Hall soon realised that Bennett was a compulsive liar, but he was convinced Bennett had not murdered his wife. He went to great lengths at the trial, even calling jewellery experts to create an element of doubt over the chain in the photograph, claiming it was of a different design to that found at Bennett's lodgings. The problem was that those

FULL STORY

OF THE

Yarmouth Murder Case.

(ILLUSTRATED.)

Portrait of the accused man, HERBERT BENNETT.

ONE PENNY.

Left: One of a number of pamphlets and newspaper supplements produced to cover the trial of Herbert Bennett.

Below: Letter written by Bennett from the condemned cell at Norwich Prison.

From *H.J. Bennett*

H. M. Prison,
Norwich
March 14th 1901.

Dear Sir I wish to inform you that I am not allowed to write to the Editor of the "Sun," but as it is my desire that something should be done for my child, I shall be glad if you will let the Editor know that I shall be thankful if he will open a subscription list for her benefit,

No. 24 I have sent in my petition as requested, I

have also wrote to Allen asking him to send the £17 balance, due to me, on to my Father for the benefit of my child, I shall be obliged to you if you will see that my Father gets the cash safely.

I must again thank you for all you have done for me & my parents,

Yours Faithfully
H. J. Bennett

who Bennett had cited as drinking with him on the night of the murder vehemently denied being with him. Then in a strange twist, another witness came forward claiming to have been with Bennett beyond the time the last train had left for Yarmouth from London – but Bennett claimed he could not recall meeting the man. Other witnesses also claimed to have seen Bennett at Yarmouth both before and after the murder, looking agitated as he waited on the railway platform for the London train.

The trial lasted six days. Due to Bennett's track record of lying, Marshall Hall did not ask him to take the stand, he excused it by saying Bennett was 'too unreliable to put in the witness box'. But as Hall's biographer Edward Marjoribanks put it: 'from this abstention an overwhelming inference was drawn… if only Bennett could have gone into the box to corroborate. Such a powerful argument might well have caused the jury to doubt, and Bennett might have escaped.' Even so, Marshall Hall's summing up speech was both eloquent and compelling, but it was not enough. The jury returned a verdict of guilty against Herbert John Bennett (22). Returned to HMP Norwich, Bennett was executed by James and Thomas Billington on 21 March 1901.

There is a strange postscript to the case. When the black flag was hoisted to proclaim Bennett's execution at Norwich Prison, the flagstaff gave way and fell; an event construed by some as a sign of Bennett's innocence. No black flag was hoisted to announce the capital sentence had been carried out at Norwich again. Almost twelve years later, early on the morning of Monday, 15 July 1912, the body of a young lady was discovered on Yarmouth's South Beach. The victim, Dora Grey, had been strangled with a bootlace from one of her own shoes and tied with a knot exactly of the type used to kill Mary Bennett. The murder of Dora Grey remains unsolved.

137
THE FELTWELL AXE MURDER

James Nicholls, 2 December 1908

Charles Wilson and his wife, Susan, lived a quiet existence in an isolated cottage just outside the village of Feltwell. Mr Wilson was a travelling umbrella salesman, while his wife (a woman of seventy and some seventeen years older than her husband) kept house. Mr Wilson returned from a sales trip on Sunday, 11 October, walking into his cottage he was horrified to find wife lying on the floor; she had been battered to death with an axe.

As Mr Wilson was making his horrible discovery, another local man, a labourer named James 'Jem' Nicholls (35), came stumbling into Maggee's Farm, where he blurted out, to two people he knew there, that Mr Wilson had just murdered his wife. Obviously shocked by the event, Nicholls was taken to the local pub. Police investigations soon found two witnesses who shed light on the events of that Sunday afternoon. After reporting the discovery of his wife's body to the authorities, Wilson went to his friend, Mr Southgate, to await the arrival of the authorities. Southgate recalled he had seen Jem Nicholls, accompanied by his dog, walking through the village in the direction of Wilson's cottage at about 2.20 p.m. Another witness soon came forward, a fourteen-year-old local lad named Banham. While playing in the fields near the Wilson residence, he had seen a man he 'knew by sight and name' as Nicholls enter the cottage. After about five minutes, the boy's attention was brought to the house when he heard screams for help from Mrs Wilson. Looking across the field, the boy saw the old woman being dragged into the road. Nicholls briefly let go of her and she stopped screaming – but then Nicolls leapt at her and dragged her back inside the cottage. When Nicholls finally exited the cottage, the boy Banham saw Mr Wilson coming up the road in his cart.

The police lost no time in arresting Nicholls at the local pub. The trial was held later the same month at the Norfolk Winter Assizes, before Mr Justice Grantham. The defence counsel questioned how the boy Banham could be so sure of the identity of the man seen entering the cottage, which was over 700 yards from where he was standing. The boy was not intimidated and clearly stated that he knew Nicholls and that he recognised him on that fateful afternoon by the clothes he typically wore and the dog he had with him. After demonstrating what time Mr Wilson returned home and how long it would take Nicholls to travel to Magee's farm, the prosecution pointed out that only Nicholls could have known about the murder of Mrs Wilson at the time he first reported it. The jury took fifteen minutes to find James Nicholls guilty of the murder of Susan Wilson. Nicholls was executed at HMP Norwich by brothers Henry and Thomas Pierrepoint,

Major Fowler, the Prison Governor and the staff of Norwich Prison, c. 1905.

on 2 December 1908; he was the last man to hang in Norfolk with members of the press present to witness the entire procedure. The reporter from the *Eastern Daily Press* vividly recorded what he saw:

At about six o'clock Nicholls was awakened from sleep and given breakfast. A more exemplary occupant of the condemned cell has never been. He had listened attentively to the ministrations of the Gaol Chaplain (the Revd R.M. Boys) who has been in daily attendance ever since the condemnation and who was by his side all the time from breakfast onwards; he has given the prison officials the least possible trouble and he looked forward to the end with calmness and resignation.

A few minutes before eight the executioner (H.A. Pierrepoint) and his brother (T.W. Pierrepoint) for assistant, entered the cell and pinioned his arms, the work of less than a minute. The officials and attendants then rapidly fell into processional order with the culprit in their midst and passed at a brisk step along the main corridor of the central block, out into the prison yard and so to the place of execution, a distance of some fifty or sixty yards. The apparatus of death had been constructed in the coach house and was as little as possible obtrusive to the sight, the doors of the trap being upon the floor level. At the head of the procession came the Chaplain, reading the usual sentences from the Burial Service; then the condemned man with Warders Chesterton and Mitchell walking closely by his side, one at each arm; next the Governor of the prison (Major Fowler), Chief Warden Fenwick, the Prison Surgeon (Dr Starling), the Under Sheriff (Mr Walter Hansell), two more warders and two representatives of the press. The central figure in this progress of death was a fairly stalwart figure of a man, looking fully his age of 35, or

Norwich Shirehall, c. 1908.

perhaps a little more. He walked slouchingly but firmly with his head well held up. The only sign of interest that he showed in external things was when he emerged into the thick foggy air of the prison yard where he cast around a weary indifferent look. His cheek was a little blanched and his lips were parted but he showed no trace of faltering, not even at the crucial moment when, on crossing the threshold of the coach house, he became confronted with the instrument of his departure. He squared his feet upon the trapdoor. The executioner threw over his face the white cap and by a simple movement adjusted the leg straps. Then he pulled the lever and the body disappeared into the pit beneath. The rope oscillated a moment or two but not more than must have been caused by the sudden strain thrown upon it. There was no sign of conscious or involuntary muscular movement. This was one of those cases in which it may be said with literal exactitude that death was instantaneous... The interval that elapsed between the time when Nicholls left his cell to the time of his passing into the land of death must have been well inside a minute. The prison surgeon having descended into the pit and made a momentary examination, the doors of the coach house were then closed.

The body was left hanging for an hour and the inquest held was at 10 a.m. before Mr Coroner Ladell, with Mr R.G. Self, appointed chairman of the jury. The Prison Governor, Major Fowler, identified the body. Dr H. J. Starling, Medical Officer of the prison, said the cause of death was dislocation of the vertebrae and confirmed 'death was instantaneous.' A verdict of death from hanging in accordance with the law was returned. Shortly afterwards the body was interred within the precincts of the prison.

138
'END MY MISERY?'

Robert Galloway, 5 November 1912

On the night of 16 July 1912, seaman Robert Galloway (27) walked from Walsoken to Wisbech, where he found Police Sergeant Jacobs in the Market Place. He confessed that he had strangled a woman 'owing to jealousy,' and claimed 'I am ready to suffer for what I have done' and gave directions to where her body lay on Burrett's Lane, off the Walsoken to Lynn road. Tragically, he was telling the truth and the body of Minnie Morris (21) was found exactly where Galloway had said, lying on her back, strangled with her own neck scarf, a reefer knot pressing on her throat and a cap placed over her face. Galloway explained that this was an attempt to lead people to think she was asleep. When in custody, Galloway gave a voluntary statement revealing how he had been living at Walsoken and had met Minnie when she came up from London for the fruit picking. They had been drinking heavily over the previous few days at the Bell and later at the Black Bear pub. On 16 July, Minnie's aunt had already left for London, leaving Minnie stranded at Walsoken;

The staff of Norwich Prison, in 1912.

Galloway claimed Minnie had become morose and said she would 'rather die' than walk back to London. Galloway then claimed Minnie asked him, 'Have you the pluck to end my misery?' He said he would do so and swore to give himself up to the police afterwards. Galloway certainly did do the latter, but what really passed between the couple may never be known. It was far more likely to be an attempted sexual attack or an argument over another man she was seeing, one William Tucker.

Witnesses bore the latter out with what they had heard pass between Galloway and Morris on the days leading up to the murder. By the time of his trial at the Norfolk Assizes, before Mr Justice Darling, on 19 October 1912, Galloway was claiming he had no recollection of what had happened and his counsel attempted to argue his mind had been unhinged by alcohol. He certainly had been suicidal before; in 1905, while serving in the Royal Navy, he had attempted to hang himself while in Lewes Prison. After the murder, Galloway had gone into The Bell and spoken to Walsoken gardener Henry Newman, exclaiming, 'I'm going to spend up, as I've only another six weeks to live.' The two spoke about a recent suicide in the village where a man had hanged himself. Galloway said he had once been tempted to throw himself under a train but could not bring himself to do it, nor could he hang himself – he would rather be hanged. Dr Starling, the Medical Officer at Norwich Prison, was called to give his opinion about the sanity of Galloway and was quite frank in stating, 'I have observed nothing in the prisoner's behaviour to suggest his mental condition was in any way abnormal.'

The jury retired for just five minutes before returning a verdict finding Galloway guilty of murder. The judge donned the black cap and the sentence of death was passed. Galloway listened to the sentence apparently unmoved, betraying no signs of fear or emotion when he was hurried from the dock into the cells below. He was executed at HMP Norwich by Thomas Pierrepoint, with George Brown as assistant.

139
DOUBLE MURDER AT SWAFFHAM

Herbert George Bloye, 12 November 1925

Swaffham man Herbert George Bloye (27), also known as Herbert George Whiteman, had been separated, by order, from his wife Alice (23) in May 1925; she had taken the children and moved in with her parents William and Clara Squires at Swaffham. He had developed a real hatred for his mother-in-law and attributed the split in his marriage to her; he had threatened to 'do the old bitch in'. On 15 June 1925, Bloye had been drinking at the Horse & Groom when he decided to track down his mother-in-law, who was working in a field about a mile outside the town, on Town Farm, known as Heath Lands. The time was about 1 p.m. Bloye's estranged wife, Alice, had taken her mother some lunch and he encountered her first, but when she dismissed his suggestion of a reconciliation he picked up a double-headed spanner and battered her to the ground. Alice's father, who was working nearby, came over to investigate and found her lying unconscious in the lane; she would later die from the wounds she received.

Alice's mother Clara was working in a nearby field and ultimately suffered the same fate. Bloye hit her so hard about the head that he left a ragged wound about 5in long, and fractured her skull on her left temple, leaving brain matter protruding. She died of her wounds at Swaffham Cottage Hospital on 3 August. Clara had screamed during the attack and her husband had come running, but he only arrived in time to see his wife crumple to the ground and Bloye run off. Bloye went to his mother's house at Great Thorns, Swaffham, and confessed, 'I have done them both in. They have gone to a better world.' He then gave his mother the bloody spanner and she threw it in a pile of wood. Next, Bloye went to his step-brother, who was working nearby, and said, 'I have killed Mrs Squires and my wife and I have come to kiss you goodbye'. He then returned to the house and awaited the arrival of the police. Bloye was brought before Lord Chief Justice Hewart at Norfolk Quarter Sessions on an indictment for the murder of his mother-in-law, with a further indictment for the murder of his wife (who died of her wounds after her mother); the first charge was the only subject of the prosecution.

The trial lasted the whole day and Bloye sat in the dock throughout in 'a perfectly composed manner.' Mr A.S. Leighton, Bloye's counsel, focussed his defence upon Bloye's mental health. Prison doctors considered him of 'low intelligence' and he was prone to epileptic fits and fits of hysteria. He was found fit to stand trial nonetheless and was fully culpable for his actions; he was found guilty of murder and sentenced to death. Herbert Bloye was executed at HMP Norwich by Robert Baxter, with Edward Taylor as assistant.

140
DEATH AT THE DOCK

Walter Smith, 8 March 1938

On the afternoon of 22 October 1937, the barge *East Anglia*, owned by the London & Rochester Trading Co., loaded with a cargo of barley, berthed at Felixstowe dock. Old school friends skipper Albert Edward Baker (28) and his mate Walter 'Ginger' Smith (33) had been for a drink at the Pier Hotel over lunchtime and returned to the barge in the afternoon. The following morning, Skipper Baker was discovered in his cabin by dockhands. He had suffered three bullet wounds, one to the head and two in the heart. A single-loading, long-barrelled pistol was lying nearby and his empty wallet was found under a pillow.

Smith, the mate, was nowhere to be found. A search was organised and he was picked up the same evening at the nearby British Lion pub. He requested he be allowed to finish his drink, which he was. Then he was promptly taken to the police station. Questioning had hardly begun when Smith enquired, 'You say he was shot dead?' though no mention had been made of how Baker had been killed. Initially, he concocted a story about how he had seen Baker quarrelling with a woman; however, the following morning, having had a chance to sleep on it, Smith made another statement in which he claimed there had been a struggle. Baker's gun had gone off, killing him. The problem was the revolver had to be reloaded after every shot, and there was no sign of a struggle in the cabin.

Tried before Mr Justice Singleton, at the Ipswich Assizes, the defence constructed a picture of an unstable man; medical evidence for the defence argued Smith had acted under a 'mania' or 'acute alcoholic insanity', and witnesses, including Smith's sister, spoke of how he had suffered two or three days unaware of his behaviour after a drinking binge. It also emerged his father was an alcoholic, his mother had suffered epileptic fits and his aunt had died in an asylum. Counter argument came from Dr I.D. Dickson, Medical Officer at Norwich Prison, who stated he had observed Smith from 25 October until 4 December and had found no evidence of mental deficiency. Neither judge nor jury were convinced by the insanity plea; in his summing up, the judge even asked the jury, 'Can you see any proof of insanity or anything like it?' The jury retired for forty minutes and returned a guilty verdict. Before pronouncing the death sentence, Justice Singleton said; 'After everything has been said that can be said on your behalf. The jury convict you upon the evidence and rightly so.' An appeal was lodged and complaint made that the judge had led the jury: the appeal was dismissed, and Smith was executed at HMP Norwich by Thomas Pierrepoint.

THE ELLOUGH WAAF MURDER

Arthur Heys, 13 March 1945

WAAF Aircraftswoman Winifred Mary Evans (27) was found battered, raped and asphyxiated in a ditch at Ellough, near Beccles, Suffolk on 9 November 1944. RAF and WAAF personnel at her camp were questioned; detectives also visited an Italian prisoner-of-war camp. The suspect, who soon emerged, was LAC Arthur Heys (37), the father of a young family, who lived in Colne, Lancashire, before he was called for war service. The evidence of the case was examined by the notable Dr Keith Simpson. Forensic evidence placed Heys in the ditch, and hairs from the victim were found on his uniform, but the most damning evidence came from the accused himself. Heys went to the trouble of smuggling an anonymous letter out of prison to his commanding officer, purporting to come from another man who had actually committed the murder, but he tripped himself up with the transposition of events and by revealing details only the murderer would have known; it was as good as a confession.

Heys was tried at the Suffolk Assizes held at Bury St Edmunds, on 22-24 January 1945. The jury were forty minutes reaching their verdict in finding Heys guilty of the murder and he was sentenced to death. As he was taken away, Heys looked towards the gallery, where his wife sat weeping. He was executed upon the gallows at HMP Norwich. Immediately after the execution, the official notice of 'judgement of death this day was executed' was posted on the prison gates, signed by witnesses: Mr Thomas Wilson, the Under Sheriff of Suffolk; Mr A. A. Rice, Justice of the Peace for the City of Norwich; Mr Sidney T. E .P. Ennion, Governor of the prison and Revd S. Merrifield, the prison chaplain. The inquest was conducted by the City Coroner, Me L.G. Hill, accompanied by his officer, PC W. Hoskins, and sat with a jury of seven, all but one of whom expressed a wish to view the body. Dr Ian Dunbar Dickson, the Medical Officer of the prison, who was also present at the execution, gave evidence that death was instantaneous; the jury recorded a verdict in accordance.

142

MURDER OF THE CHAMBERMAID

Stanley Joseph Clark, 18 November 1948

Yarmouth couple Stanley Clark (34) and widow Florence Bentley (32) had been going out together for some time when he asked her to marry him, but she refused. So incensed was pig-dealer Clark that he swore, in front of witnesses, that he would murder her. On 16 June 1948, Florence was at her usual place of employment, working as a chambermaid at a guest house at No.1, Camperdown, which was run by Clark's married sister, Mrs Miriam Prior. Clark came to see Florence at the guesthouse, and they met in the kitchen, but she soon went upstairs to carry on with her work. Minutes later Clark followed her and suddenly a terrible scream was heard by Mrs Prior, who ran towards the stairs: she arrived in time to see Florence running down the stairs followed by Clarke with a knife in his hand.

Florence had been stabbed about the head and chest and collapsed; the stab wounds to her chest had punctured both lungs and she died a short while later. As Mrs Prior tended to Florence, Clark walked out onto the street, almost as if nothing had happened. He travelled to a telephone box at Burgh Castle and contacted the police, confessing to what he had done. He said he was filled with remorse and was determined to 'soon be reunited' with Florence.

Clark brought drama to his hearing at Great Yarmouth Magistrates. When the knife he had used to kill Mrs Bentley was produced in court, he suddenly bolted from the dock and disappeared down the steps. Chief Constable Charles Jellif and other police officers seized Clark, brought him back and then sat beside him for the rest of the session gripping his wrists. Clark pleaded guilty and continued to do so at the Assizes before Mr Justice Cassels. The trial was over in four minutes, no appeal was lodged and there was to be no reprieve.

Clark soon found religion and was confirmed in the condemned cell by Dr Percy Mark Herbert, the Bishop of Norwich. At Clark's personal request, the Bishop spent the last half hour with him before the execution at HMP Norwich. There had been no execution in Britain since February; while the Criminal Justice Bill was being debated in the House of Commons, the Home Secretary had reprieved a number of murderers. The Bill, with the 'no hanging' clause omitted, had become law at the end of July 1948 and Clark went to the gallows.

143

THE BECCLES SCHOOLGIRL MURDER

James Frank Rivett, 8 March 1950

James Rivett (21), a Beccles bricklayer's labourer, had been going out with schoolgirl Christine Ruth Cuddon (17) for about three years. Christine was a very able student and showed great promise as she set out to train as a teacher. Caring about her future, her father, Blyburgate newsagent Ronald J. Cuddon, had advised her 'not to take courting too seriously' and both her parents had asked her to choose between the training or carrying on the relationship; which, if she chose the latter, would mean she would have to leave school. She chose her career but she continued to meet with ex-sailor Rivett. On the evening of 5 November 1949, Christine went to see a film at the Regal cinema but also arranged to meet Rivett. The couple were seen together between 8.30 p.m. and 8.45 p.m.; Rivett was next seen alone at 10 p.m. as he walked home to his father's house. A short while later, he went out with a shotgun and cartridges with the intention of killing himself – he had strangled Christine with her own headscarf and had left her lying in a cycle shed at the Sir John Leman school, where she had gone with Rivett for the purpose of intercourse. Rivett changed his mind about suicide and went to the house of his friend Rowland Gibbs and confessed, 'I have done the girl in.' He then calmly went to the police station and declared he had strangled his girlfriend and told them where her body was.

Rivett pleaded guilty but his defence counsel, Sir Charles Doughty, entered a plea of not guilty, so that his mental condition could be inquired into. At his trial before the Suffolk Assizes, at Ipswich, on 20 January 1950, the jury were sworn to specifically try the issue of whether Rivett was fit to plead or not. Medical officers Dr John E. M. Matheson and Dr Basil Tracey, of Brixton and Norwich prisons respectively, argued against Rivett's sanity and pointed out there had been a marked deterioration in his mental state since his incarceration. But after an hour's deliberation, the jury agreed he was fit to plead. The trial was then adjourned to the Norfolk Assizes and having heard the case, the new jury took just ten minutes to return a verdict of guilty. Rivett had always maintained he did not want to 'get off' and smiled as the death sentence was pronounced. An appeal was launched again to argue the plea of insanity but this was rejected by a third jury and Rivett was executed at HMP Norwich.

'TO THE GREAT CONCERN OF ALL PRESENT'

Norman Goldthorpe, 24 November 1950

Norman Goldthorpe (40) had suffered a tough life, interspersed with regular periods of unemployment; he had become depressed, and violent, to the degree that he attempted to take his own life. During the Second World War, he suffered battle exhaustion; his wife, Lily, had divorced him in 1946 and by 1950 the married woman he had taken up with (and moved to Great Yarmouth to be with) had left him. The furious Goldthorpe vowed he would 'have' other women.

On Wednesday, 9 August 1950, he had a day off from his work, at the kitchen at Caister Holiday Camp, and picked up mature prostitute Emma Elizabeth Howe (66) from the bar of the Great Eastern Hotel on Howard Street. She took him back to her flat in Owles Court, off Row 52, where they had sex. On Friday 11 August, Goldthorpe returned to the Great Eastern Hotel looking for Emma. Unsuccessful in finding her there, he went to Owles Court; he could not remember which of the flats was occupied by Howe, so he knocked at the door of one her neighbours and they directed him. Once inside Howe's flat, it seems that the years of frustration and anger came to a head; Goldthorpe snapped and strangled Emma Howe. Her body was discovered the following morning by her insurance agent when he came to collect the premium. The police were called immediately and DS Walter Painter was first on the scene; he knew Howe and was aware of her profession. The neighbour did not take long to identify Goldthorpe as the man who had come to the flats looking for Emma. It seems that Goldthorpe awaited his fate, drinking in the bar of the Great Eastern Hotel; the police arrested him there. He came quietly and when taken to the police station confessed to his crime. Questions over the sanity of Goldthorpe were raised at his trial, but the expert medical opinion was that he was not insane and that he knew right from wrong. The jury retired for less than an hour and then returned a guilty verdict. Before he passed sentence, Mr Justice Hilbery asked Goldthorpe if he had anything to say. He replied: 'No, only that I thank my counsel and respect the prosecution – they had a rotten job.'

When it came to arranging the executioners, both senior, experienced hangmen Albert Pierrepoint and Steve Wade had been engaged for a job in Scotland leaving Harry Kirk, an experienced assistant executioner to carry out his first execution as 'No.1'; Syd Dernley was employed as assistant. Dernley recalled in his memoirs that Norwich had been stigmatised by generations of executioners as the 'graveyard of hangmen' since the 'Goodale Mess' of 1885. Dernley's experiences at the execution of Norman Goldthorpe did nothing to negate that belief.

The murder scene at Owles Court. (TNA:PRO)

Arriving on the afternoon before the execution, Kirk and Dernley checked and prepared the gallows; Kirk decided on a drop of 7ft 8in for the 145lb, short (he stood just 5ft 1½in tall) and thick-set Goldthorpe, who was noted for having 'a muscular neck.' Taking up their lodgings in an apartment situated, curiously and uniquely to Norwich Prison, above the condemned cell, the execution team settled down for the evening. Joined by a young warder, they enjoyed a few jokes and ditties until their laughter was abruptly curtailed by a knock on the floor. The warder froze and explained, 'Oh, bloody hell! It's the condemned cell down below; they must be knocking on the ceiling with something.' The group's fun was over. Dernley and Kirk spent the rest of the evening very quietly and turned in early. During the night they clearly heard Goldthorpe singing in his cell below.

Having risen early, Kirk and Dernley set up the execution chamber then went and had breakfast. At the appointed hour the execution party entered the cell. Goldthorpe came quietly and the execution appeared to go smoothly, the gallows trapdoors opened, Goldthorpe plummeted through but then, as Dernley recalled, 'From the pit came a snort… and then another snort… and another and another… It's gone wrong! Christ, he's still alive.' The sound, rather like snoring, continued to emanate from under the hood. The Governor was horrified, 'and the little Under Sheriff had gone from ruddy red to green.' Dernley rushed into the pit beneath the trap, and grabbed the steps: as he lifted them into position near the hanging feet, however, the sounds ceased. He continued to rush up the steps and ripped open Goldthorpe's shirt, so that the Medical Officer could apply his stethoscope. The surgeon announced, 'He's dead, He's dead' and there was no mistaking the relief in his voice. In the official Minutes to Head Office after the execution, countersigned by both the Prison Governor and Basil Tracey, the Medical Officer present at the execution, records the following comments:

We had the impression that he [Kirk] was over-anxious and not altogether sure of himself. After the drop we were very concerned when we heard several deep breaths taken noisily; the body was, however, quite still. The Medical Officer was satisfied that death had taken place instantaneously by dislocation of the vertebrae, but he was in the pit for some time to make quite sure.

Both the Medical Officer and I were present when the body was taken down. We found that the noose had not drawn tight and that the rope was round the back of the neck but the ring was in front at the point of the chin. At least four inches of the hood had been drawn into the ring and in our opinion had jammed it. This state of affairs had failed to cause a constriction around the air passages and had allowed air to pass in and out noisily, to the great concern of all present... Mr Kirk is a bluff, breezy sort of man but underneath we consider that he is nervous. We think that he lacks the calmness and self-assurance which is necessary in an executioner. We should both be apprehensive if he were required to carry out this duty again.

When Kirk and Dernley returned to their quarters to collect their effects, a warder brought them a packet of cigarettes; Goldthorpe had left them for his executioners. Kirk would not take them and gave the pack to Syd; his parting comment, before he bade Dernley farewell was: 'It was a bad job.' Harry Kirk never worked as executioner or assistant again.

145

THE LAST TO HANG IN NORWICH

Dennis Moore and Alfred Reynolds, 19 July 1951

Dennis 'Denny' Moore (22) was born, raised and educated in the Norwich suburb of Old Catton, where he lived with his family on Woodcock Road. He had been courting Eileen Rose Emily Cullen (21) since they met on a trip to Great Yarmouth in June 1950. They became a devoted and loving couple, but when Ellen fell pregnant her father suggested Moore should act responsibly. Moore readily agreed, the couple became engaged and they set the date of their marriage as 17 February 1951.

On Saturday 3 February, with the wedding a couple of weeks away, and the baby due in the near future, Dennis and Ellen went to the market in Norwich, where his father kept a

Albert Pierrepoint, executioner.

stall, after which they went to see Dr Champion on Magdalen Road for a check up. The doctor was to go on record saying what a devoted couple they appeared to be. The couple walked along St Clement's Hill, then Spixworth Road, where they turned off to walk back to Old Catton via Oak Lane. Dennis asked Eileen to accompany him to a secluded cattle shed a little way off the road. Once inside, Moore asked for sex but she refused. In his statement Moore claimed:

> We were kissing and cuddling …I put my arms around her and squeezed her to me very tightly. The next thing I realised she had fallen to the floor and her mouth was bleeding. I then realised I had hold of her throat and just could not let go. After that I took her scarf, put two knots in it and tied it round her neck very tight. I then took my own scarf off and wrapped it round her mouth. I also took my rain mack off and laid over her… There was something in me and I just could not leave go. I loved her too much and I would not have hurt her for anything in the world.

Moore then went to The Park House pub on Catton Grove Road. It was a rough, cold and wet night and Moore drew attention because he 'looked untidy' and was not wearing any coat or mackintosh. Moore bought some cigarettes and left the pub shivering, simply saying 'It's bloody cold.' He then ran home. Once inside, he said he wanted a pencil. his mother asked where Eileen was, to which he replied 'outside'. Moore then went out again, through the kitchen, where he grabbed a bread knife. Curiously, Moore then returned to the shed and made a superficial attempt to cut the dead girl's throat.

After lingering with the body for about ten minutes, Moore resolved to give himself up. He went to the telephone box at the bottom of Woodcock Road and called the police. He was told to wait at the phone box and led them to the cattle shed when they arrived. After picking their way up the muddy path to the cow shed, Moore evaded restraint and threw himself on the body, crying, 'I love you. I love you!' He was rapidly pulled away and the officers checked that life was extinct. When taken into custody Moore was cautioned and made a full statement. Asked if he had anything else to add Moore replied, 'No, sir' but then, after a short pause, added very quietly, 'I'm sorry I've done this and hope I've not caused too much worry on either of our parents.'

By a curious coincidence, just five days later another young man also killed his pregnant sweetheart in Norfolk. Alfred Reynolds (25) and Ellen Ludkin (19) both lived in East Dereham and had been going out for two and a half years. Ellen was pregnant but her parents did not approve of their association and would not allow her to marry Reynolds unless he held down a job. Reynolds called at Ellen's home, where she lived with her parents, at Park Farm Cottages, at about 2 p.m., on 8 February 1951. Ellen answered the door and stood on the step talking for about twenty minutes. The pair then went across to the bicycle shed. Mrs Ludkin went out to get some wood and saw the couple standing just inside the shed and kept an eye out as she went about her housework. She next saw Reynolds walk out from the shed to the field and return with a gun. About ten minutes later, Ellen's mother heard her daughter shout 'Alfie' and a shot rang out. Ellen's mother ran out of her house but was held at bay by Reynolds, who said, 'If you go into the shed where she is I will shoot you too.' He then walked up the garden path and Mrs Ludkin ran to her neighbour, Herbert Mayer, and told him what had occurred. Mr Mayer went to the back of the Ludkin's house, where he saw Reynolds standing near the entrance to the shed with the shotgun in his hand. Mayer walked towards the shed and said to Reynolds, 'Put that gun down, Alfie.' Reynolds did not move, so Mayer repeated himself. Reynolds then replied, 'Get you out of this or I'll blow your brains out,' and pushing the gun against Mayer's hip said, 'Go on, get out'. Mayer backed off and Reynolds walked off. Mrs Ludkin then went to the shed. She had seen Ellen's body lying within, but only at that moment did she see the full extent of her injuries – the result of a blast from a shotgun at point-blank range. The police were soon on the scene, and as a precaution they set roadblocks up around Dereham and ordered all buses to be searched county wide – but Reynolds had simply returned home to No.14, Northgate, where he confessed what he had done to his parents. Later he returned to the scene of crime where he saw Ellen's father in the garden. As Reynolds came down the side of the hedge, at the back of the shed, he called out, 'There have been four or five of the buggers running after me and they haven't got me yet.' At that moment PC Albert Freeman got hold of Reynolds, saying, 'All right, Alfie'. Reynolds replied, 'I know I've had it, I want to give myself up,' and he was taken into custody. When asked to account for his actions, Reynolds claimed that he was going to kill himself; but Ellen had suggested they make a suicide pact, and that he should shoot her first.

The trial of Dennis Moore opened at the Norfolk and Norwich Assizes on 31 May. Moore's defence counsel contended that, although Moore undoubtedly committed the

DECLARATION OF SHERIFF

AND OTHERS

(31 Vict. Cap. 24)

We, the undersigned, hereby declare that

Judgement of Death was this Day executed on

DENNIS ALBERT REGINALD MOORE in His Majesty's Prison of

NORWICH. in our presence.

Dated this 19th day of July, 1961.

R. W. Ketton-Cremer Sheriff of NORFOLK.

Justice of the Peace

for NORWICH

Governor of the said Prison.

Chaplain of the said Prison.

No. 280

(60017) WL47776/80 280 5/50 A.& E.W.Ltd. Gp.688

Execution notices posted on the gate of HMP Norwich after the execution of Dennis Moore. (TNA:PRO)

CERTIFICATE OF SURGEON

(31 Vict. Cap. 24)

I, BASIL MARTIN TRACEY the Surgeon of His

Majesty's Prison of NORWICH hereby

certify that I this day examined the Body of

DENNIS ALBERT REGINALD MOORE , on whom Judgment of

Death was this day executed in the said Prison;

and that on that Examination I found that the

said DENNIS ALBERT REGINALD MOORE was dead.

Dated this 19th day of July, 1961.

(Signature) Basil M. Tracey

M.B. B.S. F.R.C.S.

No. 279

280 5/50 A.& E.W.Ltd. Gp.688

murder, he was 'labouring under such a defect of reason as not to know the nature and quality of the act he was doing.' Evidence of Moore's violent temper and how he could not recall what he had done after such outbursts was presented by a former girlfriend, a comrade from his time in National Service, but the medical officials who had examined Moore were of the opinion he was not suffering from any disease of the mind. The jury returned a verdict of guilty and he was sentenced to death.

Alfred Reynolds appeared at the Assizes on 4 June. Firearms experts agreed it was physically impossible for Ellen Ludkin to fire the gun at herself. Psychiatrist Dr. J.V. Morris stated that he believed Reynolds 'was not a mental defective, but was not far removed in intelligence from being one.' In cross-examination, however, Dr Morris could not state Reynolds had a diseased mind. Dr Matheson, the Chief Medical Officer of Brixton Prison, concurred with Morris that Reynolds was not suffering from a diseased mind and felt Reynolds had the 'emotions of a man of twenty-four controlled by the mentality of a boy of twelve.'

After the summing up by learned counsels and the judge, the jury retired and deliberated for forty minutes. They returned a guilty verdict against Reynolds and he was sentenced to death. Appeals for both Reynolds and Moore were rapidly lodged but were dismissed. Moore's father never gave up hope and organised a petition to the Home Secretary for a reprieve for his son. This also failed and the date for the execution of Moore and Reynolds was set.

Moore's execution was conducted by Albert Pierrepoint, with Syd Dernley as assistant; Harry Allen and Robert 'Les' Stewart attended for Reynolds. Pierrepoint observed the two men at exercise and worked out their respective 'drops'. The condemned men were in separate cells, one in the usual condemned cell, and the other in a cell almost opposite.

Les Stewart recorded some of the events of what was to be his first execution. During the evening, Reynolds was heard to sing 'Danny Boy' twice; he played the Governor at crib and won two legs to one, winning the prize of a bottle of beer. His minister visited him at 10 p.m. and said prayers. Reynolds requested his executioner would not to use the cap. In the execution chamber, Stewart recalled, 'Moore entered and placed his own head in the noose. It had to be removed and adjusted properly.' But the professionalism of the execution team maintained their efficiency. All preparations complete, assistants clear, Albert Pierrepoint pushed the lever; the two condemned went through the gallows trap and thus ended Norfolk's long history of executions.

APPENDIX 1

The Prisons of Norwich

NORWICH CASTLE GAOL

Parts of Norwich Castle were used as a prison from the time of its completion. In 1220, a gaol was made here for the county, and state prisoners were confined here in 1264 and 1274. It was formalised as a public gaol for the county of Norfolk by the Act of Parliament in 1340. By the eighteenth century, the old stone of the castle was blackened, its battlements decayed and overgrown and the castle ditch used as stinking receptacle for rubbish. Buildings were added to the east side of the castle to act as a new gaol in 1793, at a cost of £15,000. Norwich Castle and was finally vested in the Magistrates of Norfolk as a county gaol by Royal Grant, confirmed by Act of Parliament in 1806. Further improvements ensued soon after: the old Shire House and gaol buildings were demolished and the site cleared to allow for the construction of the new County Gaol and House of Correction, completed in 1828 at a cost of £50,000. The Governor's house was octagonal and contained apartments for his family, along with the prison chapel and committee room, and commanded a view over all wings and yards. Branching from it were three radiating wings, each containing a double row of cells on the ground floor, with a day room next to the Governor's house and double rows of cells on the upper floor. The prison was run on the separate system, and there were 240 cells in these wings with a further thirty-six retained in the old keep. The diagonals, crossing the radiating wings at right angles, contained a single row of cells; each had an arcade for the use of the prisoners when the weather would not permit their walking in the yard. Behind these were three more diagonal wings of larger dimensions, with arcades below and double rows of cells on the upper floor. A mill house containing a treadwheel was installed to the right of the entrance; prisoners employed on it pumped water for use in the establishment. The labours for the prisoners included weaving matting, and making sacks, prison clothing and shoes. In 1862, the average daily number of prisoners confined with its walls was 134 and a total of 862 through the year, 103 of them were debtors. There were usually twenty officers of the gaol; including the Governor, surgeon, Chaplain, schoolmaster, engineer, matron, turnkeys, taskmaster and porter. Felons sentenced at the Norfolk Assizes were usually hanged upon the gallows erected on the bridge behind the entrance lodges to the castle. After the introduction of the Anatomy Act (1832) brought an end to the bodies of executed felons being automatically handed over to the surgeon, the burial of those who had been executed was then conducted either 'within the castle precincts' or at St Michael-at-Thorn. The notable exception to this being Peter Taylor, who was executed on 23 April 1836 for his complicity with the Burnham Poisoners. Taylor's body was acquired by Norfolk & Norwich Hospital Surgeon Mr Donald Dalrymple and turned into a skeleton used for the instruction of anatomy.

Norwich Castle County Gaol and Shire House, with Gaoler's House to the right in 1778.

Charles Daines, 'The Hempnall Poisoner', was the last the last executed felon to be buried at St Michael-at-Thorn, in April 1837. All of those subsequently executed in public, upon the Castle Hill or privately within were buried within the walls of the castle in an open area between the granite walls and the brick buildings. Only a stone, let into the wall above, marked the grave, with the initials of the executed and the date of their execution. A total of sixteen such burials took place at Norwich Castle. After the last public execution in Norfolk in 1867, executions were conducted within the walls of Norwich Castle Gaol upon a gallows erected on the north side of the keep. George Harmer was the last man to be executed at Norwich Castle Gaol on 13 December 1886. On 2 August 1887, all prisoners from Norwich Castle were transferred to a new purpose-built HMP Norwich on Prison Road. Norwich Castle became a museum and remains so today.

NORWICH CITY GAOL
The earliest recorded prison, specifically for felons, in the City of Norwich was the Tolbooth (otherwise known as the Tolhouse) in the market place. Originally built for the collection of market tolls, it was used for court hearings and as a prison from the thirteenth century until it was replaced, on the same site, in 1413, by the Guildhall. The court was held here and prisoners detained in a purpose-built gaol at the east end of the Guildhall known as 'Little Ease.' In 1597, the City's new 'Common Gaol' was established at a new location nearby in the former Lamb Inn on St Giles Street. Those condemned by the City of Norwich Assizes were executed upon the city gallows, usually on the Castle Ditches, until the new City Gaol was opened.

The new City Gaol was erected outside St Giles Gates, technically in Heigham Hamlet; begun in 1824, it received its first prisoners from the old City Gaol on 7 August 1826 and

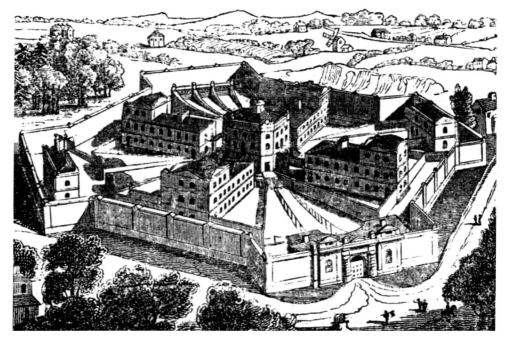

Norwich City Prison from the tower of St Giles's Church, 1827.

was fully completed in 1827. Built to the design of architect Mr Brown of Wells Street, Oxford Street, London and plans of local architect Philip Barnes, it cost about £30,000 and enclosed an area of just over an acre. The prison was run on the Separate System; it contained 120 cells and eight yards divided into fourteen airing yards, six of which were sunk 3ft below the others, so the Governor could command a full view of the whole site from the inspecting gallery in the Governor's house.

The main gatehouse contained a porter's room, press room, hot and cold baths and a room with an oven for the purpose of purifying foul linen. The upper story over the entrance gate contained the 'drop room' over which, on the lead flat of the roof, the scaffold would be erected for public executions. The prison was built around the Governor's house in the centre, which also contained the chapel. Four wings radiated from this; viewed from the main gate, the first wing on the right contained two wards, one for common debtors and the other for men awaiting trial for non-capital offences. The second wing contained another two separate wards, one for unconvicted male felons and the other for unconvicted female felons awaiting trial for capital offences. The first wing on the left contained one ward for master debtors and another for debtors from the court of conscience. The further wing, on the left, contained male misdemeanours; the other contained convicted male felons. There were two day rooms in each of the four wings, four condemned cells and four solitary cells in the back towers.

Two further separate bastions were built. To the right, the building contained a wash house and laundry on the ground floor, with separate male and female infirmaries above. The bastion, to the left, contained a mill house, stable and coach house for the Black Maria. Over these were the mill chamber and hayloft. On the roof was a large wind vane, which turned by a mechanism connected to the treadwheel and was engaged to give employment for the prisoners when there was no corn to grind in the mill.

The treadwheel was used to pump water into the cisterns of four water towers and thence to the various apartments. The prison was built with exercise yards at varying levels, so the Governor could command a view of the whole from the inspection gallery in his residence. The first, and only, public execution conducted there was that of John Stratford, 'The Norwich Dumpling Poisoner', who was hanged by William Calcraft on 17 August 1829. The only other man to be executed at Norwich City Gaol was William Sheward, who was privately executed by William Calcraft on 20 April 1869; the scaffold was erected at the extreme end of the south-east angle of the prison by Mr Foyson, who also supplied the 'drop' used for executions at Norwich Castle Prison. Norwich City Gaol was closed in May 1878 and the prisoners removed to the County Gaol at the Castle. The site was sold off and demolished to make way for the Roman Catholic Cathedral, built 1884 – 1910.

HMP NORWICH

Built to replace Norwich Castle and Norwich City Gaols as a prison for both county and city, on a strip of land between Plumstead Road and Mousehold with its own thoroughfare, originally known as Prison Road (now Knox Road), off Plumstead Road. HMP Norwich was designed by the Surveyor to the Prison Department and built by Messrs W. and T. Denne of Walmer, Kent. Work commenced in 1886 and was completed on 16 July 1887, with the first prisoners transferred there from Norwich Castle on 2 August 1887. Standing in extensive walled grounds, the building was constructed in red brick along the lines of Wormwoods Scrubs on the 'approved system' of one long building with three floors of cells. The upper floors were reached by galleries so that complete supervision could be exercised. An account published at the time of the opening of the prison recorded:

> The grounds in which the prison is situated are enclosed by a red brick wall 18ft high, with only the massive wrought iron double gateways allowing entrance or exit. These are flanked by the gate-porter's lodge and a waiting room, between which every person entering the prison has to pass. The court-yard, immediately within the precincts, is exceedingly spacious. A straight pathway runs through it to the doorway of the prison proper, within which are constructed numerous offices, stores, etc. Passing between these the visitor enters a central corridor, 180ft long and 16ft wide, lighted by a glass and iron roof, 50ft overhead. From the ground floor, which is paved with buff and black tiles, a view can be obtained of each of the doors of the 145 cells, which are arranged in four tiers, the upper tiers opening on to balconies protected by a light iron railing 4ft 6ins in height and supported by iron cantilevers. Access is gained to the balconies by iron staircases rising from the centre of the floor of the corridor. The cells are 13ft deep, 7ft wide and 9ft high and have iron plated doors fitted with Hobbs, Hart and Co's self-acting locks and

inspection glasses through which the warders can view the occupant. Those who have visited the old prison must have been struck with the immense bunches of keys of various sizes and shapes carried by each official. In the new prison the number allotted to the warders is very considerably reduced.

Each cell is fitted up and ventilated in the most approved style. Additional fresh air can be obtained by the prisoners by means of ventilators in the windows of the cells, but the general ventilation is self acting. The cells have a flooring of wood and can be lighted with gas when required but the jet is of course out of the prisoner's reach and is contained in an aperture fitted with a small square of thick glass. Old offenders, which in former days amused themselves by carrying on a conversation with their neighbour in the next cell, will find that, however loudly they call, their voice will not be heard. They can communicate only with the warders and the means provided to enable them to do this, is a little lever within the cell, which on being raised, sets machinery in motion that sounds a gong, and at the same time a disc bearing a corresponding number to that of the cell is projected from the wall. The officer in charge is thus enabled to see at a glance by whom his services are required.

Some of the cells are fitted up as punishment cells and very different to those wretched apartments used in the Castle for that purpose. There is no such thing as a dark cell in the new prison. Other cells will be employed for the medical treatment of the occupants. In

HM Prison Norwich, c. 1950.

the basement is situated is a boiler supplied by Galloway & Sons of Manchester for the heating of the building. The water is supplied from a cistern in the roof, up to which it is pumped by the tread wheel.

The out-buildings consist of a tread-wheel house at the rear of the main block the tread-wheel will accommodate 30 prisoners and is entirely covered in. A large building on the right of the entrance is used as a kitchen fitted with steam jacketed boilers, a brick oven for baking bread, a large flour store and a small kitchener for general use. The building also contains a laundry and a small building nearby is fitted up as a bathing house. Two large boilers supply the hot water for the washing of linen and the bathing of prisoners. The bath house was fitted with seven full length baths with washing boxes constructed in such a way each of the prisoners will be under the surveillance of the officer. The work yet to be completed is the erection of a prison for females and a chapel. These will be built by prison labour. Private dwelling-houses are no in course of construction for the Governor and chief warder in the outer grounds.

HMP Norwich became an all male prison in December 1924 and the remaining female prisoners were transferred to Holloway Prison, London. The new HMP Norwich constructed its first gallows in a coach house, on the east side of the building. To reach it, the convict would have to walk about 50 yards from the condemned cell in the central corridor, out into the prison yard and into the coach house. The second, more up to date execution suite had a more modern layout of condemned cell with execution chamber immediately next door.

The number of prisons where executions could be carried out was gradually reduced throughout the twentieth century. Norwich remained a hanging prison and after the closure of Ipswich Prison in 1925, male prisoners were transferred to Norwich. Those who were capitally convicted for offences committed in Suffolk were executed at Norwich. A total of twelve executions were conducted at HMP Norwich for murders committed in both Norfolk and Suffolk. All of those executed at Norwich Prison were buried within the prison grounds. The last execution in Norfolk was conducted here on 19 July 1951. HMP Norwich remains a prison to this day, with an operational capacity of 767.It accepts male prisoners (adult men and young offenders) whether convicted (Category B, C or D) or on remand.

APPENDIX 2

Norwich Executions 1727 to 1951

Execution Date	Name	Crime	Location	Comments
19 Aug 1727	John Hitching	Highway Robbery	Castle Hill	
19 Aug 1727	Robert Clark	Burglary	Castle Ditches	
19 Aug 1727	William Mallows	Burglary	Castle Ditches	
19 Aug 1727	William Winter	Felony	Castle Ditches	
31 Aug 1728	James Canham	Horse Theft	Castle Ditches	
31 Aug 1728	Deborah Harris	Arson	Castle Hill	
28 Aug 1734	William Morris	Robbery	Castle Hill	
16 Aug 1735	Timothy Wood	Housebreaking	Castle Ditches	
16 Aug 1735	John Mann	Housebreaking	Castle Ditches	
21 Mar 1737	James Blade	Horse Theft	Castle Hill	
21 Mar 1737	John Painter	Horse Theft	Castle Hill	
21 Mar 1737	William Wright	Highway Robbery	Castle Hill	
27 Aug 1737	Charles Grimmer	Horse Theft	Castle Hill	
15 Apr 1738	Robert Mays	Burglary	Castle Hill	
19 Aug 1738	William Gotts	Horse Theft	Castle Hill	
12 Apr1740	Robert Blake	Horse Theft	Castle Hill	
23 Aug 1740	Andrew Lister	Riot	Castle Hill	
23 Aug 1740	Robert Bezett	Riot	Castle Hill	
8 Apr 1741	Jonathan Mattox	Housebreaking	Castle Hill	
8 Apr 1741	Benjamin Smith	Housebreaking	Castle Hill	
8 Apr 1741	Peter Latten	Horse Theft	Castle Hill	
8 Aug 1744	Robert Capps	Murder of Joseph Laughter	Castle Hill	
12 Apr 1746	Jeremiah Pratt	Horse Theft	Castle Hill	
5 Sep 1747	Francis Cooper	Rape	Castle Hill	
8 Apr 1749	John Ambrose	Robbery	Castle Hill	
8 Apr 1749	John Jarvis	Burglary	Castle Hill	
1 Sep 1750	Thomas Clarke	Murder of John Bonney	Castle Ditches	
10 Apr 1751	William Cann	Highway Robbery	Castle Hill	
15 Aug 1752	Daniel Wilson	Theft	Castle Ditches	
8 Sep 1753	James Palmer	Sheep Theft	Castle Hill	
31 Aug 1754	Samuel Agar	Burglary	Castle Ditches	
16 Apr 1755	John Hall	Horse Theft	Castle Hill	
30 Sep 1757	Richard Taylor	Burglary	Castle Hill	
26 Apr 1758	Ambrose Towler	Housebreaking	Castle Hill	
1 Sep 1764	Samuel Creasy	Highway Robbery	Castle Hill	
1 Sep 1764	John Carman	At Large	Castle Hill	

Execution Date	Name	Crime	Location	Comments
20 Oct 1764	John Holloway	At Large	Castle Ditches	
10 Jan 1767	David Long	Riot	Castle Ditches	
10 Jan 1767	John Hall	Riot	Castle Ditches	
4 Apr 1767	John Jermy	Housebreaking	Castle Hill	
4 Apr 1767	George Woodbine	Housebreaking	Castle Hill	
20 Apr1768	Gibbon Houghton	SheepTheft	Castle Hill	
13 Aug 1768	John Sherwood	Arson	Castle Hill	
5 Aug 1769	Cornelius Green	Housebreaking	Castle Hill	
6 Apr 1771	Joseph Barber	Highway Robbery	Castle Hill	
12 Sep 1772	Edward Plumb	Highway Robbery	Castle Ditches	
28 Aug 1773	Jacob Cooper	Burglary	Castle Ditches	
16 Apr 1774	Jonathan Jex	Housebreaking	Castle Hill	
16 Apr1774	Henry Jex	Housebreaking	Castle Hill	
12 Apr 1775	Thomas Green	Burglary	Castle Hill	
19 Mar 1777	John Rye	Murder of Joseph Snelling	Castle Hill	
12 Apr 1777	John Manning	Burglary	Castle Hill	
3 Apr 1779	Thomas Bell	Shot and Maimed a Gamekeeper	Castle Hill	
3 Apr 1779	Thomas Boddy	Burglary	Castle Hill	
3 Apr 1779	Miles Bridges	Burglary	Castle Hill	
3 Apr 1779	Zorobabel Partridge	Burglary	Castle Hill	
3 Apr 1779	John Griffin	Burglary	Castle Hill	
7 Apr 1781	Michael Moore	Highway Robbery	Castle Hill	
7 Apr 1781	William Fletcher	Highway Robbery	Castle Hill	
7 Apr 1781	William Skipper	Highway Robbery	Castle Hill	
8 Sep 1781	Samuel Creasy	Robbery and Rape	Castle Hill	
5 Apr 1783	Abraham Carman	Burglary	Castle Hill	
5 Apr 1783	Henry Cabell	Burglary	Castle Hill	
10 Apr 1784	William Green	Burglary	Castle Hill	
10 Apr 1784	James Trundle	Burglary	Castle Hill	
4 Sep 1784	Simon Tuffs	Horse Theft	Castle Hill	
24 Mar 1785	James Cliffen	Murder of Peter Seaman	Castle Hill	
2 Apr 1785	Robert Randall	Highway Robbery	Castle Hill	
2 Apr 1785	Robert Cadamy	Sheep Theft	Castle Hill	
2 Apr 1785	John Ferrett	Burglary	Castle Hill	
2 Apr 1785	William Newland	Forgery	Castle Hill	
22 Jul 1785	Francis Vandergoose	Murder of his wife	Castle Ditches	
6 Aug 1785	Peter Bullard	Horse Theft	Castle Hill	
6 Aug 1785	Joseph Loads	Burglary	Castle Hill	
13 Aug 1785	William Westrupp	Burglary	Castle Ditches	
25 Mar 1786	John Shilling	Murder of John Raven	Castle Hill	
8 Apr 1786	Edward Land	Burglary	Castle Hill	
26 Aug 1786	Joseph Moore	Horse Theft	Castle Hill	
26 Aug 1786	Robert Sutton	Horse Theft	Castle Hill	

Execution Date	Name	Crime	Location	Comments
26 Aug 1786	Henry Cross	Horse Theft	Castle Hill	
30 Mar 1787	William Hawke	Murder of Henry Scarle	Castle Hill	
30 Mar 1787	Thomas Mayhew	Murder of Henry Scarle	Castle Hill	
16 Apr 1787	Benjamin Pearcey	Highway Robbery	Castle Hill	
16 Apr 1787	Benjamin Tungate	Highway Robbery	Castle Hill	
16 Apr 1787	John Camp	Highway Robbery	Castle Hill	
16 Apr 1787	John Teasdale	Burglary	Castle Hill	
18 Aug 1787	John Clarke	At large	Castle Hill	
25 Aug 1787	John Crome	Highway Robbery	Castle Ditches	
20 Mar 1788	Joseph Wakefield	Murder of Thomas Thwaites	Castle Hill	
20 Mar 1788	Henry Sell	Murder of Elizabeth Clark	Castle Hill	
5 Apr 1788	Richard Young	Highway Robbery	Castle Hill	
5 Apr 1788	John Jacob	Horse Theft	Castle Hill	
5 Apr 1788	Richard Greenwood	Burglary	Castle Hill	
26 Jul 1788	Timothy Hardy	Murder of John Aggus	Castle Ditches	
11 Apr 1789	Christopher Galloway	Burglary	Castle Hill	
11 Apr 1789	Ralph Dawson	Burglary	Castle Hill	
11 Apr 1789	Daniel Goose	Burglary	Castle Hill	
11 Apr 1789	James Ayers	Burglary	Castle Hill	
22 Aug 1789	James Banks	Robbery	Castle Hill	
19 Mar 1790	John Beckett	Murder	Castle Hill	
3 Apr 1790	Thomas Jackson	Robbery of the Mail	Castle Hill	
31 July 1790	Aaron Fakenham	Murder of his Wife	Castle Ditches	
9 Apr 1791	Robert Mullinger	Burglary	Castle Hill	
9 Apr1791	Mary Adams	Arson	Castle Hill	
3 Sep 1791	William Bales	Horse Theft	Castle Hill	
3 Sep 1791	John Turner	Burglary	Castle Hill	
24 Mar 1792	William Anthony	Murder	Castle Hill	
6 Sep 1794	Cook March	Highway Robbery	Castle Ditches	
24 Mar 1797	William Suffolk	Murder of Mary Beck	Castle Hill	
15 Apr 1797	Robert Scott	Cattle Theft	Castle Hill	
9 Aug 1797	Rebecca Howard	Murder of her Illegitimate Child	Castle Ditches	
26 Aug 1797	John Witham	Burglary	Castle Hill	
26 Aug 1797	Jonathan Green	Burglary	Castle Hill	
3 Aug 1799	James Fleming	Rape	Castle Hill	
3 Aug 1799	Samuel Windham	Rape	Castle Hill	
12 Apr 1800	Samuel Wright	Uttering Forgery	Castle Hill	
15 Aug 1801	Henry Lawn	Burglary	Castle Hill	
28 Aug 1802	William Rix	Sheep Theft	Castle Hill	
6 Apr 1805	Leeds Mays	Horse Theft	Castle Hill	
4 Apr 1807	William Carter	Horse Theft	Castle Hill	
31 Jul 1807	Martha Alden	Murder of Samuel Alden	Castle Hill	
9 Apr 1808	John Chapman	Shooting at a Gamekeeper	Castle Hill	

Execution Date	Name	Crime	Location	Comments
9 Apr 1808	William Fuller	Shooting at a Gamekeeper	Castle Hill	
9 Apr 1808	Thomas Sutton	Arson	Castle Hill	
10 Apr 1813	Charles Harper	Burglary	Castle Hill	
10 Apr 1813	Edmund Impson	Burglary	Castle Hill	
6 Apr 1816	Edward Lea	Uttering Forged Notes	Castle Hill	
31 Aug 1816	Daniel Harwood	Riot	Castle Hill	
31 Aug 1816	Thomas Thody	Riot	Castle Hill	
31 Aug 1816	Thomas Moy	Sheep theft	Castle Hill	
23 Mar 1818	James Johnson	Murder of Robert Baker	Castle Hill	
10 Apr 1819	James Belcham	Burglary	Castle Hill	
16 Aug 1819	John Pycraft	Murder of his Infant Child	Castle Hill	
28 Aug 1819	Edward Fisher	Stabbing William Harrison	Castle Hill	
1 Apr 1822	William Hardiment	Murder of Robert Baker	Castle Hill	
13 Apr 1822	Noah Peak	Arson	Castle Hill	
13 Apr 1822	George Fortis	Arson	Castle Hill	
24 Aug 1822	James Smith	Housebreaking	Castle Ditches	
24 Aug 1822	Henry Carter	Housebreaking	Castle Ditches	
5 Apr 1823	William Bray	Burglary	Castle Hill	
18 Apr 1829	John Wood	Sheep Theft	Castle Hill	
18 Apr 1829	Thomas Butler	Sheep Theft	Castle Hill	
18 Apr 1829	Richard Everitt	Horse Theft	Castle Hill	
17 Aug 1829	John Stratford	Murder of John Burgess	Castle Hill	
10 Apr 1830	William Lovet	Robbery	Castle Hill	
10 Apr 1830	John Simmons	Robbery	Castle Hill	
9 Apr 1831	Richard Nockolds	Arson	Castle Hill	
12 Apr 1834	William Pye	Arson	Castle Hill	
12 Apr 1834	Gilpin Reynolds	Arson	Castle Hill	
12 Apr 1834	William Thirkettle	Attempted Murder	Castle Hill	
18 Apr 1835	James Clarke	Arson	Castle Hill	
10 Aug 1835	Frances Billings*	Murder of Mary Taylor	Castle Hill	(Last women executed in Norfolk)
10 Aug 1835	Catherine Frarey*	Murder of Mary Taylor	Castle Hill	(Last women executed in Norfolk)
23 Apr 1836	Peter Taylor	Incitement to Murder Mary Taylor	Castle Hill	
29 Apr 1837	George Timms*	Murder of Hannah Mansfield	Castle Hill	
29 Apr 1837	John Smith*	Murder of Hannah Mansfield	Castle Hill	
27 Apr 1839	Charles Daines	Murder of Elizabeth Daines	Castle Hill	
22 Aug 1840	John Randalsome*	Murder of Mary Randalsome	Castle Hill	
14 August 1841	John Self*	Murder of Jemima Stimpson	Castle Hill	
11 Apr 1846	Samuel Yarham*	Murder of Harriet Candler	Castle Hill	
21 Apr 1849	James Rush*	Murder of Isaac Jermy and Jermy Jermy	Castle Hill	
16 Aug 1851	Henry Groom*	Murder of John Ayton	Castle Hill	

Execution Date	Name	Crime	Location	Comments
8 Apr 1854	William Thompson*	Murder of Lorenz Beha	Castle Hill	
26 Aug 1867	Hubbard Lingley*	Murder of Benjamin Black	Castle Hill	(Last Public Execution in Norfolk)
20 Apr 1869	William Sheward	Murder of Martha Sheward	Norwich City Gaol	
1 May 1876	Henry Webster*	Murder of Sarah Webster	Norwich Castle	
20 Nov 1877	Henry March*	Murder of Henry Bidewell and Thomas Mays	Norwich Castle	
22 May 1882	William Abigail*	Murder of Jane Plunkett	Norwich Castle	
30 Nov 1885	Robert Goodale*	Murder of Bathsheba Goodale	Norwich Castle	
10 Feb 1886	John Thurston*	Murder of Henry Springall	Norwich Castle	
13 Dec 1886	George Harmer*	Murder of Henry Last	Norwich Castle	
12 Jul 1898	George Watt**	Murder of Sophia Watt	HMP Norwich	
21 Mar 1901	Herbert Bennett**	Murder of Mary Bennett	HMP Norwich	
2 Dec 1908	James Nicholls**	Murder of Susan Wilson	HMP Norwich	
5 Nov 1912	Robert Galloway**	Murder of Minnie Morris	HMP Norwich	
12 Nov 1925	Herbert Bloye**	Murder of Clara and Alice Squires	HMP Norwich	
8 Mar 1938	Walter Smith**	Murder of Albert Baker	HMP Norwich	
13 Mar 1945	Arthur Heys**	Murder of Winifred Evans	HMP Norwich	
18 Nov 1948	Stanley Clark**	Murder of Florence Bentley	HMP Norwich	
8 Mar 1950	James Rivett**	Murder of Christine Cuddon	HMP Norwich	
24 Nov 1950	Norman Goldthorpe**	Murder of Emma Howe	HMP Norwich	
19 Jul 1951	Dennis Moore**	Murder of Eileen Cullen	HMP Norwich	(Last Execution)
19 Jul 1951	Alfred Reynolds**	Murder of Ellen Ludkin	HMP Norwich	(Last Execution)

*Buried within the walls of Norwich Castle
** Buried at HMP Norwich

SOURCES & SELECT BIBLIOGRAPHY

The known extant records of the Norfolk Assizes are held at The National Archives at Kew; the details of Norfolk executions before the eighteenth century are manuscript records but sadly a complete run of these does not survive and those that do tend to record only very brief information of trial date, accused, crime, sentence and date, if a capital sentence was passed and carried out. With the coming of newspapers and broadsides, the stories of the crimes, the criminals, their trial and fate may be compiled in far more detail. This book examines a selection from some of the earliest known surviving records from the thirteenth century with the last 200 years of executions in Norwich recounted in more detail up to and including the final execution at HMP Norwich in 1951. Executions conducted outside the City of Norwich are not included in this volume.

The photographs and documents in this volume are mainly from originals in the author's archive, unless otherwise annotated to Norfolk Library and Information Service (NLIS), The Norfolk Record Office (NRO), The National Archives at Kew (TNA) or Stewart P. Evans. The death masks illustrated are on display at Norwich Castle Museum and were photographed by the author with permission. Any omissions in acknowledgement or infringement of copyright are unintentional and no offence was intended.

RECORDS CONSULTED AT THE NATIONAL ARCHIVES

ASSI 33/1 - 15 Assizes: Norfolk Circuit: Gaol Books: Summer 1734 – Lent 1863

ASSI 36/29 Assizes: Home, Norfolk and South-Eastern Circuit: Depositions. Accused: R. Goodale. Offence: Murder 1885.

ASSI 36/30 Assizes: Home, Norfolk and South-Eastern Circuit: Depositions. Accused: G. Harmer. Offence: Murder 1886.

ASSI 36/38 Assizes: Home, Norfolk and South-Eastern Circuit: Depositions. Accused: F. Bloye alias Whiteman. Offence: Murder 1925.

ASSI 36/103 Assizes: Home, Norfolk and South-Eastern Circuit: Depositions. Murder: Rivett, James Frank. 1949.

ASSI 36/126 Assizes: Home, Norfolk and South-Eastern Circuit: Depositions. Murder: Moore, Dennis Albert Reginald. 1951.

ASSI 36/127 Assizes: Home, Norfolk and South-Eastern Circuit: Depositions. Murder: Reynolds, Alfred George. 1951.

DPP 2/2006 Director of Public Prosecutions: Case Papers, New Series. Goldthorpe, Norman: Murder. 1950.

PCOM 9/1576 Prison Commission and Home Office, Prison Department: Registered Papers: Series 2 Goldthorpe, Norman: convicted at Norfolk on 11 October 1950 of murder; sentenced to death; executed on 24 November 1950

Books

Anon., *Narrative and Trial of James Blomfield Rush* (Norwich, 1849)

Anon., *A Full Report of the Trial of James Blomfield Rush* – Clarke's Edition (London, 1849)

Atholl, J., *Shadow of the Gallows* (London, 1954)

Atholl, J., *The Reluctant Hangman* (London, 1956)

Beecheno, F.R., *Notes on Norwich Castle* – Revised Edition (Norwich, 1896)

Berry, J., *My Experiences as an Executioner* (London, 1892)

Blomefield, F., *An Essay towards a Topographical History of the County of Norfolk: vol. 3: The History of the City and County of Norwich, part I* (London, 1806)

Brend, W.A., *A Handbook of Medical Jurisprudence and Toxicology* (London, 1919)

Browne, P., *The History of Norwich* (Norwich, 1814)

Butcher, B.D., *A Movable Rambling Police – An Official History of Policing in Norfolk* (Norwich, 1989)

Capon, P., *The Great Yarmouth Mystery* (London, 1965)

Chapman, P., *Madame Tussaud's Chamber of Horrors* (London, 1984)

Church, R., *More Murder in East Anglia* (London, 1990)

Church, R., *Murder in East Anglia* – New Edition (London, 1993)

Cockburn, J.S., *A History of English Assizes 1558-1714* (London, 1972)

Daynes, J., *The History of Norwich* (Norwich 1848)

Dent, J., 'The Norwich Tollhouse and De Tolhus' in *The Annual: The Bulletin of the Norfolk Archaeological and Historical Research Group* (CEAS/UEA 1999/2000)

Dernley, S. & Newman, D., *The Hangman's Tale* (London, 1990)

Eddleston. J.J., *The Encyclopaedia of Executions* (London, 2002)

Evans, S.P., *Executioner: The Chronicles of James Berry Victorian Hangman* (Stroud, 2004)

Fielding, S., *The Hangman's Record – vol.I 1868-1899* (Beckenham, 1994)

Griffiths, Major A., *Mysteries of Police and Crime* – Special Edition (London, 1920)

Hopkins, M., *The Discovery of Witches: In Answer to Severall Queries, lately Delivered to the Judges of Assize for the County of Norfolk* (Norwich, 1647).

Hudson, Revd William & Tingey, J.C., *The Records of the City of Norwich* (Norwich, 1906)

'One of his Fellow Citizens' [Joseph John Gurney], *Some Account of John Stratford who was Executed after the Last Assizes for the City of Norwich* (Norwich, 1829)

Ketton-Cremer, R.W., *Norfolk in the Civil War* (London, 1969)

Lambton, A., *Echoes of Causes Celebres* (London, 1931)

Leigh Hunt, A., *The Capital of the Ancient Kingdom of East Anglia* (London, 1870)

Lipman, V.D., *The Jews of Medieval Norwich* (London, 1967)

Mackie, C., *Norfolk Annals* (2 vols.)(Norwich, 1901)

Martin, T., *The History of the Town of Thetford* (London, 1779)

Morson, M., *Norwich Murders* (Barnsley, 2006)

Morson, M., *Norfolk Mayhem and Murder* (Barnsley, 2008)

Muskett, P., 'Riotous Assemblies' *Popular Disturbances in East Anglia 1740-1822* (Ely, 1984)

Page, William (ed.) *A History of the County of Suffolk: Volume 2* (London, 1975)

Pierrepoint, A., *Executioner Pierrepoint* (London, 1974)

Rawcliffe, C. & Wilson, R. (eds), *Medieval Norwich* (London, 2004)

Rawcliffe, C. & Wilson, R. (eds), *Norwich Since 1550* (London 2004)

Robbins, R.H., *The Encyclopedia of Witchcraft and Demonology* (New York, 1959)

Smith-Hughes, J., *Unfair Comment, Upon Some Victorian Murder Trials* (London, 1951)

Sotherton, N., *The Commoyson in Norfolk* (c.1549) republished and edited by Susan Yaxley, (Guist, 1987)

Storey, N.R., *A Grim Almanac of Norfolk* (Stroud, 2003)

Storey, N.R., *Norfolk Murders* (Stroud, 2006)

Storey, N.R., *Norfolk Tales of Mystery and Murder* (Countryside, 2009)

Taylor, S.T. *The Diary of a Norwich Hospital Medical Student* (Norwich, 1930)

Teignmouth Shore, W. (ed.) *Crime and Its Detection* (London, 1932)

Teignmouth Shore, W. (ed.), *Trial of James Blomfield Rush* (Glasgow, 1928)

Wallace, E., *The Trial of Herbert John Bennett* (London, 1929)

Newspapers And Journals

The *Criminologist*

Daily Express

Diss Express

Daily Mirror

East Anglian Magazine

East Anglian Notes and Queries

Eastern Counties Collectanea Evening News

Eastern Daily Press

Famous Crimes

Family Tree Magazine

Gentleman's Magazine

Illustrated London News

Illustrated Mail

Illustrated Police News

News of the World

Norfolk Chronicle

Norfolk Fair

Norfolk Journal & East Anglian Life

Norfolk & Suffolk Notes & Queries

Norwich Annual

Norwich Gazette

Norwich Mercury

Penny Illustrated Paper

Police Gazette

Reynolds News

The *Strand Magazine*

The *Tablet*

The *Times*

Thetford and Watton Times

Yarmouth Mercury

Other titles published by The History Press

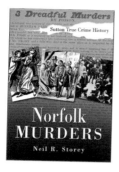

Norfolk Murders

NEIL R. STOREY

Norfolk Murders features the stories behind some of the most notorious murders in Norfolk's history. The cases covered here record the county's crimes, as well as famous murders that gripped not just Norfolk but the whole nation. This is an examination of the darker side of the county's past.

978 0 7509 4366 6

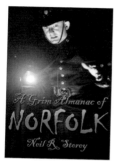

A Grim Almanac of Norfolk

NEIL R. STOREY

This almanac explores dreadful deeds, macabre deaths, strange occurrences and grim tales from the shadier side of the county's past. Jostling for position in this cornucopia of the criminal and curious are diverse tales of highwaymen, smugglers, murderers, bodysnatchers, duellists, footpads, poachers, rioters and rebels.. If it's horrible, if it's ghastly, if it's strange, it's here — and if you have the stomach for it, then read on…

978 0 7524 5688 5

Prisons & Prisoners in Victorian Britain

NEIL R. STOREY

Prisons & Prisoners in Victorian Britain provides an illustrated insight into the Victorian prison system and the experiences of those within it – on both sides of the bars. Featuring stories of crime and misdeeds, this book includes chapters on a typical day inside a Victorian prison. Richly illustrated with a series of photographs, engravings, documents and letters, this volume is sure to appeal to all those interested in crime and social history in Victorian Britain.

978 0 7524 5269 2

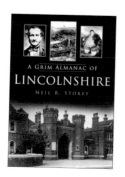

A Grim Almanac of Lincolnshire

NEIL R. STOREY

A Grim Almanac of Lincolnshire is a day-by-day catalogue of 365 ghastly tales from around the county dating from the twelfth to the twentieth centuries. Full of dreadful deeds, macabre deaths, strange occurrences and heinous homicides, this almanac explores the darker side of Lincolnshire's past. If you have ever wondered about what nasty goings-on occurred in the Lincolnshire of yesteryear, then look no further — it's all here, and if you have the stomach for it, then read on… if you dare!

978 0 7524 5768 0

Visit our website and discover thousands of other History Press books.

www.thehistorypress.co.uk